SUSAN LEVIN provides the first full-length study of Dorothy Wordsworth's prose and poetry, focusing on the textual strategies she adopts, the way words appear together in her work, and the determining factors of her narrative voice. In two appendixes, Levin includes a collected edition of all of Dorothy Wordsworth's poetry, some published for the first time, and the first published version of her short story, "Mary Jones and her Pet-lamb."

Levin shows how Dorothy Wordsworth's technique of cataloguing seemingly trivial events defines a particular narrative of self-development. She employs the models of major figures in feminist psychological theory—Carol Gilligan, Nancy Chodorow, and Jean Baker Miller—to explain Wordsworth's concentration on domestic, family, and community themes within traditionally female realms. She also shows how Dorothy Wordsworth sets the structures of her own imagination against those of her brother to describe herself as a woman who goes out to seek experience.

Levin compares passages from Dorothy's writings to similar passages from the work of William Wordsworth, Coleridge, and De Quincy to show how identical words and phrases and similar scenes are put to different uses. Her fine analyses of journal passages and poems, and her discussion of the work of Margaret Fuller, Mary Shelley, Susan Coo[

SUSAN M. LEVIN tea
stitute of Technolo;
published work has been in romanticism and women's studies.

Dorothy Wordsworth & Romanticism

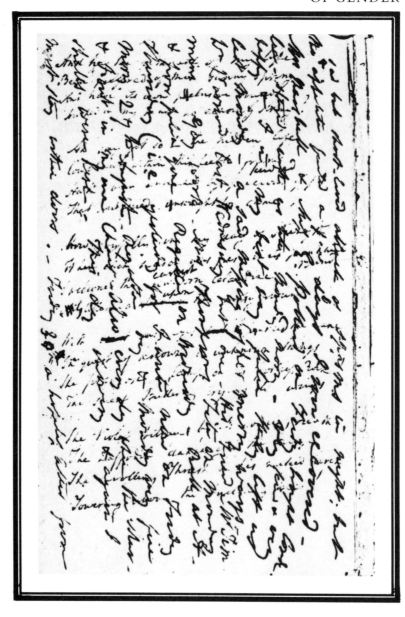

✢   ✢   ✢   ✢   ✢   ✢   ✢

Susan M. Levin

Dorothy Wordsworth & Romanticism

RUTGERS, THE STATE UNIVERSITY

New Brunswick and London

Library of Congress Cataloging-in-Publication Data

Levin, Susan M., 1950–
Dorothy Wordsworth and romanticism.

(The Douglass series on women's lives and the
meaning of gender)
Bibliography: p.
Includes index.
1. Wordsworth, Dorothy, 1771–1855—Criticism
and interpretation.   2. Women and literature—
England.   3. Romanticism—England.   I. Title.
II. Series.
PR5849.L48   1987   828'.703   86-6711
ISBN 0-8135-1146-1

British Cataloging-in-Publication Information Available

Frontispiece: Page near end of Dorothy's journal of February 12, 1831–September 7, 1833. The poem "Thoughts on my sick-bed" appears under the journal entry. Photo courtesy of Wordsworth Collection, Cornell University

CONTENTS

A complete list of the poems collected in Appendix One is provided on p. 177.

ACKNOWLEDGMENTS

The Grasmere journals of Dorothy Wordsworth have long been in print, accessible to generations of readers, but her other works have been more difficult to come by. It was not until I happened upon one of her poems about twelve years ago that I began to be aware of the scope of Dorothy Wordsworth's writing, but few of her poems had been published and just obtaining texts was often difficult. There were other problems too, including what to call her. Mere "Dorothy" sounds patronizing but "Wordsworth" means William and repeating the full name at every reference is awkward. (In this book I do whatever sounds best at the time.)

The more I worked on this project the more help and encouragement I received. My first debt is to Stephen Parrish, who has been guiding me in the study of English romanticism since I was a sophomore at Cornell. His knowledge and tact are instrumental in supporting so many students of the nineteenth century, among whom Carl Ketcham, James Butler, and Paul Betz have been particularly helpful to me. Jonathan Wordsworth has generously provided access to the materials I needed. Carl Woodring, Margaret Homans, Leslie Mitchner, and Susan Wolfson have offered invaluable advice about the manuscript. Anyone anxious about entrusting her deathless prose to a word processor should be as lucky as I was to have the help of Mary Adelman and her staff at Osner Business Machines in New York.

Grants from the NEH and ACLS and a sabbatical from Stevens Institute of Technology financed travel to the various archives where Dorothy Wordsworth material is preserved and also gave me time to write the book. As for time, my family has spent almost as much of it with Dorothy Wordsworth as I have. I must thank my children, Jonathan and Freda, and especially my husband, Robert.

My essay "Subtle Fire: Dorothy Wordsworth's Prose and Poetry," which appeared in the *Massachusetts Review,* Vol. XXI, 2 (September 2, 1980), explored many of the ideas elaborated in this book, and I thank the editors of the *Review* for allowing me to reprint them. I am grateful to Jonathan Wordsworth and the Trustees of Dove Cottage; Donald Eddy, Lucy Burgess, and the Wordsworth Collection, Cornell University; Robert C. Brandeis, Freda Gough, and the Coleridge Collection, Victoria University Library, Toronto, for help in studying manuscripts in their collections and for permission to publish them. For permission to cite material in their collections I thank the Pierpont Morgan Library in New York and the Bodleian Library, Oxford. Also I wish to thank Oxford University Press for permission to cite materials from Mary Moorman's edition of the *Journals of Dorothy Wordsworth;* the six volumes of *The Letters of William and Dorothy Wordsworth;* Ernest de Selincourt's editions of *The Poetical Works of William Wordsworth, Journals of Dorothy Wordsworth,* and *George & Sarah Green, A Narrative;* and Samuel Taylor Coleridge's *Poetical Works* edited by E. H. Coleridge.

Even as this book was being printed, colleagues were suggesting possible readings of Dorothy Wordsworth's manuscripts. I wish to thank Eleanor Wedge, Andrew Rubenfeld, and J. R. de J. Jackson.

Dorothy Wordsworth & Romanticism

I.

Introduction:
Reading Dorothy Wordsworth

❖ ❖ ❖ ❖ ❖ WHAT HAVE WE KNOWN ABOUT DOR-
othy Wordsworth's writing? Among the figures of English romanticism she has generally been seen as a background presence
whose writing often evinces a positive will not to put itself forward among the momentous energies of the early nineteenth
century. Yet generations of readers who have gone to Dorothy's
journals and letters to find out about William Wordsworth and
his circle have come away with a sense of the woman as herself
an artist. Revealing both joy and rage at her choice of life, Dorothy's writing organizes traditionally female realms of concern in
its concentration on the domestic, on family, and on community. What we can know about Dorothy Wordsworth's writing is
its quality as work of unique value, both in its own right and in
the study of English romanticism.

She wrote throughout her life. Born in Cockermouth in 1771,
one year after William, she was the third eldest and the only girl
of the family's five children. When Dorothy was six, her mother
died, and she went to live with her aunt at Halifax for nine years
that seem to have been happier, according to the letters, than the
next year and a half, spent with her grandparents at Penrith.
Grateful when her uncle took her into his family at Forncett, she
was elated when in 1795, she finally established the home with
William about which her letters so continually fantasize.

Her writing collected at Dove Cottage provides some idea of the shape of her life as well as the extent of her work. In 1797 William and Dorothy moved to Alfoxden House, which gives its name to Dorothy's Alfoxden journal. In 1798 Dorothy, Coleridge, and William went to study in Germany, a trip recounted in her *Journal of Visit to Hamburgh and of Journey from Hamburgh to Goslar*. Four volumes of the Grasmere journals, kept from May 1800 to December 1802, contain her best-known writing and tell of life at Dove Cottage where she lived with William and his family. A Grasmere misfortune provides the material for her *A Narrative Concerning George and Sarah Green*. She traveled frequently and wrote about her trips in *Recollections of a Tour made in Scotland, Excursion on the Banks of Ullswater, Journal of a Tour on the Continent, Journal of my Second Tour in Scotland*, and *Journal of a Tour in the Isle of Man*. Her later journals kept from 1824 to 1835 contain more accounts of her travels as well as writing about life at Rydal Mount, the home to which the family moved in 1813. At Rydal, Dorothy continued her voluminous correspondence, wrote out notes on her readings, transcribed a children's story she had written, and kept a commonplace book containing notes, recipes, and newspaper clippings as well as many poems of her own composition.

In 1829, while making an extended visit to her nephew at Whitwick, she contracted a fever that was nearly fatal. Her health never completely returned, and from 1835 until her death in 1855 at the age of eighty-three, she slipped in and out of sanity, the victim perhaps of arteriosclerosis, perhaps of some kind of cerebral accident. During the last years of her life, she took particular pleasure in reciting and copying her poems, many of which were sent to friends and relatives.

A few of her poems were published during her lifetime; some of her journals and most of her letters are now in print.[1] A great deal of her work, however, remains in manuscript, perhaps because her writing is distinct from institutionalized literary categories. Her texts frequently do not conform to canonical no-

---

1. For a discussion of Dorothy Wordsworth's publication history, see my Selected Bibliography.

tions of literature, often seeming weirdly idiosyncratic. Yet, the critical questions her literary output raises can be generalized to issues involving women's writing and twentieth-century literary criticism, issues involving romanticism as a literary phenomenon, the artistic acceptability of various genres, and the publication and availability of certain texts. Working in awareness of the great Western myths of masculine power, of authority and fulfillment—helping, in fact, to create one such myth—she presents an alternative to them. It is not what we are accustomed to reading.

Recent theories of language and of psychology provide help in reading Dorothy Wordsworth. Because her work demonstrates characteristics now recognized as typical of writing by women, it is illuminated by contemporary feminist critics. Like many women writers, Dorothy Wordsworth constantly denigrates herself and her talent in a manner that goes far beyond common protestations of modesty. While she does find her own forms in a community of male writing that she proceeds from and revises, the process reflects guilt and torment as she asserts her own passivity in the active world of letters in which she participated. Introducing some basic essays on feminist literary theory collected in *The New Feminist Criticism,* Elaine Showalter characterizes "the second phase of feminist criticism" as "the discovery that women writers had a literature of their own, whose historical and thematic coherence, as well as artistic importance, had been obscured by the patriarchal values that dominate our culture" (6). Showalter's comment accents both the history of Dorothy Wordsworth as a writer and the way she needs to be read. Dorothy Wordsworth is one perfect example of a woman writer whose work has been neglected, whose literary forms are "uncertain," whose development cannot be accounted for in terms of the conventional paradigms derived from men who write.

The literary quality and importance of the Grasmere journals are finally being recognized, but much of Dorothy Wordsworth's work is still unknown. Reactions to it frequently focus a traditional response to writing by women: But really, is it any good? The conventions of this response proceed through several stages. First, the journals, letters, and travel books that form the largest part of her canon are considered suspect as literature. They are not of the approved genres, are not, in any case, "quality work." Second, her texts are deemed worth reading, but chiefly for what they reveal about the psychology of the frustrated, neurotic spinster. The writing of Dorothy Wordsworth, Emily Dickinson, and Christina Rossetti has been so interpreted. Third, these women are not seen as primarily neurotic. Rather, they are said to have chosen a life that allowed creation of their art, a life, reflected in their literature, that permitted certain freedom from conventional familial restraints and thus in part enabled their creativity. The first and second reactions speak their own inadequacy, but this third response remains of some use in that it conducts the reader to a fourth reaction that does, I think, realize the significance of Dorothy Wordsworth's writing. This is that the choice was never made easily, that the writing contains a certain rage at the limitations imposed on the life of the woman artist, as well as recognition of the glory of that life.

Her writing exists as a positive articulation of a negative situation. It is writing characterized by refusal: refusal to generalize, refusal to move out of a limited range of vision, refusal to speculate, refusal to reproduce standard literary forms, refusal to undertake the act of writing. The personal journals, especially, reject, even while they seem to operate according to, conventional narrative sequence. Dorothy sets down various progressions in her life, but she refuses to make connections. Her writing does not engage the world in the usual manner. She often appears a mere cataloguer of irrelevant detail, a person strangely fixated on the minutiae around her.

One way of explaining Dorothy's faithfulness to objects, her continual cataloguing, is as a kind of perpetual reality testing. This process and the particular texts it produces—the relations to the external object world set out in Dorothy Wordsworth's writings—correspond in part to paradigms of feminine development advanced by such theorists as Nancy Chodorow, Jean Baker Miller, and Carol Gilligan. A drawing together of feminist and psychoanalytic analyses provides a further way of understanding what Gilligan would term Dorothy Wordsworth's "different voice." The way her writing places her in a world of objects calls into focus those "issues of merging and separation" and "attachment" that Chodorow sees as basic female "involvement" (166). On the one hand, her writing expresses an equipoise of self and the phenomenal world that challenges the notion of assertive self advanced by so many romantic writers. On the other hand, her insistence on detail, on naming and minutely describing what goes on around her, may indicate a fear of being absorbed and thus annihilated. Her writing of herself in her journals, the language and the structure of her work, reveals both her love of nature and the joy she takes in the surrounding world as well as her fears and successes at maintaining herself in that world. This is not to deny that male romantic writers exhibit many of the same concerns. They too write of annihilation and engulfment, of separation and attachment, but their expression and emphases are different. Dorothy Wordsworth and other women writing in the early nineteenth century simply do not sound the same as their male contemporaries. And, their differences are frequently similar.

In listening to "the stories we tell about our lives" (2), the kinds of stories that constitute Dorothy Wordsworth's writing, Carol Gilligan adds to the model of human development that Western culture has accepted as standard. By considering the ways the feminine self is differentiated, especially in relation to the mother, Gilligan and other theorists clarify women's growth, the processes of separation and ego formation, the relationships of the self and the external world, that Dorothy Wordsworth presents in her writing.

Now perhaps no concern is so basic to romanticism as this narrative of self-development, as the story of the growth of the self and its relationship to the external world. For from Rousseau's *Confessions* on, the defining characteristic of romanticism may be the taking of the individual self as the primary literary topic. Dorothy Wordsworth's writing offers a female version of that narrative, of the complexities surrounding woman's psychological development. Carol Gilligan points to the different forms male and female narratives of this maturation process take. "From the different dynamics of separation and attachment in their gender identity formation through the divergence of identity and intimacy that marks their experience in the adolescent years, male and female voices typically speak of the importance of different truths, the former of the role of separation as it defines and empowers the self, the latter of the ongoing process of attachment that creates and sustains the human community" (156). Dorothy Wordsworth provides one woman's voice to tell this story.

In a certain sense, Dorothy Wordsworth's writing literally exists to serve a community. She begins her Grasmere journal because it will "give Wm Pleasure" (15),[2] and in it she collects material that forms the basis for some of his best-known poems. In the travel journals she often presents herself as a recorder of material to be used by her friends in their work. In a more general sense, Dorothy makes an investment in the community of romantic writers, an investment in the communal effort of Grasmere and the Lake District, of herself and such writers as her brother, Coleridge, Southey, and De Quincey. Grasmere was first of all a community of men and women in nature; it was a community of language; and it was finally a community of writing, a mutuality of writing energies in which each shared in his or her way. Of all the Lake District writers, Dorothy most obviously incorporates the various parts of this community in her work because she is the most willing to write as a consciousness existing in nature. Furthermore, her writing typically uses community to define individualism. Her writing exhibits those "relational capacities" characteristic of female development. "Because of their mothering by women," Chodorow asserts, "girls come to experience themselves as less separate than boys, as having more permeable ego boundaries. Girls come to define themselves more in relation to others" (93). It is, of course, a matter of degree, for William's writing certainly demonstrates constant involvement in the Grasmere community.

And finally, this was a community of male romanticism. In her essay "Feminist Criticism in the Wilderness," reprinted in

---

2. Quotations from the Grasmere and Alfoxden journals are from Mary Moorman's edition.

The New Feminist Criticism, Showalter describes some of the implications of this fact for Dorothy as a woman writer in her discussion of "muted and dominant groups." Both groups "generate beliefs or ordering ideas of social reality at the unconscious level, but dominant groups control the forms or structures in which consciousness can be articulated" (262). Existing in an intertextual relationship with the work of the men around her, Dorothy's writing explores these texts at the same time as it revises them. Her writing moves between the polarities of community and isolation. To maintain herself in the natural world of Grasmere as well as in its authorial community she needs to write. Ultimately, however, Dorothy finds little space within the field of language offered and experiences a breakdown of mind and voice.

Various romantic constructs—most obviously that of the appropriating self—are alien to her. Her journals are a form of romantic literature in which the central energies of romanticism—the will and the imagination—are radically subordinated to the presence of the receptive mind created by the natural scene before it. Dorothy's Grasmere journals in many ways move in that mode of consciousness William Wordsworth named "wise passiveness," but which he himself knew only fitfully and problematically. Dorothy's work represents the suspension of male romanticism as well as the suspension of its literary forms; hers is an antigenre, a wholeness of perception within incomplete/complete form. The romanticism of Dorothy's group often involves a coming to knowledge of the self through conscious appropriation of the object or through a pained recognition of the total otherness of the subject. Either way, the primacy of individual selfhood is insisted upon. Dorothy's writing, however, does not as habitually project this typically romantic dialectic of self and other. I am not, I should emphasize, setting up a simple opposition between Dorothy Wordsworth and the men of romanticism. To various extents, what I term Dorothy's "feminine consciousness" inheres in the writing of her male contemporaries, possibilities fully worked out by the current critical work on romantic writers that shows how apparent meanings involve their own opposites, how romantic faiths are subject to their own doubts, how, in short, texts encompass a play of ideas. But the quality and emphases of Dorothy's romanticism are as different from those of the men around her as is her writing from theirs.

The formed/formlessness of her work forces us to rethink our assumptions about the designs of a text, about the differentiations between language and lived experience, and about the relationship of a particular field of language to the words that surround it and from which it is drawn but from which it seeks to distinguish itself. The personal journals are narratives and rejections of narrative, a perpetual unfolding, an essentially formless sequence of words that nonetheless suggests structure and closure. The journals are not a simple series of happenings; events are emplotted and through sequence make various statements about the emotional life of the narrator. At the same time, however, as the journals contain the open-endedness of the form (journal as day-by-day, indefinitely continuous account), they also each seem to tell a story that can be read as an enclosed narrative: the story of William's marrying in the Grasmere journal or the story of a particular trip in the travel journals.

Above all, Dorothy Wordsworth needs to be seen as a person who makes stories, as a writer, as a woman passionately concerned with putting words together. My readings of Dorothy Wordsworth's prose and poetry concern themselves with the textual strategies she adopts, the way words appear together in her work, as well as the possible determining factors of her narrative voice. Because Dorothy Wordsworth, like so many other women writers, often chooses to work in the journal form, the tendency has been to slip into biographical summary in discussing her writing. The relationship of lived events to the text is in fact problematic, as is the relationship of the "I" telling the story of each journal to Dorothy Wordsworth the writer. What we have to work with, however, is not Dorothy Wordsworth but Dorothy Wordsworth's writing.

One approach to this writing is to place it in its social context, and that is what many biographers of Dorothy, usually writing about her as part of her brother's life, have to some extent done. Working from a Freudian model, Margaret Homans sees much of Dorothy's writing as following a "conventional psychic pattern of femininity" "in which the girl, mirroring the Oedipal pattern, must turn from her mother to her father as the object of her love, through finding a 'lack' both in herself and in her mother. This turn entails a repudiation of origins, which males never perform, and a consequent debasing of identity" (43). Homans distinguishes between sections of the journals and letters that contain "family news and domestic details" and passages in which Dorothy "takes up a traditional poetic project, such as the construction of a myth of origins, or the identification of a self, creative or not, in relation to the phenomenal world" (44). My approach is to consider all of Dorothy's writing as a text about a woman living in England in the early nineteenth century. Because nineteenth-century relationships were not the same as ours, twentieth-century theories of literary criticism and of human psychology cannot be taken as totally transhistorical. Most obviously in Dorothy Wordsworth's case, her involvement with her brother and his household is not one that would be currently common. On the other hand, certain constants do exist in interpersonal relationships in Western culture. Texts describing these relationships are illuminated by the analyses and models of human development that our contemporary theorists of language and psychology provide, especially since they take into consideration structures of dominance and subordination that have defined Western societies. Though Dorothy no doubt internalized the models of women that Freud describes, paradigms built around incompleteness and lack, her writing often voices the continuities and power inherent in feminine growth as outlined by feminist analysts.

The works I consider in Chapter II under the title "Home" in part project this development. These writings pertain to her life with William and his family, especially Lake District existence: the Alfoxden and Grasmere journals, *A Narrative Concerning George and Sarah Green,* "Mary Jones and her Pet-lamb," and certain of her letters. Some of the complexities in these works come from their expression of both the way Western culture has traditionally viewed women—the model Freud puts together—and the way women naturally view themselves, as outlined by schemes of feminine development that do not work from a masculine model. And if, as modern language theorists tell us, language is a system of differences and writing ensures difference, then the very setting down of words is at odds with the way Dorothy needs them to bring about presences of self and natural objects. Other complexities in her work come from the way she both asserts and displaces herself as subject in her writing.

I then consider the travel journals that compose so much of her output. Setting the structures of her own imagination against those of her brother, she describes herself as the woman who goes out to seek experience, as the woman who makes unconventional life choices. The self-definition of her journals is also evident in her poetry, which I discuss in Chapter IV. Her poetry, especially that written in the 1820s and '30s, is at once more personal and more willed than her other work. The dialectical relation of her poems to her brother's poems produces some extraordinary moments that revoke the usual wisdom about her relationship as a writer to her brother. Unlike her journals, her poems are determined, at times even aggressive.

As a creator of poetry and prose, Dorothy wrote as part of the great movement of English romanticism. My concluding chapter, "Dorothy Wordsworth and the Women of Romanticism," shows some of the ways in which Dorothy and other women of the period deal with this tradition. The writing of these women exhibits a pattern of subversive pressure within the male-dominant romantic movement that results in creation of a kind of feminine romanticism. Appendix One collects her poems for the first time. Appendix Two provides the first published text of "Mary Jones and her Pet-lamb." My recovery of these texts was itself a study in subversive pressures, but finally, here they are. The as yet unpublished later journals produce an unavoidable gap in the effort to provide a fuller account of her work. Even so, what we can know of Dorothy Wordsworth's writing is a good deal more than we may have thought.

II.

Home

✤ ✤ ✤ ✤ ✤ DESCRIPTIONS OF DOROTHY WORDS-
worth inevitably focus on her eyes. Neither "soft," nor "fierce,"
nor "bold," De Quincey writes, in "Literary Reminiscences,"
"they were wild and startling, and hurried in their motion"
(2:238). Coleridge sees "—her eye watchful in minutest observation of nature—and her taste a perfect electrometer—it bends,
protrudes, and draws in, at subtlest beauties & most recondite
faults" (*Letters* 1:330). Seated above Tintern Abbey, her brother
tells her he can "read / My former pleasures in the shooting
lights / Of thy wild eyes" (ll. 117–119). As Dorothy Wordsworth's eyes are a main personal characteristic, so they enable the
most obvious characteristic of her journals: minute detailing of
the natural world in the context of daily life in the country with
her friends and family.

Her vision seems disturbingly narrow at times. She does not
write of the world outside of Grasmere; she does not write of
the great philosophical and political issues of the day. She seems
to say little of her own feelings. At one point in the Grasmere
journals she writes of an apple core thrown aside by William,
"Oh the Darling! Here is one of his bitten apples! I can hardly
find in my heart to throw it into the fire" (97). Now the sense of
self of a women who writes lovingly of her brother's garbage
must be as unsatisfactory to the modern reader as to the late

nineteenth-century editors, who found in Dorothy's journals an embarrassing amount of detail about the Wordsworth household.

So extreme have been the responses that some of the journal manuscripts have disappeared altogether. Coverings were sewn over sections of the Grasmere journals and parts were inked over with heavy black lines. These intense reactions perhaps complement the intensity of the responses to her surroundings that characterize Dorothy Wordsworth's personal journals. They reveal a writer who insistently and coherently puts down what she sees. Her obsession exists, however, in the context of a communal order. Her writing organizes itself around the continually inverting oppositions of community and that which is set apart from the group, around unity and fragmentation, around the telling of personal and communal coherence and isolate autism.

Although entries for only about three and one-half months remain of her Alfoxden notebook, they nonetheless reveal how Dorothy worked through certain traditional techniques to arrive at the unique mode of her subsequent journals. The countryside of Alfoxden, her brother William, her friend Samuel Taylor Coleridge—these are the prime components of her text. The naming by later readers of Dorothy's journals according to the place where they were kept is not arbitrary identification, as revealed by the first entry of this notebook, which demonstrates the depth of her relationship to her surroundings. The notebook opens with a description of how winter was losing its hold on the countryside and includes both natural and cultivated landscape.

Alfoxden, *20th January 1798.* The green paths down the hill-sides are channels for streams. The young wheat is streaked by silver lines of water running between the ridges, the sheep are gathered together on the slopes. After the wet dark days, the country seems more populous. It peoples itself in the sunbeams. The garden, mimic of spring, is gay with flowers. The purple-starred hepatica spreads itself in the sun, and the clustering snow-drops put forth their white heads, at first upright, ribbed with green, and like a rosebud; when completely opened, hanging their heads down-wards, but slowly lengthening their slender stems. The slanting woods of an unvarying brown, showing the light through the thin net-work of their upper boughs. Upon the highest ridge of that round hill covered with planted oaks, the shafts of the trees show in the light like the columns of a ruin.(1)

Woods and hillsides coexist with the garden that "mimics" spring and planted oaks whose shafts "show in the light like the columns of a ruin," a simile that brings Dorothy's description close to the aesthetics of the picturesque tradition.[1] She does not place herself in the text until the second entry, when she assumes a physically superior position from which to view her material, the natural scene. Similarly, some entries later, in what is almost a cliché of Burkean sublimity, she describes walking "to the top of a high hill to see a fortification. Again sat down to feed upon the prospect; a magnificent scene, *curiously* spread out for even minute inspection, though so extensive that the mind is afraid to calculate its bounds" (8). The mind's fear before notions of in-finity generated by the view is an element of the doctrine of the sublime, as is her general approach to the "prospect."

Frequently in line with the attitudes and diction of writers on the sublime and picturesque, Dorothy's text also often shares language with her brother and with Coleridge. Here, most ob-viously, the idea of "feeding" on the scene corresponds to a statement like the one William makes at the end of *The Prelude* when the prospect before him becomes "The perfect image of a mighty mind, / Of one that feeds upon infinity" (13:69–70). The words that compose the Alfoxden journal also compose William's and Coleridge's poems, raising several possibilities. Because of William's prominence and dominance, the tendency is to see Dorothy as linguistically dependent: surely she cannot come equipped with the language her brother possesses. What

1. The standard treatment of Dorothy Wordsworth's relationship to the pic-turesque tradition is John Nabholtz's "Dorothy Wordsworth and the Pictur-esque." Nabholtz discusses Dorothy's descriptions of natural scenes in the con-text of writing by William Gilpin, Uvedale Price, and Richard Payne Knight.

the early journals may evidence, however, is the mutual development of a vocabulary that Dorothy eventually uses in her own
way in the journals and to which she reverts years later in her
poetry. Often Dorothy works with words or subjects well before William. The one manuscript bit of the Alfoxden journal is
a copy William made of the opening entry, probably, Mary
Moorman speculates in her introduction to the journals, to use
in his current verse (viii). Coleridge, too, depended for language on Dorothy's journal, as the evidence of *Christabel* shows.

Some textual intersections are obvious. Dorothy writes, "At
once the clouds seemed to cleave asunder, and left her in the centre of a black-blue vault" (2). In "A Night-piece" William writes,
"—the clouds are split / Asunder,—and above his head he sees /
The clear Moon, and the glory of the heavens" (ll. 11–13). Or
she writes of taking shelter "under the hollies, during a hail-
shower. The withered leaves danced with the hailstones" (10).
William writes in "A Whirl-blast from behind the hill," "I sat
within an undergrove / Of tallest hollies, tall and green; / A
fairer bower was never seen. / From year to year the spacious
floor / With withered leaves is covered o'er, / And all the year
the bower is green. / But see! where'er the hailstones drop / The
withered leaves all skip and hop;" (ll. 6–13). Dorothy writes,
"One only leaf upon the top of a tree—the sole remaining leaf—
danced round and round like a rag blown by the wind" (9). In
Christabel, Coleridge writes, "The one red leaf, the last of its
clan, / That dances as often as dance it can" (1:49–50). Dorothy
writes "The spring continues to advance very slowly" (11). Coleridge writes in *Christabel*, "And the Spring comes slowly up this
way" (1:22). The list could be continued, but perhaps more interesting are the less overt parallels, the places where the textures
of various works approximate each other, rather than places
where the actual words are the same. When Dorothy views
clouds spread over water as she stands on a hill—"The clouds
beneath our feet spread themselves to the water, and the clouds
of the sky almost joined them" (5)—or when she focuses on
"The moon crescent" (14) or "the waving of the spiders' threads"
(6) or when she writes "heard the nightingale; saw a glow-worm"

(14), we can hear *The Prelude* or "Peter Bell" or *The Rime of the Ancient Mariner* or "The Nightingale" or "The Glow-worm."

In the Alfoxden journal, Dorothy begins the autobiography that is so different from, yet so much a part of, the life-writing of her brother. William's prospects are finally most riveting as they grow in the mind, as they take on imaginative life, becoming "a dream, / A prospect in my mind" (*Prelude* 2:369–370). Dorothy keeps the object before her, describing the coexistence of her own being and the world of objects around her. Her opening lines tell of the countryside as "It peoples itself in the sunbeams." Here the verb helps tie nature as process to the journal keeper's moment of writing that process.

Dorothy's insistence on keeping the world in front of her presents a consciousness existing on account of all that passes before it. Her frequent cataloguing may be a seeking of resistant objects against which she can set herself, not only to define herself but also to keep herself from feeling overwhelmed by what she calles "expansion" in the Alfoxden journal. Her descriptions of the season's change in terms of "multitudes" inevitably "advancing" and "expanding," her insistence on minute description, could point to a certain fear of what is happening around her, of nature's autonomous process, and a need to control it through naming. She often appears to be testing for what is real; perhaps objective description is one way she has of defining her own subjectivity, of arriving at those distinctions between herself and all that is not the self that constitute the formation of an individual ego. The infant discovers resistant objects that help her comprehend her own separateness from the external world. The continuation of this testing process characterizes Dorothy's writing and so defines the self her writing constructs.

One conventional view might find in this writing a being stuck in some kind of infantile state. To read Dorothy Wordsworth in terms of a male developmental model is to see her caught in the primary differentiation process most often characterizing the very young child; she gives voice in her writing to this arrested development. When William writes in "Tintern Abbey" that he can see his former self in his sister, he represents the idea of Dorothy as childlike, naïve, respondent: "and in thy voice I catch / The language of my former heart, and read / My former pleasures in the shooting lights / Of thy wild eyes. Oh! yet a little while / May I behold in thee what I was once, / My dear, dear Sister!" (ll. 116–121). The development he describes for himself does not occur in Dorothy's case. Isabella Fenwick's note to the "Immortality Ode" clarifies this "normal" maturation process. William tells of how at times he was drawn back into a state of oneness with the external world, a state of undifferentiated selfhood characterizing preexistence or the newborn infant. "I was often unable to think of external things as having external existence, and I communed with all that I saw as something not apart from, but inherent in, my own immaterial nature." Fearful of such absorption, he grasps a tree or wall to "recall" himself to reality. He asserts himself, finding a resistant object that assures his own existence. "In later periods of life," he continues, "I have deplored, as we all have reason to do, a subjugation of an opposite character" (PW 4:463). The aggressive ego subjugates all that is not the self. But what if we don't "all have reason" to deplore this subjugation? The generally accepted paradigm William sets out fails to materialize in Dorothy's case. But if she does not fit the pattern, it may be not because she is somehow underdeveloped but rather because she possesses a consciousness that is simply not aggressive in the usual manner of Western, masculine humanity, a consciousness that does not enter into that "subjugation" her brother deplores, a consciousness that is in the continual process of realizing not only *what* it is but *that* it is. The writing of this particular consciousness would demonstrate the relationship with the world that we see recorded in so much of Dorothy Wordsworth's work.

Although this consciousness might be conventionally regarded as "immature," another possibility is offered if we read Dorothy Wordsworth in the context of models of development that emphasize certain differences between male and female maturation. From birth, children are physically and emotionally attached to their mothers. Women mother; fathers are generally absent. This dynamic, feminist psychological theorists have shown, has a profound effect on how people grow up. Because women are identified with their mothers, attachment remains part of their separation process. For women, ego formation occurs in the context of differentiation from an other that is yet the same, a process charged with possibilities not present in the clearer path along which boys proceed towards the culturally well defined opposite of masculinity. The identification of the mother and her female child allows feminine growth to contain a kind of continuity that our culture has chosen to devalue; we have made male sexual difference from the mother positive. But women, Nancy Chodorow points out, do not need to "define themselves in terms of the denial of preoedipal relational modes to the same extent as do boys. Therefore, regression to these modes tends not to feel as much a basic threat to their ego" (167). Manifestation of earlier behavior—reality testing, for instance—may be seen as continuity rather than regression. And as Carol Gilligan demonstrates, the model that equates development with separation is both reductive and falsely linear (151). Maintaining what Gilligan calls a "reiterative counterpoint in human experience," Dorothy provides the record of an ego existing in the natural world even as it continually sets itself against the exterior to create and define itself. William characteristically writes of his relationship with the world in terms of interchange, interpenetration, or subjugation. Dorothy, on the other hand, does not tell the story of her life to create a personal myth of self but rather describes the natural world and her own being as they exist together. Journal writing, detailing the surrounding world, becomes for Dorothy a process of consciousness formation.

As she defines herself in her journals, Dorothy describes herself literally as part of a group. She walks with her brother or with Coleridge; the first-person pronoun is usually plural: "we were in the wood;" "when we left home;" "The wind blew so keen in our faces that we felt ourselves inclined to seek the covert of the wood" (3–4). The examples need not all be listed. The singular "I" is strangely absent and is not usually part of the fragmented, elliptical phrases she masses in her descriptions. One possible explanation for this trait is that Dorothy's "I" is so tenuous that she cannot assert it as she writes. That possibility also contains its opposite: the writing of "I" must displace the presence of the writer as it substitutes itself for it, thus making the form of Dorothy's sentences indicate a kind of negative assertion through her refusal to displace by signing.

The first two uses of "I" in the Alfoxden journal appear in the context of seemingly opposite phenomena. During her walk on February 3 she says, "I never saw such a union of earth, sky, and sea" (5). The next day, walking to Stowey with Coleridge, she remembers, "I saw one solitary strawberry flower under a hedge" (5). The observing "I" perceives extreme coherence and unity; it also perceives isolation and singularity. Yet the strawberry flower, though solitary, is allowed its very solitariness by the hedge and the flowers that surround it, literally as well as structurally, in Dorothy's description. "Midges or small flies spinning in the sunshine; the songs of the lark and redbreast; daisies upon the turf; the hazels in blossom; honeysuckles budding. I saw one solitary strawberry flower under a hedge. The furze gay with blossom" (5). The isolate objects Dorothy focuses on are defined in part by their larger contexts.

Though it lacks the emphasis provided by the first-person pronoun, another entry further defines this opposition. "The whole appearance of the wood was enchanting; and each tree, taken singly, was beautiful" (7). The conjunction here renders the two phrases logically equivalent. The group, the wood, and each single tree are coordinate in the structure of the sentence. As the group in this observation allows that which is not part of it at the same time as it contains it, so the imagination that structures itself in and structures the Alfoxden journal both reflects and revises the community that contains it.

Though it would be misleading to draw too many conclusions from the fragmentary Alfoxden journal, much of what Dorothy does there is further developed in her best-known work—what has come to be called the Grasmere journals. The opening entry of the journals establishes the concerns and techniques of the notebooks kept through January 1803: Dorothy's life with William, his courtship of and marriage to Mary Hutchinson, his separation from Dorothy, William's poetry and the writing going on around her, the natural world of Grasmere, the observing of that world, the purpose of journal writing, the social and cultural changes in nineteenth-century England.

May 14 1800 [*Wednesday*]. Wm and John set off into Yorkshire after dinner at ½ past 2 o'clock, cold pork in their pockets. I left them at the turning of the Low-wood bay under the trees. My heart was so full that I could hardly speak to W. when I gave him a farewell kiss. I sate a long time upon a stone at the margin of the lake, and after a flood of tears my heart was easier. The lake looked to me I knew not why dull and melancholy, and the weltering on the shores seemed a heavy sound. I walked as long as I could amongst the stones of the shore. The wood rich in flowers. A beautiful yellow, palish yellow flower, that looked thick round and double, and smelt very sweet—I supposed it was a ranunculus—Crowfoot, the grassy-leaved Rabbit-toothed white flower, strawberries, geranium—scentless violet, anemones two kinds, orchises, primroses. The heckberry very beautiful, the crab coming out as a low shrub. Met a blind man, driving a very large beautiful Bull and a cow—he walked with two sticks. Came home by Clappersgate. The valley very green, many sweet views up to Rydale head when I could juggle away the fine houses, but they disturbed me even more than when I have been happier. One beautiful view of the Bridge, without Sir Michael's. Sate down very often, though it was cold. I resolved to write a journal of the time till W. and J. return, and I set about keeping my resolve because I will not quarrel with myself, and because I shall give Wm Pleasure by it when he comes home again. At Rydale a woman of the village, stout and well dressed, begged a halfpenny—she had never she said done it before, but these hard times—Arrived at home with a bad head-ach, set some slips of privett. The evening cold, had a fire—my face now flame-coloured. It is nine o'clock. I shall soon go to bed. A young woman begged at the door—she had come from Manchester on Sunday morn with two shillings and a slip of paper which she supposed a Bank note—it was a cheat. She had buried her husband and three children within a year and a half—all in one grave—burying very dear—paupers all put in one place—20 shillings paid for as much ground as will bury a man—a stone to be put over it or the right will be lost—11/6 each time the ground is opened. Oh! that I had a letter from William! (15–16)

The entry begins and ends with her brother's absence: he leaves Grasmere for Yorkshire; the wished-for letter would necessarily come from a person who is away. Given that William has been gone for less than eight hours, her exclamatory desire for a letter might be viewed as somewhat extreme. But writing, in the form of the letter and of the journal itself, is seen as evoking presence not only of a distant loved one but of the journal writer herself, who writes so as not to "quarrel with" herself, so as not to be self-divided, so as to maintain her own coherency. As in the Alfoxden journal, the moment of writing connects with the process it describes: "—my face now flame-coloured. It is nine o'clock."

The particular writing of the Grasmere journals also serves the community: it will bring William "Pleasure." Given the charged meaning of the word *pleasure* among those surrounding William Wordsworth, Dorothy asks a great deal of her writing. The "grand elementary principle of pleasure," counsels the Preface to *Lyrical Ballads,* is a force by which man "knows, and feels, and lives, and moves" (167).[2]

As she begins her work, pleasure in the sense of enjoyment is decidedly missing. The landscape reflects her mood, the lake being "dull" and "melancholy." Her eye rests on one object, this time one yellow flower in a bed "rich in flowers." Like the single Alfoxden strawberry flower, the ranunculus is named distinct from yet defined by its surroundings. This characteristic mode of viewing helps shape the journal. "Our favorite Birch tree," for instance, "yielding to the gusty wind," is "like a Spirit of water" surrounded by other birch trees but "a creature by its own self among them" (61). Or, a single foxglove looks like a star because it is surrounded by snow (72). It is, I think, appropriate to see reflected in these descriptions both Dorothy's emotional states and her position as a solitary woman seeking definition from those around her, "a creature by [her] own self among them." She describes what Carol Gilligan calls "a self delineated through connection" (35).

The position is one of extreme vulnerability, threatened from

2. For a discussion of the concept of pleasure and what it meant to the romantics, see Lionel Trilling's essay, "The Fate of Pleasure."

without and within. An entry in January 1802 images this fragility. "I found a strawberry blossom in a rock. The little slender flower had more courage than the green leaves, for *they* were but half expanded and half grown, but the blossom was spread full out. I uprooted it rashly, and I felt as if I had been committing an outrage, so I planted it again. It will have but a stormy life of it, but let it live if it can" (83). The general landscape of Grasmere, so literally and spiritually necessary to Dorothy's writing is also constantly threatened, as she emphasizes in her opening entry. The "fine houses" that have been built, the development and "gentrification" that have occurred are particularly disturbing to her view, especially saddened as she is by her brother's departure. She attempts to "juggle them away," adjust her mode of seeing to preserve the countryside she loves. The constructing of fine houses and their grounds changes the physical structure of Grasmere.

In the first entry, another kind of disruption and change is brought up by two of the figures she has encountered. The blind man with two sticks and the young beggar woman are the first of a parade of vagrants who pass through town, people affected by the economic pressures of the time, dislocated from the land by enclosure and the movement of capital to industrializing centers. The figures Dorothy observes become the solitaries of William's poems. In Dorothy's work they become a means of focusing ideas about communal charity, about her own center at Grasmere and the possible disintegration of her chosen manner of life.

For even as the Grasmere journals describe community, unity, and coherence, they also detail breakdown and discontinuity. William and John are going to Yorkshire to visit Mary Hutchinson, whose marriage to William will bring about radical change in Dorothy's life. If we wish to find a narrative structure for this text, we may say it is Dorothy's story of William's engagement and marriage to Mary Hutchinson. She tells the story not by presenting an actual analysis of her feelings but through careful delineation of details. The ways she arranges descriptions and the natural objects brought into the journal define her emotional devastation at her brother's marriage. She relates the exact time of William's departure—"½ past 2 o'clock"—and also notes that her brothers have "cold pork in their pockets." Detail distances anxiety, displaces it onto the world around her. Describing birds, trees, flowers, stars—she describes what Mary's presence may do to her life. Once the wedding occurs, the journal has for all important purposes run its course, and it is soon left off.

As 1802 progresses, she increasingly uses such endearments as "my beloved" and "my darling" to refer to William. On March 23 her description retains a perfect moment with him. "The fire flutters and the watch ticks I hear nothing else save the Breathing of my Beloved and he now and then pushes his book forward and turns over a leaf" (106). Fixed in her writing, the breath of life, time, literature, and William are unified. The next day, they walk "to Rydale for letters. It was a beautiful spring morning— warm and quiet with mists. We found a letter from M.H. I made a vow that we would not leave this country for G. Hill" (106). That Mary's home, Gallow Hill, will replace the home Dorothy has shared with William at Grasmere is one feared outcome of the marriage.

At the end of May 1802 Gallow Hill again intrudes to begin a sequence of details that organize more of Dorothy's feelings about the marriage. "I was much better. I made bread and a wee Rhubarb Tart and batter pudding for William. We sate in the orchard after dinner. William finished his poem on Going for Mary. I wrote it out" (129). The poem she copies, "Our Departure" (entitled "A Farewell" when it appeared in 1807), is a poem about leaving Grasmere, "The loveliest spot that man hath ever found," (l. 6) to go fetch a woman who will love the place as much as they. The poem catalogues what must have been Dorothy's own concerns. In its focus on a place as defining a mode of existence, the poem sharpens Dorothy's own focus on Grasmere as a place that allows the life she has chosen. The metaphor of wedding—"to you herself will wed" (l. 31)—to describe the gentle maid's relationship to the place names the literal event in her own and William's life. It is all too easy, the poem points out, for one's relationship to a location to alter, since the place is "most fickle," "wayward," and "easy-hearted." The new presence must also change the particular combination of nature and people. Not having been part of the past that helps determine the present there, the newcomer will have to be taught how things are. Everything, even the past, must now be shared, but this new relationship cannot be completely happy for Dorothy. The poem's final image of creeping into the "bosom" of the place, this time with Mary in tow, must connect in Dorothy's psyche to the first great deprivation of her life, the death of her mother, which meant a loss of the maternal bosom. The new presences William provides evoke for Dorothy the greatest desolation.

Having written in her journal of copying this poem that touches on so many of her worst hidden fears, she speaks of breaking her tooth and notes, "They will soon be gone" (129). The arrangement of detail here is again most significant. Although her teeth bothered her a great deal, only at this point does she write of losing them all. Loss of teeth often refers to loss of sexual power, a connection that Dorothy indicates with the next sentence: "Let that pass I shall be beloved—I want no more." The loss of Grasmere as special home to her and William, the arrival of Mary as his wife, the content of the poem she has just copied—all relate to loss of her brother's undivided love, which she must translate into loss of power and happiness. The resolution she appears to find—"I shall be beloved—I want no more"—can be turned to its opposite: I want everything.

The next entry provides a different mode of describing her situation.

Tuesday [*1st*]. A very sweet day, but a sad want of rain. We went into the Orchard before dinner after I had written to M.H. Then on to Mr. Olliff's Intakes. We found some torn Birds' nests. The Columbine was growing upon the Rocks, here and there a solitary plant—sheltered and shaded by the tufts and Bowers of trees. It is a graceful slender creature, a female seeking retirement and growing freest and most graceful where it is most alone. I observed that the more shaded plants were always the tallest. A short note and gooseberries from Coleridge. (129)

Nests, homes, have been destroyed. But the columbine remains strong. This flower is one of those solitary objects through the description of which Dorothy organizes the description of her own state. Feminine, shy, slender, graceful—it is still independent. It is also set off by that which surrounds it, growing tallest because it is shaded. The writer finds virtue in the kind of isolation Dorothy may experience, as well as in the position of being overshadowed. Here, the content of nature allows the content of the narrator's life. The entry closes by turning to Coleridge, whose situation might be viewed as a warning of the devastating possibilities of marriage.

Coleridge's presence is an important one in the Grasmere journals, as it is in the Alfoxden journal. He supplements her brother in Dorothy's emotional and artistic life, and William is not altogether gracious about his friend's position in Dorothy's affections. Dorothy almost accuses William of lack of sensitivity when he derides her feelings for Coleridge. "C. had a sweet day for his ride. Every sight and every sound reminded me of him dear dear fellow—of his many walks to us by day and by night—of all dear things. I was melancholy and could not talk, but at last I eased my heart by weeping—nervous blubbering says William. It is not so. O how many, many reasons have I to be anxious for him" (57). One reason for her anxiousness may be the marriage Coleridge enters into, a frequent topic of discussion in the Wordsworth household.

For Dorothy, marriage, although the conventional choice, is not necessarily the proper choice for a woman or a man. She herself, as the Grasmere journal shows, makes a different kind of commitment—to life as a member of her brother's community, to helping him in his work, and to doing her own writing when she could, forsaking the possibility of her own household. Her choice may seem strange, even neurotic. Yet it did bring with it involvement in the creation of what may be the century's greatest English poetry, and it did provide material for her own writing. Still, it is not a situation she can accept easily. Of a May morning she writes: "He completely finished his poems I finished Derwent's frocks" (123). The equation of poems and frocks effected by the lack of punctuation in the sentence and by the repetition of the verb may describe a household in which everyone carries out his appointed task and in which every task is important. Given the importance placed on writing in this household, however, neither Dorothy nor the reader can be totally convinced that sewing and writing are equal. Here the relation of words in the sentence opposes what is being signified.

Dorothy's description of the specific organization of the Grasmere household at the time of her brother's wedding further reveals her pain. She cannot keep up daily entries, shifting instead to a long narrative account. Having written briefly of their last trip alone together, their journey to France to settle matters with Annette Vallon, Dorothy describes their arrival at Gallow Hill and the wedding day.

We stayed in London till Wednesday the 22nd of September, and arrived at Gallow Hill on Friday 24th September. Mary first met us in the avenue. She looked so fat and well that we were made very happy by the sight of her. Then came Sara, and last of all Joanna. Tom was forking corn standing upon the corn cart. We dressed ourselves immediately and got tea—the garden looked gay with asters and sweet peas. I looked at everything with tranquillity and happiness—was ill on Saturday and on Sunday and continued to be during most of the time of our stay. Jack and George came on Friday Evening 1st October. On Saturday 2nd we rode to Hackness, William Jack George and Sara single, I behind Tom. On Sunday 3rd Mary and Sara were busy packing. On Monday 4th October 1802, my Brother William was married to Mary Hutchinson. I slept a good deal of the night and rose fresh and well in the morning. At a little after 8 o'clock I saw them go down the avenue towards the Church. William had parted from me upstairs. I gave him the wedding ring—with how deep a blessing! I took it from my forefinger where I had worn it the whole of the night before—he slipped it again onto my finger and blessed me fervently. When they were absent my dear little Sara prepared the breakfast. I kept myself as quiet as I could, but when I saw the two men running up the walk, coming to tell us it was over, I could stand it no longer and threw myself on the bed where I lay in stillness, neither hearing or seeing anything, till Sara came upstairs to me and said 'They are coming'. This forced me from the bed where I lay and I moved I knew not how straight forward, faster than my strength could carry me till I met my beloved William and fell upon his bosom. He and John Hutchinson led me to the house and there I stayed to welcome my dear Mary. (153–154)

Her continuous illness during this time may be a physical manifestation of her uneasiness; that she would remark on sleeping
most of the night indicates she must not have expected to do so.
She interrupts her account of the wedding to detail her own
ceremony with William before his departure for the church.
The description of their ring ceremony is erased in the manuscript, indicating that somebody, perhaps Dorothy herself, was
uneasy about its implications. Her narrative during the ceremony does not focus on her own agitation but, perhaps to control or to avoid her feelings, shifts to Sara's preparing breakfast.
Her control breaks down as the men come "to tell us it was
over," phrasing that connotes the ending of something unpleasant. One cannot imagine the same phrase applied to a purely
joyous happening, especially when the narrator continues with
"I could stand it no longer." The pronoun "it," unusually im-
precise for Dorothy, includes both the wedding and things in
general. She simply will not at this point maintain her own coherency. She throws herself on the bed "neither hearing or
seeing anything." The text involutes here, going against the
rules it has established for itself, shattering the unities it has
been erecting. Seeing and writing, the main principles of the
journals, are inverted. Dorothy's ambivalence about her life in
the Grasmere community, her ambivalence about her brother's
marriage, her ambivalence about the investments she has made
in writing and in nature overwhelm her; here is the negative center from which the positive field of her journals radiate.

   Yet at the same time as she refuses to be a part of the community, she uses her brother's words to make that refusal signify,
literally becoming the "she" of "A slumber did my spirit seal."
At the same time as she is isolated from the Grasmere community, she needs their words. This momentary collapse prefigures
the reality of her later years: complete withdrawal from the
community. On the wedding morning, however, Sara's words
force her back to consciousness, if not to solid reality, and somehow—again she maintains decidedly decreased awareness of
herself—she reaches William. She is finally in the position of
standing with the groom to welcome home his bride, a version
of what she actually must do: welcome Mary into Dove Cottage.

This entry covering an extended period of time, rather than a day-by-day account, continues as the three make their way back to Grasmere. At the first stop Dorothy describes in detail, they visit a graveyard. Here she finds a message on a gravestone about how the "unfortunate woman" buried there "had been neglected by her Relations," a possibility she herself must have dreaded even more after her brother's marriage (155). On the first night of their journey home, she "prevails upon" William—a phrase that indicates strong persuasion—to leave Mary by the fire at the inn and accompany her on a walk to some ruins. She also tries to maintain something of their past relationship as they progress towards Grasmere by returning frequently in her descriptions to previous journeys she and William had made without Mary. Her own move to Grasmere with William finally takes on a certain sanctity; returning from the wedding, she writes of "our pilgrimage together" (160). Marriage interrupts that holy journey even as it maintains it through this descriptive journal. Mary's presence is finalized as Dorothy ends her journal with their unpacking, their baking of bread, and a description of "the first walk that I had taken with my Sister" (161).

Placing these events from her emotional and lived experience in the narrative structure of the journal, Dorothy allows certain images and references to pick up resonances as the work progresses. In her frequent descriptions of birds, for example, are reflections of her own situation. "Stone chats" (perhaps sandpipers) amuse her with what she hears as their "restless" but "unwearied voices," adjectives also befitting her own writing and actions during William's absences (16). Anticipating William's homecoming, she happily sees "The little birds busy making love" (24). When her brother returns, part of her joy includes an observation about how "The birds were singing, and all looked fresh, though not day" (25). Birds also help describe the holiness and harmony of her time with William in Grasmere.

When we turned the corner of our little shelter we saw the Church and the whole vale. It is a blessed place. The Birds were about us on all sides—Skobbys Robins Bullfinches. Crows now and then flew over our heads as we were warned by the sound of the beating of the air above. We stayed till the light of day was going and the little Birds had begun to settle their singing. But there was a thrush not far off that seemed to sing louder and clearer than the thrushes had sung when it was quite day. (118)

The vision is one of both unity and individual object as again she focuses on the single thrush, isolated but part of its surroundings in a parallel of Dorothy's own position.

Her fears about what Mary's presence will do to her harmonious nest are perhaps reflected in the story of the swallows that she tells in the second part of the journal. Having written of a letter "speaking to Mary about having a cat," Dorothy talks to William about "the little Birds keeping us company" (136), and he tells her how a baby bird perched on his leg. The reader must wonder exactly what the new presences—cat and woman—will do to such scenes. She describes two swallows that have arrived at their cottage. "The swallows come to the sitting-room window as if wishing to build but I am afraid they will not have courage for it, but I believe they will build at my room window. They twitter and make a bustle and a little chearful song hanging against the panes of glass, with their soft white bellies close to the glass, and their forked fish-like tails. They swim round and round and again they come.—It was a sweet evening" (137). She observes the swallows carefully, often mentioning them as she describes "sweet" times with her brother and taking pleasure in them as creatures self-sufficient to each other, singing and building a home for themselves. The happy scene is shattered when the nest falls, prompting Dorothy to retell her particular relationship with them, the way they had built the nest, sat on it side by side, the way she watched them hour after hour, especially when William was away. A missing manuscript page evidently describes the rebuilding of the nest; four days later Dorothy goes "out on purpose to see their faces" and is pleased to see them sitting "side by side both looking down into the garden" (142). A week later in phrasing of double domesticity she notes: "The swallows have completed their beautiful nest. I baked bread and pies" (145). Two days later, however, she must leave both beautiful homes for Gallow Hill. In prose that fragments, perhaps with her distress, she writes her sadness also in terms of the swallows. "O beautiful place! Dear Mary William. The horse is come Friday morning, so I must give over. William is eating his Broth. I must prepare to go. The Swallows I must leave them the well the garden the Roses, all. Dear creatures!! they sang last night after I was in bed—seemed to be singing to one another, just before they settled to rest for the night. Well, I must go. Farewell.——" (146). In this last entry before Mary is brought to Grasmere, the moment of writing again becomes part of the telling of the story, and language allows what coherence can be managed.

The swallows are not the only repeated reference that helps organize Dorothy's emotions about her life with William and Mary. A similar use is made of the moon and moonlight in the Grasmere journal. Superb descriptive artist that she is, Dorothy often uses moonlight to enhance her effects. Thus description takes on added depth when she writes "moonlight lay upon the hills like snow" or of the moon shining "like herrings in the water" (41, 49). Like the swallows, however, the moon is also an object that bears upon Dorothy's emotional state. Her joy at reading *Lyrical Ballads* exclaims itself through "Blessings on that Brother of mine! Beautiful new moon over Silver How" (98). Having received a letter from William and Mary, she starts home, walking with Thomas Wilkinson, whom she sees as mercilessly questioning her, "like a catechizer."

> Every question was like the snapping of a little thread about my heart I was so full of thoughts of my half-read letter and other things. I was glad when he left me. Then I had time to look at the moon while I was thinking over my own throughts. The moon travelled through the clouds tinging them yellow as she passed along, with two stars near her, one larger than the other. These stars grew or diminished as they passed from or went into the clouds. (108)

The feminine moon, seen with two stars, appears as Dorothy mulls over her own thoughts. Characteristically, she does not analyze her emotions but, rather, focuses on a natural image that may relate to her concerns. No direct equations should be set up between Dorothy and the moon and between William and Mary and the big and little star. The moon is, however, a traditional symbol of feminine psychology, of virginity, of the Diana figure, woman of the forest—all of which associations apply to Dorothy. And here the moon is dominant. It is the one constant of the trio, changing the sky when it passes, as Dorothy's narrative voice, in the context of the journal, shifts the focus from the human to the natural, controlling the scene. Here the moon accompanies Dorothy's self-collection, but in another reference, the moon reveals disruption and disunity. Having read a letter from Mary, Dorothy notes she has a headache and then returns to a description from several days before: "On friday evening the moon hung over the Northern side of the highest point of Silver How, like a gold ring snapped in two and shaven off at the ends it was so narrow" (99). The circle snaps; harmony is broken. Dorothy thus portrays her pain and one possible consequence of William's marriage, the breaking of their circle.

The journals can thus be seen as a story—the story of William Wordsworth's courtship and marriage. Yet the perfectly plausible narrative structure I have been imposing on the Grasmere journal does not fully account for various sections of the text, for the particular way the journal is put together, or for certain passages analyzed in that context. It especially does not account for certain kinds of discontinuities in the journal or for the massed phrases of detail presented. Most obviously problematic is what ought to be the climax of such a narrative, the wedding ceremony. This passage is literally a nondescription. To have a narrative structure, to order the elements of a text into a narrative, there must be a center, but Dorothy provides a noncenter. At the point when the story of her brother's marriage should be moving to the ceremony, she literally and figuratively blacks out.

Moreover, Dorothy blurs the borders of the text, setting it up as a perpetual unfolding. Units of "entries" rather than chapters or verses compose the journals. These, in turn, are composed of sequences that signify by implication or repetition rather than through direct authorial indication of relationship. She confuses the conventional interaction in narrative of the reader and the text by projecting the continuous presence of an already situated reader, William. All these characteristics of Dorothy's writing in the Grasmere journals militate against the kind of reading I have been doing.

Consider, for example, the following entry, which demonstrates something more of how Dorothy's writing resists imposition of conventional narrative codes:

Friday 12th. A very fine bright, clear, hard frost. William working again. I recopied the Pedlar, but poor William all the time at work. Molly tells me 'What! little Sally's gone to visit at Mr. Simpson's. They say she's very smart she's got on a new bed-gown that her Cousin gave her. It's a very bonny one they tell me, but I've not seen it. Sally and me's in Luck.' In the afternoon a poor woman came, *she said* to beg some rags for her husband's leg which had been wounded by a slate from the Roof in the great wind—but she has been used to go a-begging, for she has often come here. Her father lived to the age of 105. She is a woman of strong bones with a complexion that has been beautiful, and remained very fresh last year, but now she looks broken, and her little Boy, a pretty little fellow, and whom I have loved for the sake of Basil, looks thin and pale. I observed this to her. Aye says she we have all been ill. Our house was unroofed in the storm nearly and *so* we lived in it for more than a week. The Child wears a ragged drab coat and a fur cap, poor little fellow, I think he seems scarcely at all grown since the first time I saw him. William was with me—we met him in a lane going to Skelwith Bridge. He looked very pretty. He was walking lazily in the deep narrow lane, overshadowed with the hedge-rows, his meal poke hung over his shoulder. He said he was going 'a laiting'. He now wears the same coat he had on at that time. Poor creatures! When the woman was gone, I could not help thinking that we are not half thankful enough that we are placed in that condition of life in which we are. We do not so often bless god for this as we wish for this 50£ that 100£ etc. etc. We have not, however to reproach ourselves with ever breathing a murmur. This woman's was but a *common* case.— The snow still lies upon the ground. Just at the closing in of the Day I heard a cart pass the door, and at the same time the dismal sound of a crying Infant. I went to the window and had light enough to see that a man was driving a cart which seemed not to be very full, and that a woman with an infant in her arms was following close behind and a dog close to her. It was a wild and melancholy sight.—

William rubbed his Table after candles were lighted, and we sate a long time with the windows unclosed. I almost finished writing The Pedlar, but poor William wore himself and me out with labour. We had an affecting conversation. Went to bed at 12 o'clock. (89–90)

The entry divides itself into four parts. Two are what I shall call narrative moments: the story of the woman begging rags and that of the family and the cart. Both sequences have the elements of a narrative, but the author does not pursue this possibility. Having detailed what it indicates is a problematic state in each instance, the narrative voice pulls back and frames a comment on and contrast to that state. The second part of the passage may also be viewed as a repetition of the first part. In both cases poverty, disintegration, and desolation contrast with the domestic, vocational, and personal coherence of the narrator's situation. The opposition of inner and outer works throughout the entry. Outside lies destruction and disintegration: a cold, hard brightness, illness, a woman once beautiful, now broken, forced to beg for old, used-up materials to care for her husband's wound, unable to keep her child from becoming thin and pale, and then darkness, a crying infant, a family with all their meager possessions in a cart. Inside is warmth and sustenance: literary productivity, a cheerful servant, an intelligent young boy, glowing warmth from a polished table and lighted candles, "affecting conversation," a bed for the night, domestic, personal, vocational, and fraternal assurance. From the female space of her household, the narrator views the outside through a window that frames and thus protects.

There is no real narrative progress in the passage but instead the repetition of narrative moments and the comments upon them. The first time, the comment takes the form of a rather banal, moralistic statement about her relationship with the beggar woman. Then, almost as if to provide an antidote to her "common" reflection on this "common case," Dorothy provides a description that renders the common quite extraordinary. The second part of the passage juxtaposing a "wild and melancholy sight" to a scene of inner warmth and prosperity is

Dorothy's idiosyncratic writing at its most interesting. Here no formal connection is made between the narrative and the comment on it. The incident touches the journal writer's life contiguously rather than being made metaphorically representative of her state. The opposition of Dorothy's unified home at Grasmere and the itinerant, deracinated existence of the people outside is established through sequence. Writing metonymically, she does not draw the connections typical of metaphoric writing.

Part of the problem with reading Dorothy Wordsworth has been a failure to deal with this metonymic quality of her writing. As Jonathan Culler explains in *The Pursuit of Signs,* metaphor has become "the figure of figures," and readers tend to value it over metonymy (188–209). Yet Dorothy at her best, as in the second part of this passage, refuses metaphor. She writes in a lateral sequence of associations rather than a narrative unit that can synecdochically represent the whole. Writing structured this way can frustrate the reader's desire to know why the author chooses the details that she does. The passage we have been examining, however, demonstrates one impulse in the will to coherence that generates the journal.

The details of the passage also provide an important point of self-reference in the journal. The form the impulse takes—writing, articulation—is everywhere in the passage, even providing a point of convergence for the sides of the inner–outer opposition. The sequences are related in terms of different kinds of articulation: people relate incidents in their lives and the lives of their relatives; earlier conversations are reproduced, complete with dialect; brother and sister converse "affectingly." Dorothy and William are writing, copying, revising "The Pedlar." This poem, mentioned frequently in the Grasmere journals, brings the subject of "a ruined cottage," a home destroyed, into Dorothy's home, as does the beggar woman's tale of the "unroofing" of her house. In setting up the opposition of inner and outer, Dorothy's own writing in the journal attempts to control this intermingling while validating a certain moral and fraternal order. What happens here, however, is that writing creates an outside, which turns into a view of the inmost, the infant's cry (another kind of articulation) being a kind of primal wail introducing a landscape of the most feared inner possibilities—dislocation, disintegration, destruction.

Throughout the Grasmere journals, Dorothy Wordsworth responds to the same "outside" as the other writers around her. Solitary figures, frost at midnight, a single cottage are her materials. Her handling of the material is, as we have been noting, very different. These distinctive structures of Dorothy's imagination are particularly evident in her well-known description of the daffodils, especially in contrast to William's handling of the same topic.

That William Wordsworth continually mined his sister's journal for subjects and observations is well known. If she wrote to give William pleasure, the pleasure he took was at least partly professional, for in writing such poems as "A Night-piece," "Beggars," "Resolution and Independence," "Alice Fell," "To a Butterfly," "To the Small Celandine," "The Redbreast chasing the Butterfly," it pleased him to interact with her journals. Take, for instance, the case of the daffodils.

> When we were in the woods beyond Gowbarrow park we saw a few daffodils close to the water side. We fancied that the lake had floated the seeds ashore and that the little colony had so sprung up. But as we went along there were more and yet more and at last under the boughs of the trees, we saw that there was a long belt of them along the shore, about the breadth of a country turnpike road. I never saw daffodils so beautiful they grew among the mossy stones about and about them, some rested their heads upon these stones as on a pillow for weariness and the rest tossed and reeled and danced and seemed as if they verily laughed with the wind that blew upon them over the lake, they looked so gay ever glancing ever changing. This wind blew directly over the lake to them. There was here and there a little knot and a few stragglers a few yards higher up but they were so few as not to disturb the simplicity and unity and life of that one busy highway. We rested again and again. (109)

Now William's version:

I wandered lonely as a cloud
That floats on high o'er vales and hills,
When all at once I saw a crowd,
A host, of golden daffodils;
Beside the lake, beneath the trees,
Fluttering and dancing in the breeze.

Continuous as the stars that shine
And twinkle on the milky way,
They stretched in never-ending line
Along the margin of a bay:
Ten thousand saw I at a glance,
Tossing their heads in sprightly dance.

The waves beside them danced; but they
Out-did the sparkling waves in glee:
A poet could not but be gay,
In such a jocund company:
I gazed—and gazed—but little thought
What wealth the show to me had brought:

For oft, when on my couch I lie
In vacant or in pensive mood,
They flash upon that inward eye
Which is the bliss of solitude;
And then my heart with pleasure fills,
And dances with the daffodils.
                              (*PW* 2:216–217)

In his poem, William embellishes the description, placing himself in the text to demonstrate how he discovers something about himself and his profession as a poet through use of the external world. William is alone in his version, which shows him in the very process of the typically romantic act of appropriating nature to create a myth of self—in this case the myth of the working, romantic poet. For William the scene provides an opportunity to elaborate the concerns of the Preface to *Lyrical Ballads,* the creation of poetry "from emotion recollected in tranquillity" (173). The natural scene becomes an "investment" upon which the viewer can realize a "return." Behind William's poem also lies the assumption that the speaker has the basic right to appropriate the world for use in this way. Dorothy's version characteristically refuses this kind of appropriation, seeming to come from an imagination that exists to perceive what passes before it. For Dorothy, writing is not a vehicle for the attempt to arrive at a "truth." There is a certain amorality in her writing. Her eye and her words affirm a natural world without categories of fault or truth.

To function as it does, William's "I" must be a preexistent secure entity, an ego that Dorothy perhaps lacks for some of the reasons we have been discussing. Yet to phrase her vision as a "lack" indicates one cultural bias we bring to the text. Dorothy may not have the identity that allows reaction to the world in William's way, but his way is not necessarily more valuable. The absence of the "I" in Dorothy's passages is as characteristic of her vision as is the speaker as isolate individual in William's poem. In his recounting the "I" becomes twice removed from any community, not only "lonely" but "as a cloud"—remote, above, disconnected from the scene at hand. He ends up on his couch, also alone we may assume. But Dorothy writes of "we," the plural pronoun appearing six times in her description. The walk is a communal activity; the flowers themselves are part of a group. Her view locates a society engaged in a communal act of perception. Her Grasmere journals are in part the recording of that act.

In this community, Dorothy herself appears as a facilitating rather than a competitive presence, constructing a nonaggressive rather than an ego-dominant self. Both William and Coleridge use her words; she offers them gladly. But the process may not be so simple. Her words imprison and sometimes stifle her brother. In one instance, for example, she reads to him an entry that is two years old about "a very tall woman, tall much beyond the measure of tall women," and her sons (26), in the hope her brother can use the description in his poem. But as she records, William "could not escape from those very words, and so he could not write the poem" (101). She terms the influence "unlucky" but may not be totally apologetic.

The Grasmere journals tell of writing as a family matter, a

community product, but that it also produced tension is clear. Writing is surrounded with hypochondria: William's eyes and chest and back hurt; Dorothy has constant headaches. The context in which William's use of her material is described raises the possibility that his borrowing is less than a purely positive act. One entry starts out well enough. "A beautiful morning. The sun shone. William wrote a conclusion to the poem of the Butterfly—'I've watch'd you now a full half-hour'. I was quite out of spirits and went into the orchard" (113). The notion of watching works several ways here. In one sense, Dorothy herself has been watched because she can watch or see things. Or perhaps she is upset because she too has watched but she too does not write the poem. Her own attempt at poetry she dismisses. "I had many very exquisite feelings and when I saw this lowly Building in the waters among the Dark and lofty hills, with that bright soft light upon it, it made me more than half a poet. I was tired when I reached home. I could not sit down to reading and tried to write verses but alas! I gave up expecting William and went soon to bed" (104). Giving up the attempt at poetry here also describes giving up William's presence. Here he is a negative muse, whose absence revokes her own writing.

The way the journals become a medium for the social and communal understanding of the self in nature is more clearly defined in the entry of the day following the experience of the daffodils.

> When we came to the foot of Brothers water I left William sitting on the Bridge and went along the path on the right side of the Lake through the wood. I was delighted with what I saw. The water under the boughs of the bare old trees, the simplicity of the mountains and the exquisite beauty of the path. There was one grey cottage. I repeated the Glowworm as I walked along. I hung over the gate, and thought I could have stayed for ever. When I returned I found William writing a poem descriptive of the sights and sounds we saw and heard. There was the gentle flowing of the stream, the glittering lively lake, green fields without a living creature to be seen on them, behind us, a flat pasture with 42 cattle feeding to our left the road leading to the hamlet, no smoke there, the sun shone on the bare roofs. The people were at work ploughing, harrowing

and sowing—lasses spreading dung, a dog's barking now and then, cocks crowing, birds twittering, the snow in patches at the top of the highest hills, yellow palms, purple and green twigs on the Birches, ashes with their glittering spikes quite bare. The hawthorn a bright green with black stems under the oak. The moss of the oak glossy. (111)

Here Dorothy separates from William momentarily and assembles nature, poetry, and vision to generate "delight." She sets off one point of suspension in which she can watch herself and finds this state so amenable that she seeks to stay there permanently. It is the property of the journal, however, to delineate passage; the "I" rejoins William and the description becomes a panoramic vista of the productive unity of the countryside. The people farming allow work as a continuous, communal process. Dorothy's description makes the writing of poetry part of that communal activity when her view places William's writing in the context of all the other productive activity going on. For a moment, in fact, Dorothy's "there"—perhaps the synecdochical word in her descriptive lexicon—elides the specific work of poetry with the specificity of Lake District agriculture: "William writing a poem . . . there was the gentle flowing . . . green fields . . . a flat pasture with 42 cattle." Dorothy's work is the organizing of "sights and sounds" into a vision of coherent, communal livelihood that includes "the highest hills" and the "black stems under the oak," the people plowing and the writers writing.

As much, however, as it interests itself in the unity of the life around her, Dorothy's journals, as we have seen, also details breakdown and fragmentation. Community and disintegration figure simultaneously in the descriptions not only of her brother's wedding but also of her many encounters with beggars and wanderers. These vagrants exist in the journals both as personal possibilities for Dorothy herself and as victims of social change. The way she tells their stories and the support she provides them allow these people to be part of the communal relationships that so concern her. She sees the members of her group as bound to aid the increasing number of poor people whose wanderings indicate a general breakdown of English society.

Still "stout and well dressed," the woman of the opening entry has never had to ask for aid before. A whole new class of poor people seems to be appearing because of "these hard times" (16). The woman encompasses both individual and general upheaval. She, like so many others, wanders without a home. Her family has dissolved. Even death is affected by economic breakdown, as Dorothy emphasizes by including the inflated economics of burial. Because of "an alteration in the times," there will soon be "only two ranks of people, the very rich and the very poor, for those who have small estates," a friend says, "are forced to sell, and all the land goes into one hand" (19). Those thrown off their land are forced to wander.

The rich, too, contribute to the general disintegration, by amassing land. Estates are being rearranged, Grasmere itself taken apart. "They are making sad ravages in the woods. Benson's Wood is going and the wood above the River" (97). "They are slashing away in Benson's wood" (99). Words like *ravages* and *slashing* reveal the depth of her feeling and the violence of the upheavals that Dorothy seems to describe with such cool observation. Generally avoiding large social and historical concerns, she deals only by implication with the world that sends these people past her door.

Her home is a solid center for Dorothy against the dislocation occurring around her. The poverty-stricken wanderers she describes both contrast with and reinforce her own way of life and therefore are part of the ego definition so much of her journal entails. In one particularly telling encounter, surrounded by her men and her community, she gives money to a woman and her two daughters. After working on the "Leech Gatherer," Dorothy and William meet Coleridge on their morning walk.

We came down and rested upon a moss covered Rock, rising out of the bed of the River. There we lay ate our dinner and stayed there till about 4 o'clock or later. Wm and C. repeated and read verses. I drank a little Brandy and water and was in Heaven. The Stags horn is very beautiful and fresh springing upon the fells. Mountain ashes, green. We drank tea at a farm house. The woman had not a pleasant countenance, but was civil enough. She had a pretty Boy a year old whom she suckled. We parted from Coleridge at Sara's Crag after having looked at the Letters which C. carved in the morning. I kissed them all. Wm deepened the T with C's penknife. We sate afterwards on the wall, seeing the sun go down, and the reflections in the still water. C. looked well and parted from us chearfully, hopping up upon the side stones. On the Rays we met a woman with 2 little girls one in her arms the other about 4 years old walking by her side, a pretty little thing, but half starved. She had on a pair of slippers that had belonged to some gentleman's child, down at the heels— it was not easy to keep them on but, poor thing! young as she was, she walked carefully with them. Alas too young for such cares and such travels. The Mother when we accosted her told us that her husband had left her and gone off with another woman and how she '*pursued*' them. Then her fury kindled and her eyes rolled about. She changed again to tears. She was a Cockermouth woman 30 years of age—a child at Cockermouth when I was. I was moved and gave her a shilling—I believe 6^d more than I ought to have given. We had the crescent moon with the 'auld moon in her arms'. We rested often always upon the Bridges. Reached home at about 10 o'clock. The Lloyds had been here in our absence. We went soon to bed. I repeated verses to William while he was in bed—he was soothed and I left him. 'This is the spot' over and over again. (120–121)

The passage progresses through various kinds of community, breakup, and family, the juxtaposition of detail again important. Three women in the passage—Dorothy, the farm woman, and the beggar woman—describe different possibilities of feminine and familial existence.

Frequently a ritual of togetherness, mealtime here first takes the form of an idyllic union of food, friendship, nature, and poetry. The farm woman Dorothy encounters when she later drinks tea, has a conventional way of life, complete with house and nursing baby but seems out of sorts, especially when described by Dorothy from her own ecstatic state. Dorothy displays her emotions in a way that must be different from that of the woman at the farmhouse: she kisses letters, the initials at Sara's crag. In the abstract, it would seem strange to go around kissing stones instead of nursing babies, but Dorothy's gesture serves to exalt the writing community of herself, William, and Coleridge. Even the breaking up of their group is happy here as Coleridge hops off along the stones.

The woman they then meet on the Rays, like the farm woman, has invested in a conventional sort of family life, but she has been betrayed, she and the children left for another woman. The situation is at once clichéd and terrifying, especially for Dorothy who must feel her brother is in some sense leaving her for another woman, Mary. This woman is Dorothy's potential counterpart, even to having spent her childhood in the same place, as Dorothy observes in a typically fragmented, elliptical statement. The poverty-stricken, slightly demented condition of the woman as well as the contrast of the classes—carried out through detail about the child's shoes—particularly interests Dorothy. William and she accost the wanderers, a reversal in the usual process of begging, and fascinated, Dorothy pursues the story. She encircles it with what she has, the household of solidarity and literature of which she is a part. But the possibility of the other woman remains not only for those who take the conventional oath of marriage but for any dependent woman.

The personal terror is partly controlled by placing this woman in the context of all the other beggars. Dorothy gives a dry, numerical account of her gift, questioning her own generosity. The money she gives to wanderers tends to increase the more she identifies with them. Her gift here indicates the depth of the relationship she feels to this woman. The gift is also a statement of her position on charity: the community must support these people. At the same time as Dorothy catches these people in movement, she refers them to a larger social coherence, again demonstrating the way things hold together. She gives a sense of these stragglers as part of the whole, not as alien presences. As much as it differentiates the emotional states of Dorothy Wordsworth, the Grasmere journals construct the community that entitles them.

The obligations and power of the Grasmere community as a cohesive social force are further elaborated in Dorothy's *A Narrative Concerning George and Sarah Green of the Parish of Grasmere.* The well-known events leading to the piece can be briefly told. In March 1808 George and Sarah Green perished in a snowstorm while trying to return home to Easedale from a sale in

Langdale. They left eight children under the age of sixteen, and the people of Grasmere organized to care for the orphans. A story of Grasmere's "united efforts" (61), Dorothy's narrative delineates various forces of community: charitable obligations, nuturing of children, familial structures and their possible mutations, the disruption and continuity of life in a rural village. Once again, a community of writing figures here, for Dorothy's is but one of three accounts of the tragedy. The way she tells the story of the Greens allows their lives to comment on her own existence in Grasmere.

The deaths of George and Sarah Green cause extreme disruption in both the personal and communal life of the town. They also bring the villagers together in a fierce concentration of unities and loyalties. Nothing else can be "thought of." During the search for the bodies "—the first question was, 'Have you heard anything from the Fells?'" (51). Even economic considerations take second place, as Dorothy emphasizes in a mildly surprised but proud way by including her conversation with a neighbor who says he will continue searching for the bodies even though he must leave his profitable employment as a shoemaker. Of course, one of the larger idealizations of the story mythicizes the economic stability of a community thus able to absorb trauma to its own poor: existence suddenly rendered marginal is resecured within the economic wholeness of Grasmere.[3]

The funerals themselves provide continuity as neglected burial customs are resurrected for the ceremony. Giving a small loaf of bread to each guest before the bodies are taken to the graves, "an ancient custom now much disused" (55), is one tradition that reasserts itself as the Greens are buried. This connection with the past of the village goes beyond even the Wordsworths

---

3. In *The Making of a Tory Humanist,* Michael Friedman elaborates this idea. Friedman also points to letters regarding the Greens in which William emphasizes that *too* much money ought not to be given the children because it might unfairly raise their expectations as well as make the other poor envious. "What emerges from his explanation," Friedman writes, "is a Tory humanist conception of a community structured by traditional rank and degree and a belief that such a hierarchic community must be preserved" (181). Dorothy's own narrative plays down the paternalism of their charity.

as people of Grasmere: Mary tries to refuse the bread because of the orphans' poverty and accepts it only when she fully realizes the significance of the gesture. The funeral ceremony of Dorothy's description generates still more unity among the mourners. She remarks that "all the people who were gathered together appeared to be united in one general feeling of sympathy for the helpless condition of the Orphans" (56).

Caring for the children brings together disparate elements of the village; contributors come from all classes: "With five guineas, ten guineas, three guineas, is intermingled a long list of shillings and sixpences, and even one threepence—many of these smaller contributions from labouring people and Servants" (62). The dispersal of the children to their new homes, actually the breakup of the family, is also seen in terms of interconnection and unity. The woman who takes Jane and the baby is quoted as saying her connection with the late Greens makes this gesture perfectly natural. Her mother-in-law was the sister of George Green's first wife, so she sees herself as related to the children and fulfilling a natural obligation to them. The picture of Jane and the baby seated by her fireside transforms dislocation into serenity and at-homeness. Two of the little boys, taken by a woman who has lost her own child, cry at first but are then described as becoming a comfort to their foster mother. Their bonds to their new place solidified, they are last heard exclaiming, "we will never go away frae this house" (69). The last description of the children's dispersal contains all the material for a lyrical ballad. Seven-year-old John is taken by an old family friend who is "feeble and paralytic" and who had previously spent his time outdoors with "no Companion but his Dog and his Staff." John becomes like a grandson to the old man, a "faithful attendant upon his Master's course." The narrator just happens to have seen them "last night on their return homewards; little John was running here and there as sportive as a mountain lamb," keeping the old man company as he "creeps at a slow pace, with tottering steps" (71). Continuing to emphasize the felicitous outcome of the community effort, Dorothy also describes a visit to the old man's housekeeper, who is thoroughly delighted with the boy and is in fact knitting stockings for him at the moment of the narrator's visit. Not only are the children happily provided for, but those who take them are rewarded and rejuvenated.

Dorothy's telling of these events is also an affirmation of a certain mode of social assistance. What are the obligations of a society to those who cannot sustain themselves? How much should be spent? Who should control charity and how should it be distributed? Dorothy emphasizes the absolute necessity of fulfilling the needs of the weak and the poor in a way that preserves the autonomy and interrelations of a small, rural village; her assertions may be perceived as at once reactionary, utopian, naïve, and efficiently workable. In her view, the effort on behalf of the Greens succeeds extraordinarily well, but of course Dorothy is not an unbiased observer of these events, since she herself was so involved in their implementation. Yet she is able to judge her success by other standards, offering as proof the treatment accorded another orphan. In setting up this comparison, the narrator becomes more of an outside observer and first outlines the usual method of dealing with dependent children. "It is the custom at Grasmere, and I believe in many other places, to *let,* as they call it, those Children who depend wholly upon the Parish, to the lowest bidder" (58). Her description conveys disapproval of such treatment even before she characterizes the parish apprenticeships that they are given at age ten as "at best a slavish condition" (59). Sarah Green herself was a parish apprentice, and Dorothy hints that such a childhood may be partly responsible for her "fallen" condition and illegitimate child (78). The narrator recalls first coming to Grasmere and observing another such apprenticed child, thus making specific the comparison with the Greens. Her impression then was of a boy being ruined, a boy of "natural quickness with much good temper in his countenance" being ill-used (59). The boy had become a daily example of the failure of such charity and was on the way to becoming a social liability; "he has more than once been detected in dishonest practices, probably having been tempted to them by his desire of obtaining liquor" (60). To avoid any repetition of this situation, the Green children are placed with "respectable" families who will pass on to them the accepted values of literacy and religion.

The village participates, and everyone's help is valued. The only discord comes from Mrs. North, "sullen and dissatisfied that she had not had the whole management of the concern" (72). Dorothy characterizes her as "only recently come into the country and having no connection with Grasmere" (63), although she and her husband had purchased Rydal Mount in 1803. The trouble she causes contrasts with the way Dorothy herself fits in as a true woman of Grasmere. Mrs. North provides a negative example in Dorothy's story, appearing as one who does not understand the communal mode of charity. The narrator is particularly annoyed because Mrs. North had "engaged to place all the Children with an old Woman in indigent circumstances, who was totally incapable of the charge" (63). Now one could say that in keeping the children together, Mrs. North was finding them a more favorable situation than those Dorothy and her group had arranged. Dorothy's story, however, has it that communal and natural bonds can equal, if not replace, familial ones.

The narrative also sets out possibilities for replacing blood ties. The end of the piece speculates that the children may even be better off, since their foster parents can offer them more education than the poverty of their natural parents would have allowed. Implications of this somewhat forced consolation are continued in the notes that Dorothy appends to the manuscript. A note on Sarah Green's natural daughter tells how she insists on going to search for her mother and stepfather. "In her distraction she thought that *she* should surely find them" (90). The feelings are similar, the note goes on to say, to those of Mary Watson, who is sure that she can find the body of her drowned son. Both women feel that blood ties bind them more forcefully to the lost individuals, but in both cases, it is the villagers who succeed. Mary Watson's other son is an even more pointed denial of the force of blood ties, for he kills his mother. The villagers have continually warned her about him. Societal bonds may be more dependable and secure than ties of blood.

It is important to Dorothy that the children remain in Grasmere, "quartered in their native Vale" (61). Dorothy's story of George and Sarah Green affirms the rightness not only of a mode of charity but of a way of rural life under intense pressure from economic change. The designation of the Greens as "the poorest People in the Vale" (48) may or may not be an accurate dollars-and-cents description. Even so, the superlative helps establish that from even direst poverty can come respectable men and women, if the proper environment can be provided. Poor as they are, the Greens own some land. "The love of their few fields and their ancient home was a salutary passion, and no doubt something of this must have spread itself to the Children" (75). This type of individual ownership, as Dorothy pointed out in her journal, was becoming increasingly rare. The benefits derived from it, so important to the Greens in her view, were lost to most people. A way of life was being destroyed.

Their land provided a familial economic unity. The children, for example, could help gather peat as soon as they could walk. "In this way the Family were bound together by the same cares and exertions" (76). Dorothy theorizes that the environment can positively shape a personality. In their restricted country setting, the children find structure, regularity, and cohesion, but such nurture enhances innate characteristics, maybe "a pecular tenderness of Nature; perhaps inherited from their Father" (77), a character trait that is also finally related to the land and their life on it, as is the consolation given at the end of the story. The deaths may have kept the Greens "from that dependance which they dreaded . . . and perhaps, after the Land had been sold, the happy chearfulness of George and Sarah Green might have forsaken them, and their latter days have been tedious and melancholy" (87). Dorothy's narrative documents the power of this threatened way of life.

The story also affirms the value of a particular kind of discourse that life at Grasmere generates: "fireside talk in our Cottages" (53). Occurrences such as the death of the Greens release a perfect record of the "inner histories of Families, their lesser and greater cares, their peculiar habits, and ways of life." The unusual acts as a catalyst for the verbal organization of daily life. These biographies, so excellent according to Dorothy, are "re-

corded in the breasts of their Fellow-inhabitants of the Vale"
(53). Again, this type of community can provide something of
unique value for those who live there—a record that is "faithful"
and that possesses an authenticating power for its subjects. Dorothy favors this kind of discourse over more sophisticated biography, accounts of those "who have moved in higher stations
and had numerous Friends in the busy world . . . even when
their doings and sufferings have been watched for the express
purpose of recording them in written narratives" (53).

Her positive description of a community in which experience
and relation of that experience almost conflate, a community
that maintains itself through talk rather than through writing, is
bound up with nostalgia for the dignified but simple communal
life Dorothy portrays. Yet she produces writing, which might
appear an unwelcome supplement to the people's talk. Hence,
the narrative apologizes for itself as written text, stating that it
does not give an accurate account of the Greens, that it fails to
set out the presence of their story. The problem appears in individual phrases throughout: "I can scarcely tell you," "It would
not be easy," "I know not indeed how to find a word sufficiently
strong to express." The narrator finally summarizes her problem, again writing in the context of communal life: "I cannot
give *you* the same feelings that *I* have of them as neighbours and
fellow-inhabitants of this Vale; therefore what is in my mind a
full and living picture will be to you but a feeble sketch" (86).

Dorothy does attempt to write in elements of the people's
spoken record. She sets up her work as a familiar, chatty recounting, personalizing its content, addressing it "to a Friend,"
perhaps Joanna Hutchinson of the dedication. In a technique
reminiscent of William's in beginning "Michael," she invites the
reader into the narrator's intimate circle by immediately addressing her as one who knows Grasmere, assuming her familiarity
with the village and the people in it. "You remember a single
Cottage at the foot of Blentern Gill—it is the only dwelling on
the Western Side of the upper reaches of the Vale of Easedale,
and close under the mountain; a little stream runs over rocks and
stones beside the garden wall, after tumbling down the crags: I
am sure you recollect the spot: if not, you remember George and

Sarah Green who dwelt there" (43). Again she works with oppositions of isolation and community. Though she recalls a
"single Cottage," "the only dwelling," George and Sarah Green
sustain spoken and written being because they are "of the Parish
of Grasmere," an emphasis set out in the title at the top of the
first manuscript page: "A Narrative Concerning George and
Sarah Green of the Parish of Grasmere, Addressed to a Friend."
Dorothy integrates the vernacular of Grasmere people, including, for example, the observations of Peggy Ashburner, a poor
but favorite neighbor. The shortcomings of George and Sarah
Green—for Dorothy is not so unrealistic as to portray them as
perfect—are also spoken through the neighbors' voices, and in
fact, their failings are stated mainly in terms of their relation to
the community. They are at once not open enough to it and too
eager to be with their neighbors. "The Neighbours say that
George and Sarah Green had but one fault; they were rather 'too
stiff', unwilling to receive favours," and comment how "a love
of Sales" has proved their undoing (79, 50).

Despite these features, however, Dorothy fears she has not
created a "faithful" record and uses her brother's words to deni-
grate her effect. "I fear I have spun out my narrative to a tedious
length" (86), as in *The Excursion,* William's Pedlar says, "Sir, I
feel / The story linger in my heart; I fear / 'Tis long and tedious;
but my spirit clings / To that poor Woman" (1:777–780). Dorothy rewrites William's words to accord with her main concerns
in the narrative. "I may say with the Pedlar in the 'Recluse' 'I feel
/ The story linger in my heart, my memory / Clings to this
poor Woman and her Family'" (86). Both the individual woman
and her family group are the basis of the story. As *that* changes
to *this,* the woman becomes a more immediate presence, closer
to the narrator who tries to provide something of the "fireside
talk" she values so much.

Despite her doubts about her work, Dorothy seems to have
succeeded most fully in providing, at her brother's urging, "a
record of human sympathies" describing the Green tragedy.
William's short poem, "George and Sarah Green," and De Quincey's version of the story, "Early Memorials of Grasmere," do

not have the straightforward, substantive coherence of Dorothy's narrative. De Quincey admires her "simple but fervid memoir," mentioning it several times in his own piece and in fact borrowing liberally from it (13:125–158). Jane becomes Agnes in his version, but details such as her winding of the clock and the attitude of the shoemaker are most surely taken from Dorothy. In typical De Quinceyan fashion, the story expands and digresses, finally becoming a disquisition on death in regions of snow and mountains. Not only does De Quincey use Dorothy's version; he also includes all nine stanzas of William's poem, which emphasizes the interrelations of husband, wife, the hills, and the grave but is much too short to approximate Dorothy's treatment. The way the three accounts come together in De Quincey's version again reveals the power of the writing community at Grasmere, demonstrating once more the generative role Dorothy played in it. In this instance it is left to her to set out the story completely and directly.

The subject matter finds a particularly cogent telling in her work for several reasons. Her involvement with the people of Grasmere and their modes of expression renders her narrative well suited to a successful account of the events. Moreover, she may have been particularly attracted to this material because it can be related so closely to her own life. Dorothy herself makes such a connection near the beginning of the narrative when she describes her own near fatal experience above Easedale Tarn, the place where the Greens' footprints are discovered.

Those foot-marks were now covered with fresh snow: the spot where they had been seen was at the top of Blea Crag above Easedale Tarn, that very spot where I myself had sate down six years ago, unable to see a yard before me, or to go a step further over the Crags. I had left W. at Stikell Tarn. A mist came on after I had parted with him, and I wandered long, not knowing whither. When at last the mist cleared away I found myself at the edge of the Precipice, and trembled at the Gulph below, which appeared immeasurable. Happily I had some hours of daylight before me, and after a laborious walk I arrived at home in the evening. (45–46)

Dorothy survives; the Greens do not. The narrative becomes in part a reassertion of her own life. Separated from her brother, she is allowed to return to him and his home.

Her life with William and his family relates to another central aspect of the Greens' story: bearing and caring for children. Dorothy does not bear children; rather she spends so much of her time and energy caring for her brother's children, who are like, but not quite, her own. Perhaps Jane figures so prominently in the story because she is a type of Dorothy herself, nurturing children not her own and also caring for her brothers.

In her role as surrogate mother, Jane takes pride in being the only one who can handle the baby. William and Mary see Jane as a graceful child, beautifully dressed, "tripping over the wooden bridge at the entrance of the Valley" (65). Dorothy includes this idealized description perhaps as a contrast to her own picture of the bereft, poverty-stricken child, alone with her younger siblings in a barren cottage. William's description of the child in her dark blue cloak that goes with a pink petticoat that complements her "pink bonnet tied with a blue ribband" (66) is countered in Dorothy's tale when her brother tries to borrow a cloak so that Jane can go seek her parents. The two cloaks are objects of Jane's contrasting states.

Dorothy transfers the arranged beauty of her brother's description to Jane's actions in organizing her family.

> She had nursed the Baby, and, without confusion or trouble, provided for the other Children who could run about: all were kept quiet—even the Infant that was robbed of its Mother's breast. She had conducted other matters with perfect regularity, had milked the cow at night and morning, wound up the clock, and taken care that the fire should not go out, a matter of importance in that house so far from any other, a tinder-box being a convenience which they did not possess. (66–67)

The middle term of the last triad calls attention to itself. Winding the clock allows the regulation of time, providing structure and organization. In a parallel gesture, Dorothy too seeks organization and meaning for both the life of the Greens and her own life as she tells the story.

The main dislocation in Dorothy's own life parallels Jane's experience. She, like Jane, has lost her mother. Dorothy's narrative tells of ruptures between mother and children and the accommodations that must be made to deal with such basic catastrophes in a child's life. The Sarah Green whom Dorothy projects seems to be totally bound up in her children; in dying she commits a mother's greatest crime against a child: total, irrevocable abandonment. Surely Dorothy's feelings about her mother's death work into the narrative. Surely traces of bitterness can be detected in the narrator's attitude towards Sarah, coldly called "the Woman." Dorothy surrounds this statement with qualification but includes it nevertheless: "the Woman had better been at home" (50).

Leaving an eleven-year-old in charge of five younger children may not have been illegal then as it is today, but even then it must have seemed reprehensible, particularly when "the youngest, an infant at the breast," is also left. Dorothy's emphasis on this nursing child indicts the woman who would separate herself from one so dependent. As any mother who has nursed a child knows, the desire to escape, to get away from it, becomes overwhelming at times. But one cannot leave; the possibilities for the child are too devastating. Dorothy characterizes the infant as "robbed of its Mother's breast." Robbed by whom? By circumstances, by nature, by the mother who leaves? The exact age of the baby is difficult to ascertain from Dorothy's descriptions, suggesting that she may be manipulating them to make the child seem younger and thus more dependent. It cries "Mam" and "Dad" and was given gin for its bowels the summer before the tragedy, which would indicate an older child than the "fair and beautiful Infant [who] lay asleep in its cradle three days after its Mother's death" (51). Were the baby older than four or five months, it would also have been something of an exaggeration to depict it as "robbed" of the breast, since by that time most babies are interested in other forms of nourishment. The younger the infant appears, however, the more irresponsible Sarah seems. Such irresponsibility, in turn, is enhanced by the aura of sexual excess that surrounds Sarah. Once again qualifying her statement, Dorothy nevertheless includes a description of Sarah as a "fallen woman," though, interestingly, only towards the end of the narrative, as if some pressure to judge Sarah Green finally had to trouble Grasmere's benevolent response to the tragedy. Moreover, for one so poor, Sarah does seem to produce too many children to care for. The last three or four look malnourished; the infant appears positively unhealthy, a direct comment on Sarah's nurturing ability.

Dorothy's complex attitude towards Sarah and her fascination with the Greens may come partly from her own early loss. On the one hand, the narrative shows how an eleven-year-old girl can compensate for the loss of a mother and how a community can draw together to save a family of children when their parents have died. On the other hand, the story shows the wicked mother and the destructive world of nature conspiring to bring about unforgettable loss and devastation.

The concerns of deprivation, devastation, and parental protection are worked out in a different way in a children's story entitled "Mary Jones and her Pet-lamb," published for the first time in Appendix Two of this book. It is, in many ways, a happy version of the Green narrative as well as an exploration of some common childhood fantasies, desires, and anxieties.[4] The story may also be read as a depiction of feminine psychological development.

As the most formally conventional narrative Dorothy produced, "Mary Jones" stands in contrast to the journals and their subversion of linearity. Unlike the story of the Greens, which wanders chattily and to which Dorothy adds several codas, "Mary Jones" has a clear beginning, middle, and end. The in-

---

4. This interpretation of "Mary Jones" is partly based on work done by Yvette G. Janssen, M.D., clinical assistant professor in psychiatry, New York Medical College, and director of the Metropolitan Hospital Therapeutic Nursery.

tended audience may have something to do with the story's particular coherence and resolution: children demand clarity. The particular form of the piece may also come from the way what has been primarily a matter of style in the Grasmere journal is transformed into the theme of "Mary Jones," a work that discusses discontinuity rather than formally demonstrating it.

In this story, Dorothy works with material of general appeal. A reader of English romantic poetry recognizes the figure of the lamb from Blake, Wordsworth, and Keats. The particular relationship of Dorothy's Mary and her lamb also seems to recall the nursery rhyme "Mary Had a Little Lamb," but Dorothy wrote the story long before the poem appeared in 1830 in the American periodical *Juvenile Miscellany,* edited by Sarah Josepha Hale, who claimed its authorship. The poem describes an event said to be "partly true," but Hale herself pointed out that "the incident of an adopted lamb following a child to school has probably occurred many times" (Opie 300).

While Book 2 of *The Excursion* and Book 8 of *The Prelude* contain similar material, Dorothy's story most explicitly intersects with William's poem "The Pet-Lamb," written in 1800 (*PW* 1:245–246). Since the dating of "Mary Jones and her Pet-lamb" is problematic, it is difficult to know who is revising whom here, but the story and the poem complement each other to provide an interesting demonstration of some of the differences between Dorothy's imagination and that of her brother. Like Mary Jones, "little Barbara Lewthwaite" of William's poem cares for a pet lamb that her father brings home from the hills. William uses the material to speculate on matters of writing and narrative relationships: his poem considers the question of who can claim responsibility for literary creation. A text, he indicates, may belong not only to the poet but to his material as well. William is more concerned with the narrator/poet than with the child and her lamb. Dorothy's emphasis, however, is on Mary and her family, on the solidity and security of their relationships.

The narrator of Dorothy's story is third-person omniscient but generally unobtrusive. It is clearly the voice of a person talking to a child, entering the story once to remind the listener she has described the three-legged stool and a second time to comment on Mary's feelings. William's narrator, on the other hand, sees the girl pause after giving the lamb a drink and goes into an extended fantasy about what she might be saying to her pet. Wishing to claim the "ballad line" that results, the narrating poet decides that "'more than half'" the "song" belongs to the girl (l. 66).

Supposing that the lamb complains in some way, the narrator imagines the girl telling him what a wonderful life the pet has with her. William's poem does not specify what has happened to the mother, only that the lamb has been deserted. The narrator first has the child assert that she is just as good a parent—"the dam that did thee yean / Upon the mountain-tops no kinder could have been" (ll. 39–40). The girl then realizes that she and the lamb are not of the same "kind" and that its "mother's heart which is working so" in the lamb necessarily distances it from her. Moreover, the child's plan to harness the lamb to her cart, "like a pony in the plough" (l. 46), hints at incomplete altruism.

Dorothy's story is free from certain ambiguities in the relationship of substitute mother and her child. Mary Jones knows her lamb's mother is dead, and this is a different level of desertion from the running off possible in the poem. Given the death of the mother, Dorothy's interest lies in focusing on the enduring, protective relationships between family members and between surrogate mothers and their children, relationships William's work does not favor. In the poem, the girl reminds the lamb to be grateful for its safe home, contrasted with the frightening mountains. The lamb should be glad it does not have to contend with fearsome nature. Mary Jones's lamb returns to its own kind, however, by running back into the hills of its birth. Mary and her lamb actually experience the potentially destructive natural world, but she is able to rescue her charge and is in turn rescued by her own parents. (Unlike William's Margaret in *The Excursion,* Dorothy's Margaret can save her child.) The differences between the two stories of pet lambs point up the contrast of William's practicality and Dorothy's hopefulness. Dorothy creates a story that demonstrates both compensation for loss and the subversion of destruction. Of course, the optimism of the story may also be read as a desperate attempt to deal with what is fundamentally irreparable.

The note to William's poem brings up the subject of dead mothers as he explains his use of names by relating an incident involving the death of Barbara Lewthwaite's mother. This Barbara is not the child William overhears talking to her lamb; her name is used for other reasons. Nevertheless, she claims to remember the incident and becomes "very vain of being thus distinguished" (*PW* 1:364). William turns the incident into a warning against using the names of living persons in one's writing, a precaution Dorothy ignores in the associations her title sets up. For her title echoes the name of a recurring figure in Dorothy's life, the periodically insane Mary Lamb, another woman through whom Dorothy seems to define herself. Like Dorothy, Mary Lamb lived with her brother, Charles Lamb, and like Dorothy she was a writer. Mary Lamb, however, suffered fits of madness throughout her life, during one of which she killed her mother. The figure of the dead mother, then, has compelling presence in Mary Lamb's life and may be one reason Dorothy choses her to embody the deprivations she considers. And, Mary Lamb is a possibility that Dorothy herself fulfills when, in her own later years, she too appears quite mad.

In Dorothy's work, then, the lamb is used to consider topics having to do with familial nurture as well as the usual connotations of purity, innocence, and value. Like most fairy tales, this story lends itself to various psychological interpretations. As an only child, Mary fulfills the childhood wish of having the parents all to oneself. The family unit of three—mother, father, child—evokes the solidity of Mary's "three-legged stool," which Dorothy emphasizes by mentioning it twice. It is steady; it won't fall down; and it helps define Mary's "own place in the chimney-corner." Her family arrangement, then, contains all the security a child seeks. More generally, children often enact with animals how they wish to be treated. Mary is the ideal mother every child dreams of. She devotes herself completely to the lamb, "nursing it," fussing over it. The lamb dominates her life, even controlling her dreams, and she provides the protection it needs, searching for and finding it when it wanders off.

Dorothy's story thereby enacts another common childhood fantasy, that of a parent frantic at a child's disappearance, energies totally centered on locating her. Such a fantasy involves the child's wish for power to control the powerful adult.

Putting a Freudian construction on the story, we remember how in other fairy tales, the number three enumerates the sides of the Oedipal triangle, "Goldilocks and the Three Bears" being the most obvious example. In Dorothy's female version, the situation becomes a reality for Mary Jones when her father brings her the pet baby lamb. Thus, not only does it fulfill the child's desire for a baby of her own and for something even more helpless than she, but it also is provided by her father, who brings the daughter a baby. For Freud this fantasy has to do with a girl's growth into femininity, a heterosexual orientation she arrives at through her relationship with her father.

The way Dorothy tells the story, however, connects it more closely with the perspective of such theorists as Chodorow and Miller. Mary demonstrates how girls contain what Chodorow sees as two gender identities—a heterosexual orientation to the father and a homosexual one to the mother, who remains a love object for a girl. Chodorow recasts one kind of Freudian discontinuity. As a woman matures, the "relationship of dependence, attachment, and symbiosis to her mother continues, and her oedipal (triangular, sexualized) attachments to her mother and then her father are simply added" (129). Although Mary follows her father to his work, she first replaces him in her mother's life "when her husband was out in the fields." She is her mother's escort at church, although "Mary and her mother could only go there when the weather was fine." (No mention is made of the father's attending church.) Mary herself somewhat resembles a Victorian paterfamilias as she reads a Bible chapter to her parents every evening.

The lamb provides a means of separation from the mother with whom she inherently identifies but whom she must also fear as totally overpowering, as having the tendency to reabsorb her. Mary's relationship to the lamb allows her to grow away from her mother, while retaining her identification with her. The name "Mary" like her mother's name, "Margaret," is often associated with mother through the common syllable, *Ma.* Because she has a child, the lamb, who runs away, Mary literally and figuratively differentiates herself. She undergoes a trial of separation on the mountain but awakes from her adventure "to find herself in her Mother's arms." She has matured but is still attached to her mother. She never leaves home again without advising her parents, a trait that can be seen either as homebound dependency or as an example of the particular dynamic of separation, consideration, and attachment that characterizes woman's development. Instead of a fairy tale in which a girl awakes to marry a prince and live passively ever after, Dorothy creates a story in which the heroine awakes to active participation in what Carol Gilligan calls an "ethic of care." It is a natural part of female development, a demonstration of woman's "embeddedness in lives of relationship" (171). Mary tends to her parents; she "took care of them when they were infirm and old."

The story shows female children coming to mother. Even the lamb nurtures. As Mary lay on the ground weeping bitterly, "The poor Lamb lay down close to her, as if it wanted to keep her warm." Later, the lamb grew into "a fine Ewe and brought forth many Lambs." Interestingly, no mention is made of Mary's having children. Rather, she demonstrates her feminine maturity when she has "grown up to be a Woman" by becoming the caretaker of her parents. As a woman grows, she expands her care network to include first her child and then her parents. In the context of the story, this life is seen as positive and powerful, not as defined by lack of achievement.

In "Mary Jones and her Pet-lamb," as in *A Narrative Concerning George and Sarah Green,* Dorothy attempts various compensatory fantasies. Here, though, the possibility of nurture and parental protection overcomes deprivation. The obvious associations of the father's name, William, need not be elaborated. The way the protection he gives his child is detailed, however, should be noted. Being lost on the mountain means losing sight of her father's house. "It was not dark, but the day light was faded, and she could not see her Father's house, or the trees, or the fields." The exact sequence of rescue is provided: he picks his child up off the ground (without even waking her), wraps her in his cloak, and carries her home. William is also partly responsible for the protection of the cottage; generations of his family's men have "planted trees round their cottage to keep off the cold winds that blew from the mountains." William and Margaret, like the Greens, live in an isolated cottage—"the farthest house in one of the Cumberland Dales"—but nature and parents conspire to protect in this inversion of the Green tragedy.

Not only are parents able to take care of their children in "Mary Jones and her Pet-lamb," but nature, fully respected by Mary, also helps sustain life. The trees around the cottage control the destructive possibilities of storm and hot sun. The bees "never stung her"; on the contrary, they hover over, perhaps guarding, her lamb's final resting place. The time Mary spends on the mountain happens to be "the mildest night of all the year." The heather provides a dry bed for her, preventing the damp ground from affecting her. Thus does each potential natural threat provide its own natural counter. Death in nature appears only through a simile, another children's tale, that of Robin Red-Breast. In a basic narrative mode, the story rehearses one of Dorothy's most wished for and shattered fantasies.

If the mother provides a girl with her primary sense of self, then the daughter who loses her mother must continually find ways to try to make up for this deprivation. (Here I am making a distinction between her biological mother, whose death caused such a disruption in Dorothy's life, and the substitute primary care givers whose femininity has enabled my previous discussion of women's development.) The letters she writes until she refuses to write any longer form another record in language of Dorothy's struggle to provide necessary compensations for herself and to arrange her life in the Grasmere community. Though obviously a different kind of narrative from those we have been considering, the letters are particularly revealing, perhaps because they constitute one form of writing expected of her and thus totally open to her.

The concerns of the journals also appear in her letters. She continually denigrates herself as a correspondent, often maintaining to the recipient, who had to pay postage according to weight, that her letters are not worth the cost. In almost every personal letter she apologizes for her penmanship. If handwriting reflects how one feels about oneself, then Dorothy is indeed troubled about her image, and her anxiety about her handwriting parallels the statements of her own worthlessness that creep into her letters. She writes frequent self-characterizations to Lady Beaumont, who she is sure will be mightily disappointed when they finally meet. In a letter of 1805 she summarizes her view of herself as a member of the Grasmere community of writers. "I have not those powers which Coleridge thinks I have—I know it—my only merits are my devotedness to those I love and I hope a charity towards all mankind" (1:525).

The importance of establishing inviolable relationships with "those [she] loves" is a main theme of her early letters. The two dominant beings of her emotional life are Jane Pollard and her brother William, as she insists in 1793. "I am very sure that Love will never bind me closer to any human Being than Friendship binds me to you my earliest female Friend, and to William my earliest and my dearest Male Friend" (1:96). Dorothy suffers without her parents. She presents herself as a Cinderella figure, a poor orphan dependent upon the unsympathetic relatives with whom she must live. She emerges in these early letters to Jane as something of a glorified servant. She wants to visit friends but cannot leave her aunt. She has little time for herself. "As I am head nurse, housekeeper, tutoress of the little ones or rather superintendent of the nursery, I am at present a very busy woman and literally *steal* the moments which I employ in letter-writing" (1:99).

But the letters are also sometimes giggly and fluttery in tone, containing Jane Austen–like sections in which Dorothy portrays herself as a young lady concerned with gowns and balls, nervous at her first dance, unhappy when only six men are present at a gathering. She worries about being a wallflower. Yet when Jane teases her about a suspected romantic involvement, she asserts, "I can only say that no man I have seen has appeared to regard me with any degree of partiality; nor has any one gained my affections." In girlish confidentiality she goes on to assure Jane:

"believe me, *if ever I do* form an attachment it shall not long be a secret from you" (1:28).

The important man in her life is, of course, William. Connecting the loss of her mother with loss of a firm sense of her own being, Dorothy's letters describe the finding of herself in relation to other people—to Jane Pollard and especially to William. "Oh! my dear Friend, you measure my heart truly when you judge that I have at all times a deep sympathy with those who know what fraternal affection is. It has been the building up of my being, the light of my path. Our Mother, blessed be her Memory! was taken from us when I was only six years old" (1:568). In the spring of 1794 Dorothy writes of the exhilarating time spent with her brother in the Lake District. Here is a twenty-two-year-old woman who has been living as only slightly more than a servant for ten years reunited with the man she loves the most in the most beautiful country she can conceive of.

So begins the combination of William, writing, and nature that Dorothy, going against convention, makes her life. In a letter she defies her aunt's censures of her unacceptable behavior—"rambling about the country on foot," traveling without a chaperone, placing herself in an "exposed situation." Dorothy sets out her intention "to make use of the strength with which nature has endowed" her. She will remain at Windy Bow for the "beauty of the country" and "the pleasantness of the season. To these are added the society of several of my brothers friends from whom I have received the most friendly attentions and above all the society of my brother" (1:117).

The sentiments of this letter develop further as Dorothy and William, sometimes with Coleridge, go to Germany, Alfoxden, and finally Grasmere. She begins to construct a life and being for herself dependent upon her life with William and his myth of nature, the natural world providing the testing place against which she can set herself. Always possible, however, are the conventional female roles to which she cannot accommodate herself. She watches Sara Coleridge and writes to Mary Hutchinson a letter of both dismay and hostility:

She would have made a very good wife to many another man, but for Coleridge!! Her radical fault is want of sensibility and what can such a woman be to Coleridge? She is an excellent nurse to her sucking children (I mean to the best of her skill, for she employs her time often foolishly enough about them). Derwent is a sweet lovely Fatty—she suckles him entirely—he has no other food. She is to be sure a sad fiddle faddler. From about 1/2 past 10 on Sunday morning till two she did nothing but wash and dress her 2 children and herself, and was just ready for dinner. No doubt she suckled Derwent pretty often during that time. (1:330–331)

Dorothy organizes her life differently. At Racedown she too has a child to care for, Basil Montague, but of her time there she can write, "I have all my domestic concerns so arranged that everything goes on with the utmost regularity" (1:160). She deals in the letters with household and personal monetary matters, insisting on some financial independence for herself. The letters emphasize her concern with making sound investments, with not jeopardizing her money, for "if I we[re to] lose it I should forfeit my independence without having any means of reinstating myself in it" (1:387).

The "female" household tasks are still hers, but they exist in a context different from most women's. Her reading, her writing, her walking, her brother's work, their talk together are the principal components of her life. The life recorded in the journals is that of her existence with William in nature. What is perhaps her greatest work, the Grasmere journal, comes out of an alteration in that relationship. Her letters written after William's marriage express the conventions of nineteenth-century womanhood and yet describe some of the tensions in the choice of life open to a woman like Dorothy Wordsworth.

The children fill her letters. She regards them as "my Flock" (3:240), and indeed the household becomes extremely dependent upon her for care and nurture. By 1814 two of the children have died; when another of them becomes ill while Dorothy is away, William begs for her return. He and Mary cannot cope without her (3:172–173). Anyone who has raised children from infancy can fully appreciate the physical and emotional labor this work entails. "I do not read much—very little, indeed," she observes in an 1805 letter to Lady Beaumont, who becomes one of the four or five women to whom Dorothy reveals the details and problems of her life (1:664).

The content of this letter, in fact, sets out many of the oppositions characterizing Dorothy Wordsworth at thirty-four. Having begun the letter on Christmas Day, significantly her birthday and "a day of dear and interesting remembrances," she is interrupted. Mary is away, leaving Dorothy, as is often the case, with complete responsibility for house and children. Dorothy picks up the letter to Lady Beaumont the next day to reminisce about Christmas as a time of "rejoicing" in her father's house, from which she was excluded after the death of her mother.

> The Day was always kept by my Brothers with rejoicing in my Father's house, but for six years (the interval between my Mother's Death and his) I was never once at home, never was for a single moment under my Father's Roof after her Death, which I cannot think of without regret for many causes, and particularly, that I have been thereby put out of the way of many recollections in common with my Brothers of that period of life, which, whatever it may be actually as it goes along, generally appears more delightful than any other when it is over. (1:663)

The importance of community, even of its remembrance, is emphasized here. Its lack is a deprivation Dorothy seeks to correct throughout her life.

She continues in the letter to write of Coleridge, now ill and depressed, of the children John and Dorothy, and of plans to make caring for them easier. She pauses once again when the Grasmere fiddler arrives.

> I have been summoned into the kitchen to dance with Johnny and have danced till I am out of Breath. According to annual custom, our Grasmere Fidler is going his rounds, and all the children of the neighbouring houses are assembled in the kitchen to dance. Johnny has long talked of the time when the Fiddler was to come; but he

was too shy to dance with any Body but me, and though he exhibited very boldly when I was down stairs, I find they cannot persuade him to stir again. (1:664)

The letter turns to William and his poetry, to his *Lyrical Ballads* and the "Poem addressed to Coleridge," which she is transcribing. Finally both William's writing and her own, "the third part of my Journal of our Scotch Tour," are the subject of this recounting of life at Grasmere.

Her letters suggest a trade-off. She does finally find some of the familial security she longs for. In 1803 she rejoices to Catherine Clarkson: "And oh! My dear Friend, what a beautiful spot this is! the greenest in all the earth, the softest green covers the mountains even to the very top. Silver How is before my eyes, and I forget that I have ever seen it so beautiful, every bit of grass among the purple rocks (which are of all shades of purple) is green. I am writing in my own room" (1:393). Still, the beauty and solitude, and the writing, are frequently overtaken by domestic concerns—washing, ironing, cooking, tending children. There must be some resentment in her characterization of herself as having so much to do, of being one of two "able-bodied people in the house except the servant and *William,* who you know is not expected to do anything" (2:252). Another letter to Lady Beaumont to fulfill "a restless desire that you should know me better" sets out in the language of the community—here "Frost at Midnight"—the opposing poles of solitude and family life that Dorothy needed.

> The Children are now in bed. The evening is very still, and there are no indoor sounds but the ticking of our Family watch which hangs over the chimney-piece under the drawing of the Applethwaite Cottage, and a breathing or a beating of one single irregular Flame in my fire. No one who has not been an Inmate with Children in a *Cottage* can have a notion of the quietness that takes possession of it when they are gone to sleep. The hour before is generally a noisy one, often given up to boisterous efforts to amuse them, and the noise is heard in every corner of the house—then comes the washing and undressing, a work of misery, and in ten minutes after, all is

stillness and perfect rest. It is at all times a sweet hour to us; but I can
fancy that I have never enjoyed it so much as now that I am quite
alone— (1:648)

The joy and noise of family life are set against the luxury of
being totally alone, a situation few women with children get to
enjoy. Dorothy regards her time at Grasmere as "the very happiest of my life" (1:659). Yet what contributes to that happiness
also dissipates her energies, preventing her from completing
much of what she sets out to accomplish.

Not only familial security but the glory of Grasmere itself is
seen working on Dorothy in her letters. Anxious that they will
have to leave, she writes gleefully to Lady Beaumont:

> You will rejoice to hear that we shall *not* be forced to leave Gras-
> mere Vale. We are to have the Parsonage house which will be made a
> very comfortable dwelling before we enter upon it. . . . But Oh!
> my dear Friend, this place—the wood behind it and the rocks—the
> view of Easedale from them—the lake and church and village on
> the other side—is sweeter than paradise itself. For these two days we
> have again had sunshine with westerly breezes. (2:406)

Their presence in Grasmere as well as the community of the vale
must be maintained. The Green affair shows what can be done
when "all the Inhabitants of Grasmere" work together (2:235).
The move to Rydal Mount, partly because of the family situation—the inability to stay near the children's graves in Grasmere—is for Dorothy something of a loss of Eden.

Another possibility of disintegration considered in the letters
occurs during the Lowther-Brougham election of 1818. "You
will think, dearest Sara," Dorothy writes in March, "that my
head is turned with this election, that I can think of nothing
else, and true it is" (3:449). Here the mob of rabble women, the
"numbers of disgusting females shouting Brougham," threaten
to tear the communal fabric of the vale. "I could not have believed it possible that so many impudent women and girls were
to be found in Kendal" (3:454). This form of aggressive womanhood is unacceptable in its potential destructiveness. Dissolu-

tion does come for Dorothy when, adopting a different kind of aggressive self, she falls out of community back into herself. Neither William, nor nature, nor family, nor William's writing can support her.

Her letters show that Dorothy always appraised her brother's writing clearly. She believed in his work but had no blind faith in his genius. In the early years, in 1793, for instance, she does not praise him without mentioning his "many Faults, the chief of which are Obscurity, and a too frequent use of some particular expressions and uncommon words" (1:89). By 1830 she writes to Mary Lamb of how William "shrinks from his great work, and both during the last and present winter has been employed in writing small poems. . . . my sister and I take every opportunity of pressing upon him the necessity of applying to his great work, and this he feels, resolves to do it, and again resolution fails" (5:191).

Dorothy's letters are frequently about the business of writing, publishing, and selling. Marketing William is a family matter, and all take care of various details of the poetry. Dorothy is most anxious that the work sell. Finally, however, she claims to give up: "As to us *we* shall never grow rich; for I now perceive clearly that till my dear Brother is laid in his grave his writings will not produce any profit. This I now care no more about and *shall* never *more* trouble my head concerning the sale of them" (3:247). Her letters suggest both resignation to and disappointment in the return on her investment of life and energy in William's writing.

Though her letters reveal a great ambivalence about her own writing, her poetry carries her through her darkest times. She allowed William to publish some of her poems in his own collections but not to put her name on them. An 1806 letter to Lady Beaumont relates her concerns about writing.

And you would persuade *me* that I am capable of writing poems that might give pleasure to others besides my own particular friends!! indeed, indeed you do not know me thoroughly; you think far better of me than I deserve— . . . Do not think that I was ever bold enough to hope to compose verses for the pleasure of grown persons. Descriptions, Sentiments, or little stories for children was all I could be ambitious of doing, and I did try one story, but failed so sadly that I was completely discouraged. Believe me, since I received your letter I have made several attempts (could I do less as you requested that I would *for your sake?*) and have been obliged to give it up in despair; and looking into my mind I find nothing there, even if I had the gift of language and numbers, that I could have the vanity to suppose could be of any use beyond our own fireside, or to please, as in your case, a few partial friends; but I have no command of language, no power of expressing my ideas, and no one was ever more inapt at molding words into regular metre. I have often tried when I have been walking alone (muttering to myself as is my Brother's custom) to express my feelings in verse; feelings, and *ideas* such as they were, I have never wanted at those times; but prose and rhyme and blank verse were jumbled together and nothing ever came of it. (2:24–25)

Dorothy's habitual self-denigration fills the letter; she gives herself no credit. What she does do well, such as description, she dismisses as trivial. If one of the "little stories for children" was "Mary Jones and her Pet-lamb," why would she consider herself such a failure? Part of the problem might be that she sees her writing only in terms of her brother's, even to aping his method of composition. There is no recognition that other forms, more accessible to her kinds of perception, should be the basis of her literary output. Regular meter does not necessarily constitute a poem; the mixture of prose, rhyme, and blank verse that she dismisses as an impossible jumble could in another place be a perfectly acceptable, if not preferred, mode of expression. Little room for Dorothy's kind of art existed in the Grasmere community of writing, and she was able to make space for herself only accidentally and certainly never to her own satisfaction.

She did decide to go into print with her *Recollections of a Tour made in Scotland* but gave up the idea when William reinforced her anxieties by suggesting that the strain of authorship and publicity would be too much for her. Her own desire for anonymity lies behind a letter in answer to Catherine Clarkson's suggestion that she publish her story of George and Sarah Green.

My dear Friend I cannot express what pain I feel in refusing to grant any request of yours, and above all one in which dear Mr Clarkson joins so earnestly, but indeed I cannot have that narrative published. My reasons are entirely disconnected with myself, much as I should detest the idea of setting myself up as an Author. I should not object on that score as if it had been an invention of my own it might have been published without a name, and nobody would have thought of me. But on account of the Family of the Greens I cannot consent. Their story was only represented to the world in that narrative which was drawn up for the collecting of the subscription, so far as might tend to produce the end desired, but by publishing this narrative of mine I should bring the children forward to notice as Individuals, and we know not what injurious effect this might have upon them. Besides it appears to me that the events are too recent to be published in delicacy to others as well as to the children. (2:453–454)

If Dorothy did not consider herself an author, some would argue, neither should we. But her statement here is about "setting . . . up as an Author," about avoiding notoriety, not about writing itself. Hers is an anxiety many women feel at the prospect of becoming public figures, and it is enhanced by the wish she must have had to avoid any appearance of treading on her brother's turf. Her objections to publication also raise a general question about works drawn "from real life": What effect will the text have on the subject? For the romantic writer, who often takes herself and those nearest to her as the best subject available, the concern is typical. With the change in the early nineteenth century in what was considered appropriate or interesting literary material must come the sort of authorial uneasiness Dorothy here expresses, an uneasiness faced by so many romantic and modern writers.

The poetry she so denigrates indicates one part of her mind that finds expressed form during the illness that dominated her last twenty years. Although she had periods of verbal clarity, during much of that time she muttered, laughed, made weird noises, sang, and recited her poems. Information about this time must be pieced together from Dorothy's letters and late journals and from the observations that remain of those around her. Evidently, there was much to suppress or much that people felt should be kept hidden about her condition. It may be, however, that her last years were a perfectly logical end to the life she chose. It may be that a series of inversions occurred in which the isolated, hostile, aggressive underside of existence in the Grasmere community took over.

A physical change seems to have occurred when, at fifty-six, Dorothy became ill during a visit to her nephew. Although her journals often mention physical complaints, she believed—so she wrote in a letter to Henry Crabb Robinson—that this was "the first time in my life of fifty six years in which I have had a serious illness" (5:71). She insists that she is perfectly recovered, but her letters after that time focus increasingly on sickness, aging, and death. And according to William, "she will never I fear perfectly recover" from the attack of "cholera morbus" (5:394). Four years later, in 1833, she almost died, and William wrote, "No one could scarcely be brought lower and yet survive, as God be thanked she has done" (5:635). Her illness began to take various forms. William wrote of "bilious attacks"; Mary Wordsworth termed her "a strange case"; Dorothy herself wrote of "tremendous struggles." A letter of 1836 reveals both physical and mental alterations. "I have got through a mighty struggle—and thank God am now as well as ever I was in my life except that I have not recovered the use of my legs. My Arms have been active enough as the torn caps of my nurses and the heavy blows I have given their heads and faces will testify" (6:189). Dorothy ascribes both immobility and pugilism to herself, two characteristics that one would scarcely associate with her. She has always been the greatest of walkers, and the notion of her striking a servant is bizarre. Elizabeth Kincaid-Ehlers suggests that what occurs in these last years is a "crazy logic of reversal." Dorothy finally lets go and lives out the reverse of those qualities into which she has been forced.[5]

---

5. My view of Dorothy's late life has been greatly influenced by Elizabeth Kincaid-Ehlers and has grown from discussions with her as well as from reading parts of her manuscript, "Blue Woman on a Green Field: A Consideration of Dorothy Wordsworth," *DAI* 39:2291A–2292A (1977). I am not convinced by Mary Moorman's assertion in *William Wordsworth: A Biography* that Dorothy was in a "mischievous mood" and was joking when she wrote of striking her nurses. (2:513n.)

Indeed, Mary's letters portray a Dorothy who is filthy, fat, selfish, and crazed, who "never attempts to use her legs, except sometimes when two of them [her attendants] support her and make her *think* she is walking: tho' she only shoves one foot before the other without bearing the least of her own weight" (214). After years of walking in nature, she won't move. After years of helping to wash and bleach the family laundry, she requires a maid "*entirely* devoted to her" because the laundry must be done every day (164). After years of meeting those who came to visit her brother and making friends as she traveled, in 1838 she must be kept out of the way, "or she would terrify strangers to death" (218). After years of eagerly awaiting William's return from his travels, she no longer cares about his presence. Dora need not worry about detaining her father on Dorothy's account: "it is all the same to her, poor thing" (165). Mary presses her about William's absence: "'but about your Brother, I think we are not to see him yet'— 'I don't know,'" she replies and soon is singing away (180). After years of supplying words to the writers around her to help them define the world, she retreats into her own private language. After years of living for her brother and his family, she becomes totally self-involved, totally selfish. She demands service from the community she has served even as she cuts herself off from it. By 1848 she becomes, according to Mary, "so much the Master of her Brother, who humours all her waywardness as quite to enervate him—so that whether he will have the heart to deprive her of his indulgences, (which she is much happier without) by our leaving home—is doubtful" (306).

What puzzles Mary is the way Dorothy can slip in and out of madness. She writes in a letter of 1838, "—and at times if you heard her talk, without seeing her, you would think nothing ailed her. It is a strange case" (218–219). It may not be such "a strange case," however, if we look at it briefly in terms of theories of feminine psychology. Jean Baker Miller writes of how what members of a "subordinate" group like women really know and feel is bound to come into opposition with what the dominant male culture encourages them to know, feel, and do. "An inner tension between the two sets of concepts and their derivatives is almost inevitable" (11). For a long time, Dorothy holds these tensions in suspension, working out in her writing many of the ambivalences she experiences, the conflicts typically felt by women in accommodating themselves to the dominant male structure, to what society expects of them. In the later part of her life, however, perhaps because her physical illness triggers such a release, she lives the conflict, setting it out on her own terms. When Mary tries to read to her or to engage her in one of their old communal pastimes, Dorothy refuses to participate. "She says," Mary writes in a letter, "'she is too busy with her own feelings'" (157). Dorothy may not need to write anymore because she can *be* what Miller calls "authentic," holding up her ambivalences for all to view. She can be both the old Dorothy that everyone knows and loves and the aggressively unacceptable crazy lady. In a letter of 1837 Dorothy can still describe herself with the clarity that those around her accept as normal: "A Madman might as well attempt to relate the history of his doings and those of his fellows in confinement as I to tell you one hundredth part of what I have felt, suffered and done. Through God's Mercy I am now calm and easy, and I trust my dear Brother's eyes are in a fair way of perfect recovery. They all feared he would lose his sight; but now he is very much better" (6:472).

How many women who become "authentic" are considered seriously disturbed? Recognizing conventional responses, Dorothy relates herself to "a madman." But in the voice of what everyone considers her "real" self, she sets up in this letter a sequence of associations typical of the old days by connecting herself to William's eyes. She spends her life helping him to see the world; while she has been refusing to view that world, he has been sinking to blindness. In her sentence, his recovery of sight conjoins her recovery of "calm," of "normalcy."

It is a state she maintains only sporadically. Her journals, which stop in 1840, demonstrate conventional mental clarity and a particular concern with order in the number of lists and accounts they contain. She also copies and recopies her poems in them. Numbers and her own poetry constitute her final language of coherence. Her last surviving letter, written in 1838, cries of language and nature gone awry.

My dearest Dora

They say I must write a letter—and what shall it be? News—
news I must seek for news. My own thoughts are a wilderness—
'not pierceable by power of any star'—News then is my resting-
place—news! news!

Poor Peggy Benson lies in Grasmere Church-yard beside her
once beautiful Mother. Fanny Haigh is gone to a better world. My
Friend Mrs Rawson has ended her ninety and two years pilgrimage—and *I* have fought and fretted and striven—and am here beside
the fire. The Doves behind me at the small window—the laburnum
with its naked seed-pods shivers before my window and the pine-
trees rock from their base.—More I cannot write so farewell! and
may God bless you and your kind good Friend Miss Fenwick to
whom I send love and all the best of wishes.—Yours ever more

Dorothy Wordsworth
(6:528)

The lines she sends to Dora, in many ways a younger Dorothy,
are forced from her by "them," by her community. By this time
a shift in pronoun emphasis occurs. She no longer writes "we,"
but rather "I" and "they." Dorothy remembers; she can still
(mis)quote Spenser, but the protecting grove of *The Faerie
Queene* becomes for Dorothy a crazy wilderness. No light enters; no light is given off. No longer able to view and shape the
world around her, she seeks happenings to report. She dies into
the language of event, "the resting-place" of news, which here
becomes the telling of deaths. Four women are dead and faded—
Peggy Benson, her mother, Fanny Haigh, and Mrs. Rawson—
and all Dorothy's struggle ends with her planted beside a fire,
another version of the deaths she has related. Nature is caged inside and tormented outside—"shivering" and "rocking." It does
nothing for her; she does nothing for it. The letter cries the betrayal of her mind, her voice, her nature. What happens to a
woman of incredible sensibility and awareness who loses her
mother, who makes her life's choices at odds with cultural convention, who seeks to fulfill the demands of her emotions and
her talents? What happens when she is finally betrayed by the

world and the language of that world in which she has made her life? Her being was in the writing and the nature that were not hers alone, not William's alone, but she tried to speak within his language. Part of her abiding interest for women and men today rests in the modes of defense she articulated when she found out that her space within that language necessarily sealed her off not only from her brother but ultimately from the world.

III.

Travel

❖ ❖ ❖ ❖ ❖ DOROTHY WORDSWORTH DEVOTES
the most space in the canon of her writing to the recording of
her travels, an emphasis that becomes hideously ironic when the
woman of the late journals and letters is set against the one who
journeys out into the world. In a letter to Dora Wordsworth,
Maria Jane Jewsbury describes Dorothy as traveler:

> I think you would smile if you knew all she did and saw. "Panting
> Time" (that is myself) "toiled after her in vain." Churches—Mu-
> seums—Factories—Shopping—Institutions—Company—at home
> and abroad—not that I attempted to compete with her,—no I merely
> lay in bed and legislated—provided relays of friends and carriages—
> and had the pleasure of knowing that my visitor was pleased—and
> that she won all hearts before and around her. She is the very genius
> of Popularity—an embodied spell. I should be jealous of her for a
> continuance. I should be dethroned even on my own sofa—amidst
> my own circle. (Gillett xlv)

The vitality Jewsbury emphasizes complements another gloss
that the travel journals provide on Dorothy's relationship to
the Grasmere community. In them, she often makes a point of
asserting herself as an independent person, distinct from the
housebound women she meets as she goes. Yet, her travel journals reveal her dependence on and joy in a domestic life in
nature.

Ernest de Selincourt reprints seven such works: *Journal of Visit to Hamburgh and of Journey from Hamburgh to Goslar (1798), Recollections of a Tour made in Scotland (A.D. 1803), Excursion on the Banks of Ullswater (November 1805), Excursion up Scawfell Pike (October 1818), Journal of a Tour on the Continent (1820), Journal of my Second Tour in Scotland (1822),* and *Journal of a Tour in the Isle of Man (1828).* Varying in length from a few to a few hundred pages, these journals reveal the development of Dorothy's descriptive techniques and powers, and the gap of thirteen years between the first three and the last four help to differentiate the early and late phases of Dorothy's imagination.

In her earliest German journal she appears as a fairly conventional tourist, comparing the shops, houses, and food of foreign cities to those of her own country. Often she is not particularly impressed with what she sees: "there is such a constant succession of hateful smells, that it is quite disgusting to pass near the houses."[1] Already in the Hamburgh journal, Dorothy is meticulous in setting down details, but it is not until she goes to Scotland—"the country above all others that I have seen, in which a man of imagination may carve out his own pleasures" (1:214)—that she puts together the unique blend of landscape, voyage, writing, memory, stasis, and change that constitute her best travel writing.

At first, Dorothy appears to be acting as communal secretary, recording observations to be used later, mainly by her brother. In fact, in the Hamburgh journal, when she is too ill to write, the entry is in William's hand, which indicates that each day had to be noted down. The insistence on keeping detailed, accurate records, evident in all her journals, takes on a different element of necessity in the creation of a travel journal, as the texts themselves describe. The style of the travel journals combines

1. *Journals of Dorothy Wordsworth,* ed. Ernest de Selincourt. I, 30. All quotations from the travel journals are taken from this edition and are hereafter cited in the text. In publishing these journals, de Selincourt has selected material from several sources. What he entitles "Excursion up Scawfell Pike" was originally a letter to the Reverend William Johnson. "Journal of a Tour in the Isle of Man" is a selection from the late journals. "Journal of Visit to Hamburgh and of Journey from Hamburgh to Goslar" is taken from a small notebook, which Dorothy kept in Germany. Dorothy intended the records of both Scottish tours as well as that of the tour on the Continent to be separate travel books.

record and recollection to produce a minute recounting of such things as conversations held, prices paid, meals eaten, landscapes viewed. *Recollections of a Tour made in Scotland,* however, is written not from notes but from memory. "I am writing not a Journal, *for we took no notes,* but *recollections* of our tour in the form of a Journal" (1:vii). But Dorothy finds simple recollection wanting, for sometimes her memory fails. She wishes to describe several buildings but cannot and "now at this distance of time regret that I did not take notes" (1:390). In the later journals, as a consequence, she frequently rewrites notes taken on the spot. In the second Scottish tour, for instance, she describes her method as one of copying "the few notes which I took at intervals during the day, adding now and then my recollections" (2:376). When, for some reason, she does not take notes, she feels her descriptions hindered. "As I took no notes it is impossible for me to give a notion of the extensive and picturesque remains of the castle of Rheinfels" (2:52).

Yet the notes so necessary to her are frequently misplaced. She writes, "—but I had left my journal!—and the poor boy was sent back again," or, "On reaching the Inn I discovered I had left my journal; but whether in the boat, upon one of the seats, or scattered by the way I could not guess" (2:141, 90). The gestures of pushing away her work may not be wholly accidental and may reflect, in addition to Dorothy's general anxiety about writing, the problems she associates with this particular kind of writing, the composition of travel books. Both the narrative voice and the language of the journals themselves speak to the difficulties, if not the impossibilities, of creating a satisfactory travel journal. How, Dorothy continually wonders, can an image be fixed in words? How can a scene that she has viewed be brought before a reader? The very basis of a travel journal, the attempt to show a landscape to the reader, to re-create a moment, is alien to the medium of language, which reveals itself in Dorothy's work as a set of conventions that force separation and mediation. As the word displaces the thing itself, the travel journal in one sense only separates the reader from the scene described. Of a particularly striking landscape Dorothy exclaims, "I would willingly have given twenty pounds to have been able to take a lively picture of it" (1:338). Language proves inadequate to her task.

"But if I were to go on describing for evermore, I should give but a faint, and very often a false, idea of the different objects and the various combinations of them in this most intricate and delicious place" (1:274). Her work questions the notion that language allows access to the reality of things.

Verbal descriptions are problematic, she asserts, not only because of the differentiating medium involved but also because of that process by which they are arrived at. Notes can serve as reminders, but memory must be called upon in the writing of a description, and memory does not always serve, not necessarily because of a failure to remember but because Dorothy sees the material itself as alien to the faculty. The banks of Loch Lomond, an important place in any Scottish tour, give her particular difficulty. "My description must needs be languid; for the sight itself was too fair to be remembered" (1:321). Because her writing works with such direct relationships between the mind and the world, because her mind does not seek to store images from the natural world to be used later in a process of self-definition, the immediate presence of the object seems necessary to her imaginative process. Thus the exercise of memory, the delayed return to a scene, necessary to travel writing, makes this enterprise somewhat alien to her. Even after many years and many pages of such writing, she frequently worries about the problem. About the Rhine, a site central to her continental tour, she can write only, "It is impossible even to *remember* (therefore how should I enable anyone to imagine?) the power of the dashing, and of the sounds—the breezes—the dancing dizzy sensations—and the exquisite beauty of the colours!" (2:89). The question here is combined with an exclamation about the scene that attempts to re-create it even as it denies the possibility of such a re-creation. As the text continually points to such contradictions, it questions the whole possibility of presenting a natural scene in words, of writing a travel book.

Complementing Dorothy's skepticism about the possibility of accurate imaginative re-creation are the text's frequent references to "forgeries" and deceptions. In *Excursion up Scawfell Pike,* Dorothy writes of how she "espied a ship upon the glittering sea while we were looking over Eskdale." Their guide asks Dorothy how certain she is of this perception, and her compan-

ion replies for both women: "It is a ship of that I am certain."
The guide does not persist but a moment later points to the
ship, now a cloud formation of "a horse with a gallant neck and
head." Dorothy takes this incident as a warning about deception
in perception. "I hope, when again inclined to positiveness, I
may remember the ship and the horse upon the glittering sea"
(1:430). It seems more than coincidence that Dorothy's first
Scottish tour opens as she, William, and Coleridge arrive at
Carlisle on the very day that John Hatfield, the forgerer, was
condemned. Certainly her emphasis on the case is rather odd in
a travel book. Dorothy relates his story in detail, fascinated with
this deceiving writing. She specifically recounts the observation
of another tourist who declared that "we might learn from Hatfield's fate 'not to meddle with pen and ink'" (1:196). Might not
a person transferring a natural scene to the printed page also be
involved in a kind of forgery, a meddling with pen and ink?

Although the possibility remains that her writing is meddle-
some tampering with the immediacy of the universe, Dorothy
also makes a claim in her travel journals for the authenticating
power of her mode of travel writing. The journals emphasize
her uniqueness and importance as a recorder of the journeys of
men and women in nature. Aware that she sees things unavailable
to other eyes, Dorothy is "better satisfied with myself for being
able to find enjoyment in what unfortunately to many persons is
either dismal or insipid" (1:214). The insight, clarity of vision,
and independence of mind composing the travel journals are reflected in the description with which she begins *Excursion up
Scawfell Pike*. This characterization, ostensibly not of Dorothy
herself but of Miss Barker, the woman with whom she per-
forms "the feat" of climbing Scawfell Pike, nonetheless reveals
Dorothy's own particular authorial energies. Living alone in a
secluded spot she has chosen for its haunting beauty, Miss Barker is at once fiercely independent and at ease among her many
friends. "You will guess," Dorothy writes, "that she has re-
sources within herself; such indeed she has. She is a painter and
labours hard in depicting the beauties of her favorite Vale; she is
also fond of music and of reading, and has a reflecting mind;
besides (though before she lived in Borrowdale she was no great
walker) she is become an active climber of the hills" (1:425).

The parallels with Dorothy herself are numerous. Both women live independent, unconventional lives; both study extensively; most important, both are artists whose creativity is often tied to the landscape around them. Her surroundings render Miss Barker more physically active, having made her into a walker like Dorothy, and similarly, new material for a travel piece energizes Dorothy. "On going into a new country I seem to myself to waken up, and afterwards it surprises me to remember how much alive I have been to the distinctions of dress, household arrangements, etc. etc" (1:247).

Dorothy's self-characterizations contain both confidence in and surprise at her own success as a travel writer. She is proud of how fine her texts are, how superior they are to the observations of typical travelers, "our prospect-hunters and 'picturesque travellers'" (1:271). Although her work has features common to contemporary travel books, she sees herself as going far beyond these conventional descriptions. Her discussions with her brother and Coleridge, she feels, allow her to make finer distinctions in descriptive terminology than is usually done. She analyzes the very process of viewing and of writing about seeing more sophisticatedly than most travel writers. Moreover, Dorothy's travel books reveal the particular concerns of a nineteenth-century woman traveler. The imaginative structures that demonstrate themselves in this set of texts again provide an alternative view, a vision different from that of the male members of Dorothy's community of writing and journeying.

Recollections of a Tour made in Scotland and *Journal of my Second Tour in Scotland* treat the same subject nineteen years apart and provide an important record of the beginning and end of Dorothy's career as a travel writer. In 1803 Dorothy, William, and Coleridge went on a six-week tour of Scotland. They walked a lot and talked a lot and collected material that would later be used in their writing. Dorothy's account of the tour took the form of her *Recollections,* put together first for "the sake of a few friends, who, it seemed, ought to have been with us" (1:vii). Deciding to attempt publication, she revised the work extensively, producing five manuscript versions. Then in 1822 she toured Scotland for a month, this time with Joanna Hutchinson. She composed her *Journal of my Second Tour in Scotland* soon after she returned from the trip, working from notes taken while she traveled. She did not spend much time on it, however, because she was still revising her *Recollections,* which she was once again planning to publish. The *Recollections* never appeared during Dorothy's lifetime; William finally decided public authorship would be too much of a strain on his sister's delicate health. This publication history and certain comments in *Recollections* evidence both Dorothy's general anxieties about writing and the difficulties she associates with travel writing.

A passage in the *Recollections,* describing a night in the Trossachs, encompasses both the difficulty of substituting a written description for a natural scene and the desirability of illuminating a landscape through her presentation of it. On this particular night, Dorothy retires early, thus withdrawing into a private space.

> I went to bed sometime before the family. The door was shut between us, and they had a bright fire, which I could not see; but the light it sent up among the varnished rafters and beams, which crossed each other in almost as intricate and fantastic a manner as I have seen the under-boughs of a large beech-tree withered by the depth of the shade above, produced the most beautiful effect that can be conceived. It was like what I should suppose an underground cave or temple to be, with a dripping or moist roof, and the moonlight entering in upon it by some means or other, and yet the colours were more like the colours of melted gems. (1:277–278)

While the description effects a kind of unity between the man-made room and the natural cave, it allows nature's presence, somewhat artificially, through simile and metaphor. Paradoxically, death and darkness—shade-withered underboughs of a beech tree—produce the extraordinary beauty Dorothy's view elaborates. As she lies in bed, the house preoccupies her more than "the remembrance of the Trossachs, beautiful as they were." She looks at the lake, listens to the rain, but thinks of literary artifice. "I thought of the Fairyland of Spenser, and what I had read in romance at other times, and then, what a feast would it be for a London pantomime-maker, could he but transplant it to Drury Lane, with all its beautiful colours!" (1:278). The progression indicates the displacement of the natural world into words and finally into the farce of a London pantomime, a thoroughly hybrid, artificial entertainment.

The pantomime would, however, be colorful, and Dorothy's description evinces a certain eagerness for the spectacle. Similarly, the underground cave or temple into which the moonlight enters raises contradictory possibilities: preservation through isolated hiding and ruin through illuminating display. The beauty admired encompasses the destruction of substance ("melted gems"). The moist, dripping, hidden cave, an image easily associated with femininity, is illuminated by another of Dorothy's characteristic, traditionally feminine principles, the moon. The scene also allows the overseeing feminine principle of the moon the power for seduction, and the moonlight views that which its own light helps create. Dorothy's use of this imagery common to other romantic writers, particularly Percy Bysshe Shelley, here highlights the scene as one of feminine self-sufficiency and emphasizes the self-authenticating figuration of a female writer.

The domestic concerns that are a distinguishing quality of Dorothy's travel writing, often taking the form of descriptions of other women and their familial scenes, may also point to the feminine origins of the work. Kitchens, mothers and children, and family firesides appear almost as frequently in the journals as do landscapes. Her presentation of homes and hearths contrasts with what Dorothy herself undertakes in the journal—movement and travel. Unlike most women of her day, Dorothy often found travel and the work of writing that resulted from it more important than home, husband, and children. The closing description of the first Scottish tour makes one comment on Dorothy as traveler in contrast to woman as wife and mother, the woman here being Mary of Dorothy's own household. Returning from Scotland, they find "Mary in perfect health, Joanna Hutchinson with her, and little John asleep in the clothes-basket by the fire" (1:409). William's sonnet, the last words of the *Recollections,* elaborate on the mother-child relationship left behind "While we have wander'd over wood and wild—"

(1:409). Having chosen another kind of life, Dorothy describes her choice in part through the lives of other women.

Indeed, she tends to focus on the women she encounters in her travels more than on the men. The access she, as a woman, has to other women and the part she gives these contacts to play in her travel journals individualize her work. Her descriptions of women help characterize the country she wishes to describe at the same time as they help define her own being as a woman and a writer.

Her progress through Leadhills in the first Scottish tour is a good example of how Dorothy uses female contacts. Leaving William, she goes to buy some thread. While waiting for the proprietress's son to get some from another shop, she sits with the woman and has a chance to observe "the quiet manner in which they lived" (1:210). The poverty and smallness of the houses do not seem to affect their inhabitants too adversely. This particular shopkeeper, moreover, belies the popular stereotype of the uncouth country peasant. Dorothy finds "a bookishness, a certain formality in this woman's language, which was very remarkable," remarkable perhaps because Dorothy is herself a "bookish" country woman. Finally, Dorothy's description of the woman's dress becomes a general description of the way women clothe themselves in this part of the country. All this information is given in the context of her purchase of thread.

After returning to the inn, Dorothy goes into the kitchen to speak with the landlady about beds. In the journal, the time she spends chatting with the woman by the fire also provides the opportunity to describe both the kitchen and the baking of oat bread. She finds this landlady a bit ill-natured and her kitchen generally dirty, but Dorothy disapproves much more of the landlady at Loss, who does not want to give them a fire even though the night is cold.

> Her countenance corresponded with the unkindness of denying us a fire on a cold night, for she was the most cruel and even hateful-looking woman I ever saw. She was overgrown with fat, and was sitting with her feet and legs in a tub of water for the dropsy (probably brought on by whisky-drinking). The sympathy which I felt and expressed for her, on seeing her in this wretched condition (for

her legs were swoln as thick as mill-posts), seemed to produce no effect; and I was obliged, after five minutes' conversation, to leave the affair of the beds undecided. (1:250)

Dorothy's view of this woman derives in part from her own moral and class biases. Perhaps her sympathy produces no effect because it comes with disapproval and disgust evident in her view that physical discomfort is brought on by overindulgence.

She shows a similar aversion to the women in the ferry-house at Loch Curran. Faint with cold and hunger, Dorothy sits by the fire but cannot bring herself to eat anything because of the filth in the house and because "there were so many wretchedly dirty women and children" (1:318). Distinguishing herself from others of her class, she insists she might have gotten over the dirt had there not been "a most disgusting combination of laziness and coarseness in the countenances and manners of the women." The four women living in the hut are particularly repellant to Dorothy because they make no attempt to remedy their situation: "there was no work amongst them." While expressing her rage at the degradation and poverty of so many women in Scotland, Dorothy also believes in the possibility and validity of work to prevent one from being overcome by a hopeless situation.

Perhaps because of her investment in her own work and intellect, she praises the women she encounters who exhibit any signs of intelligence and awareness. She is more in sympathy, for example, with the women at Glencoe. One of them lives in a dirty house surrounded by dirty children, but her "benevolent, happy countenance almost converted her slovenly and lazy way of leaving all things to take care of themselves into a comfort and a blessing" (1:326). Another enters carrying a baby and some fish, eager to speak of her old home that Dorothy has just visited. They endear themselves further when they hurry Dorothy off to meet the grande dame of the village, a charming woman of little education, whom they respect because she is from England.

Dorothy's life is very different from that of the women she often chooses to describe. Spending the night at an inn on the way to Calendar, Dorothy sits and chats with the mistress, who is baking barley cakes. After talking about various techniques of cake making, the two women begin an extended discussion of their personal lives. Although the innkeeper deluges her with questions, Dorothy is not offended. She sees a fresh innocence in this Scotswoman and many of the others she meets, likening them to children who always want to be told more stories and who "delight in being amused without effort of their own minds" (1:382). Dorothy wryly ascribes "pious seriousness and perfect simplicity" to the woman's assurance that as a virgin Dorothy will have a special place in heaven. When this woman goes on to describe her loss of several children and the sorrows that have filled her life, we must begin to question Dorothy's delineation of her childishness and simplicity. Sympathetic though it is, Dorothy's description of her is also somewhat condescending, as if the pressures of the woman's life, though rendering her an object of concern and pity, have left her somehow underdeveloped.

Dorothy is either unable or unwilling to see the fulfillment and joy some of these women experience in their traditional female roles. She most often uses their familial situations to contrast with and reassert the felicity of her own life choices, which are certainly not without pain and ambivalence. It is obviously not easy to live a life so different from that of other women, and Dorothy focuses on those women who allow her to reaffirm her decision. She describes a family crossing Inversneyde on the ferry—a man, his wife, and child who, like the vagrant families of the Grasmere journals, must leave their home to seek work elsewhere. Concentrating on the woman to whom "every step was painful toil, for she had either her child to bear or a heavy burthen," Dorothy emphasizes that she is also walking but that for her it provides sheer pleasure. Unburdened by child and husband, Dorothy would recall even "toil" as "pleasure" (1:369). Similarly in the second Scottish tour, she reports an early morning walk near what she supposes to be a deserted lake. She is startled by the coughing of a woman who soon overtakes her. Assuming that the woman is going to work, Dorothy describes the lunch she might be carrying and recounts their conversation. "'What, you are taking a walk? It is very pleasant walking here!' So, truly, it was—and I then felt as if I were in the most beautiful, and the quietest place in the world. The Lake was very near me—it was not perfectly calm, yet moving and glittering, and broke so gently against the shore that I scarcely heard the sound without listening for it. The Robins made a constant warbling. The woman slackened her pace by my side, and we chatted together" (2:356). Here a simple question releases overpowering feelings as this feminine presence produces a new awareness in Dorothy. Why should she suddenly feel as if the place were the quietest and the most beautiful in the world, especially since the constant warbling of robins does constitute noise? Her focus remains on the woman and the landscape. Dorothy does not analyze her own feelings extensively but rather makes her description of the woman comment on herself. This woman too is able to draw overpowering feeling from a natural scene, but she is walking to work, whereas Dorothy is walking for fun; her toil is Dorothy's pleasure. As they continue to talk, the woman describes how hard her life is, especially in winter: the churches far away, schooling for the children almost impossible to afford, and travel, especially by steamboat, beyond her means. "How different her condition and ours!" Dorothy finally exclaims, startled by this view of travel. She herself, after all, is walking near Loch Lomond because for her steamboats are so cheap. In this woman, then, Dorothy finds both a catalyst for her own feelings and a defining contrast to her own life.

Another woman, Joanna Hutchinson, appears frequently in Dorothy's work as such a foil. Her life paralleled Dorothy's in many ways. An orphan at an early age, she centered family life on her siblings, keeping house for one brother or another throughout her life. Dorothy's representation of Joanna, her traveling companion in the second Scottish tour, allows her to express some of her own fears about growing older and about the inability to travel that might come with age. Timid and nervous, Joanna is also physically ill during their tour; Dorothy frequently mentions Joanna's rheumatism and catalogues her other aches and pains. The standard published version of *Journal of my Second Tour in Scotland* concludes with a reference to Joanna's deteriorating physical condition: "Poor Joanna stiff and tired, and soon very sick" (2:396). Ernest de Selincourt does not print the remaining entries, which tell of Joanna's illness in Burnfoot and of a trip to Edinburgh and Sea Field where Joanna took the baths, because he feels they "are not worth reproduction." But in fact, the entries are important for their emphasis on a sickly, frightened Joanna, whose illness underlines Dorothy's robust competence. Whereas in the first tour Dorothy depends on the male members of her group and generally defers to them, in the second she is the dominant member of the party, totally in control of the journey, undertaking responsibilities previously left to her brother, coping with luggage, missed boats, and unacceptable accommodations.

Such responsibility and independence is far from worry free, however, both because of her own feelings and because of the restrictions generally placed on women. Indeed, the journal of the second Scottish tour is in part about what it is like for two women to travel by themselves in the early nineteenth century, to be the only females "travelling for pleasure" (2:381). Their friends do not approve of the project, characterizing Dorothy and Joanna as "'two forlorn helpless creatures!'" (2:340). Well-meaning relatives lecture them about accidents that might befall them, innkeepers who might deceive them, and foreigners who might take advantage of them. Once, near the end of the trip, Dorothy's confidence collapses completely into a nightmare of female independence invaded and destroyed by male lust and power.

Walking alone with Joanna, Dorothy asks "a big strong old man" how far it is to the toll bar. His reply, "What, do you mean to *house* there?" makes her feel it was very unwise to speak to him (2:391). Perhaps she is picking up Joanna's nervousness, for her companion, who will not look up, finally cries, "How could you be so imprudent as to speak to that man in this lonely place?" They rush on, looking fearfully back over their shoulders, certain that someone is bearing down on them. A light appears in the distance, but Dorothy's fears have made her feel incapable of moving to escape danger. Joanna, she notes, is in even worse condition. Their terrors are eased only by another feminine presence, "the sight of a woman's kind face" at the farmhouse they approach. As they try to calm themselves before the fire, however, men invade the scene of feminine self-sufficiency, when two crude Scotsmen with a "rattling wild air" burst into the room demanding whiskey. The landlady throws them out but not before Joanna becomes convinced that these are the men they have seen pursuing them. Dorothy speculates that they "*had heard something* about us." Perhaps the rumor of two women traveling alone had aroused these men, or more to the point, Dorothy and Joanna assume that it has and are sure the men have come to the farmhouse because of them. Finally beginning to feel at ease with the landlady, her husband, and brother, Dorothy and Joanna decide to spend the night there, but their fear is renewed with the realization that they have made themselves utterly dependent on strangers. Dorothy experiences "one five minutes during which I was more terrified than ever before in my whole life" (2:393). After they are in bed, the brother goes out, and Dorothy becomes convinced that he is admitting the men who had "come in after us in the evening," that the four men had plotted to murder them (2:394).

Dorothy's projections demonstrate the underside of feminine independence, which, ever set against male dominance and ever in fear of male aggression, may eventually be murdered by what it opposes. It seems impossible for a woman to free herself from these terrors, no matter how competent she may be. On the other hand, Dorothy has some reason to be afraid. She is in a unique situation; Englishwomen did not venture into the wilds of Scotland alone, and Dorothy herself certainly has little experience with aggressive Scotsmen. Her class expectations as well as her fears may lead to her terrified conclusions. Throughout the second Scottish tour, she is conscious of her financial means, aware that she is of a different class from most of the people she meets.

This difference is supplemented by another, for Dorothy is also aware of the journey as a return. She is revisiting the scenes of her youth, remembered from past travels, and is understandably ambivalent about sharing with another woman scenes she had visited with William and Coleridge when all were at the height of their creative powers. Setting out up Kirkstone, along the path that used to connect them with Coleridge, she thinks, "Nothing, surely, so beautiful in Scotland!" (2:339). The second journal concentrates less on the wild beauty of the country, which Dorothy feels cultivation has diminished, than on progress, time, death, and memory as her view of the country itself mirrors her own aging process. With age that brings greater wealth, polish, and self-sufficiency comes an obvious loss of youthful energy as well as, she fears, a certain loss of imaginative power.

While she regrets "the departure of such native attractions as *must* give way to improvements in wealth and industry," she feels it "almost churlish" to do so (2:381). She now finds carefully ordered walks with "seats conveniently placed" (2:348). She can afford the expensive section of the steamboat, but her means of travel demonstrates her ambivalence about progress. Although she understands that technology makes it possible for her to take the journey with Joanna, she laments, "Alas! steam-boats are always in a hurry, and take noise and commotion along with them" (2:353). Perhaps because she is financially more secure, she focuses on the poverty of the country. As on the first tour, she finds herself sitting in a small cottage where she is surrounded by women nursing their children. At one end of the room, however, lies the dead body of a small child, its mother seated at the head of its bier. As Dorothy sits "by this humble fire-side, musing on poverty and peace, on death and the grave," she is pushed to more general considerations than she has previously recorded (2:366). Whereas it has not been a property of her imagination to generalize and to draw conclusions from a description, she does so more frequently in the second Scottish tour. She often recalls those people she met on her first tour and wonders what has happened to them, speculating on the poverty, sickness, and death that must characterize their lives.

Compare these activities of mind to her characteristic mode of expression in the following passage from the early journal, which also contrasts her view with William's:

We had three miles to walk to Tarbet. It rained, but not heavily; the mountains were not concealed from us by the mists, but appeared larger and more grand; twilight was coming on, and the obscurity under which we saw the objects, with the sounding of the torrents, kept our minds alive and wakeful; all was solitary and huge—sky, water, and mountains mingled together. While we were walking forward, the road leading us over the top of a brow, we stopped suddenly at the sound of a half-articulate Gaelic hooting from the field close to us; it came from a little boy, whom we could see on the hill between us and the lake, wrapped up in a grey plaid; he was probably calling home the cattle for the night. His appearance was in the highest degree moving to the imagination: mists were on the hillsides, darkness shutting in upon the huge avenue of mountains, torrents roaring, no house in sight to which the child might belong; his dress, cry, and appearance all different from anything we had been accustomed to. It was a text, as Wm. has since observed to me, containing in itself the whole history of the Highlander's life—his melancholy, his simplicity, his poverty, his superstition, and above all, that visionariness which results from a communion with the unworldliness of nature. (1:286)

The travelers walk in a scene of water, half-light, torrents, and mists, a scene of nature poised for a powerful moment. The walkers too are ready for something, their minds stimulated by the forces of nature. The figure that suddenly appears partakes of the natural scene itself, its solitary greyness, for he is wrapped in a grey shawl; his hooting parallels the sounding of the torrents. The figure she presents is actually much like Dorothy herself, who is also a unique, lonely presence immersed in the natural world, a person free from the common domestic scene, a kind of solitary belonging to "no house in sight." It is up to William, however, to generalize about the elements Dorothy has assembled. He makes them into a "text," placing categories of "melancholy," "simplicity," "purity," "superstition," and "visionariness" on her observations, interpreting into symbolic generalizations the scene she presents. He, moreover, focuses on the power of nature's "otherworldliness"; Dorothy notes that which is definitely in the world.

William's observations appear frequently in Dorothy's travel journals, often in the form of his poetry. The *Recollections* especially includes many of William's poems, sometimes in conjunction with Dorothy's own perceptions, sometimes to explain her observations more fully, sometimes to contradict them. But she uses her brother's words less and less in later journals as she comes to substitute her own experiences for her recounting of his.

In her account of the first Scottish tour, perhaps because William was with her, her brother's poetry, as well as the presence of other male poets, is much in evidence. When she includes such texts as "The Solitary Reaper" or "Rob Roy's Grave," Dorothy fleshes out her own observations. She also circumvents her own refusal to generalize through her use of William's poetry. "What! you are stepping westward?" remembers both William's "feelings and mine" while elaborating an instant Dorothy portrays through a characteristic distrust of her powers of description. "I cannot describe how affecting this simple expression was in that remote place, with the western sky in front, *yet* glowing with the departed sun" (1:367). Here Dorothy lets William's poem perform what she "cannot," but in other places she offers descriptions that at once complement and oppose the poem she selects.

An example of this technique occurs when she includes "Sweet Highland Girl, a very shower" after her own extended account of two young girls who helped run the inn near Loch Lomond (1:283–285). William's poem expands Dorothy's depiction of what he considers a quintessentially Scottish girl. The idealized, isolated, desexualized "highland girl" of William's poetry, however, is very different from the two individuals Dorothy presents. In her account, the girls appear swathed in grey plaids, from which only their faces emerge. Representatively Scottish, they are still differentiated: one is "exceedingly beautiful," the other "delicate and unhealthy-looking" (1:279–280). Of these two, William constructs one beautiful fourteen-year-old, who lives a life much like his Lucy's, isolated in calm surroundings, and who is almost an extension of the natural beauty around her: "Benignity and home-bred sense / Ripening in perfect innocence." Dorothy's girls are rather more human, partly because they must work so hard to keep the inn running. William's girl has "A face with gladness overspread," because she has "The freedom of a mountaineer." Dorothy's girls are viewed mainly indoors, in a hut "after the Highland fashion, but without anything beautiful except its situation; the floor was rough, and wet with the rain that came in at the door, so that the lasses' bare feet were as wet as if they had been walking through street puddles,

in passing from one room to another" (1:281). Their relationship
to Dorothy includes a particularly feminine vigor, for they dress
her up, providing her with dry clothes from their own and their
mistress's wardrobe. Dorothy is a lady in these girls' eyes, but
they treat her with affection, with both energy and diffidence.
William's girl remains remote not only because she is an idealized version of woman but also because she is characterized by
lack of speech. The terms in which he describes her silence—
"eager visitings / Of thoughts that lie beyond the reach / Of thy
few words of English speech"—also may hint at his anxieties during this time about his own possible loss of "English speech."
Characteristically, in this poem, a figure appears who tells the
poet something about himself. Dorothy's inclusion of a poem
containing this particular fear in a piece that everywhere demonstrates her control of language may indicate both sympathy and
hostility. William fantasizes about his highland girl's relationship
to men. She is so innocent, he speculates, that she doesn't even
know what flirting and coyness are. He finally imagines himself
not as her lover but rather as her older brother or father. Dorothy chooses a poem that differs from her own description
but nonetheless that includes topics of major concern to her:
William's writing and his familial relationship to women.

In addition to her brother's poetry, *Recollections* contains poetry by Robert Burns. The figure of Burns appears frequently
at the beginning of the journal as Dorothy writes of his home,
his family, his poetry, and his grave. She includes Burns's "Is
there a man whose judgment clear" (1:198–199) as well as a section of the poem William wrote to Burns's sons some years after
the Scottish tour (1:202). Here, William's poem complements
Dorothy's own concern with the effect of a notorious man's life
on his family. In fact, much of her discussion of Burns centers
not on his writing but on his family. Surely her emphasis is a
recognition of the degree to which Dorothy's relationship to her
brother was affected by their writing.

The connection Dorothy posits among herself, William,
Burns, and Coleridge through their common view of Skiddaw
typifies the relationship of friends, writers, and landscape so
operative in the first tour. The second tour shows in part how

time and age have ruptured these groupings. Her memories of youthful creativity gone with time infuse the record of the later tour with sorrow. Yet her descriptions of landscape in *Journal of my Second Tour in Scotland* emphasize that, although past, her first tour with William and Coleridge illuminates her present. Failing to find the particular lime tree under which she had sat with William and Coleridge, she is nevertheless able to recall the scene from the earlier tour in which the three of them were absorbed under the impenetrable branches of the tree. Her search for this moment from the past keeps her from the morning church service attended by the poorer people of Inverary. Perhaps in keeping with her wealthier station in the second tour, Dorothy goes to the afternoon English services at which the duke and duchess of Argyle are present. After the service, she walks out to climb Doniquack Hill but is stopped by a "sunken fence" she is sure she cannot cross. A group of local inhabitants assure her that she can continue, and they help her across. The duke's lime burner accompanies her on her walk and as she chats with him, she returns, with his guidance to scenes of her past visit with William. It is as if she had to leave the monied people of the church service to reaffirm her connection with the past through those people she would have sought out on her first tour. She is able to take the kind of "sociable walk" she would have taken in her youth. When she reaches the top of the hill, images from both tours merge to bring her a moment of real pleasure:

> We attained the summit of Doniquack hill almost insensibly, and the view that burst upon me was truly enchanting on that bright and calm day. The town and church spire most elegant, pure as alabaster, the sun shining full upon them. The pier was crowded with people watching the steam-boat, in which the Duke and Duchess were making a short excursion down the Lough. The volume of dark smoke attending the gliding vessel made a beautiful appearance in contrast with the shining water. I saw nothing, however, from Doniquack hill which rouzed in me such lively pleasure as the big form of that well-remembered mountain, Cruachin, and the road which we (William and I) had pursued thitherward over the hills to Loch Awe. (2:374–375)

Remembrances of the time of her youthful wanderings with William and Coleridge are still more treasured than the present scene.

The contrasting descriptions in the texts of the first and second tours of her visits to Arthur's Seat, a popular Edinburgh tourist spot, also help reveal what the years have meant for Dorothy's particular vision. In 1803 she and William set out on a dark, dismal morning that promises "nothing but a wet day" (1:385). At the top of the hill, they sit on a stone "overlooking a pastoral hollow as wild and solitary as any in the heart of the Highland mountains." The world, poised for some kind of revelation, is composed of Wordsworthian elements characteristic of such a moment: wind, water, and the roaring of torrents. In the language of "Frost at Midnight"—"the goings-on of trade, the strife of men, or everyday city business"—Dorothy, like Coleridge, describes these features of city life through mention of their absence. She brings the elements of the mountain scene to bear on a cityscape that is almost an inversion of the London obscured by smoke, rain, and mist, making itself known only through its sounds, that William sees from Westminster Bridge. Here, however, the by-products of industrialization, the smoke and the noise, contribute to an impression that is "grand," unified, "visionary," and magical, that connects Dorothy with a point in childhood: "the impression was one, and it was visionary, like the conceptions of our childhood of Bagdad or Balsora when we have been reading the Arabian Nights' Entertainments." The moment becomes one of coherence in time and space, a point of order that exists in opposition to the individual points that compose it. The scene works with the language of her relationship to Coleridge and William, but her method differs from theirs in that she allows her presentation to speak for itself rather than drawing extended conclusions from it. Her later visit to Arthur's Seat does not result in the same kind of visionary unity. Accompanied partway by Joanna, she feels inclined to "climb to the summit" but does not because "Joanna was waiting below." The stones around the nearby chapel "resembled wild beasts couched in stillness upon the green grass." Their hope to see the city "in peculiar splendour" is dashed by enveloping fog (2:345). Decrepitude, savagery, and sudden obscurity replace the visions of her youth.

In *Recollections of a Tour made in Scotland* and *Journal of my Second Tour in Scotland*, Dorothy Wordsworth as a woman romantic writer treats the literary subject of herself in part by writing of other women. The women of Scotland speak to the possibilities of her own devastation. In Joanna Hutchinson she finds a woman closer to her, who at once describes the possibility of her own weaknesses and the fact of her own strengths. Finally, with a wisdom that comes from recollection, Dorothy encounters her memory of herself, bringing to her existence as an older woman a kind of sad acceptance. Dorothy's travel books reveal a consistent feminine awareness of the work and writing of other women, even an awareness that certain language use may be termed feminine. Her simile, for instance, describing "a wild and singular spot" as being "like a collection of patchwork, made of pieces as they might have chanced to have been cut by the mantua-maker, only just smoothed to fit each other" points to itself as "a woman's illustration" (1:207).

Dorothy's focus on the women she meets in her travels rather than on the men complements her focus on herself as a woman who is traveling and writing. Instances occur when she is the only woman among a group of men and when she causes comment because she is a woman traveling. At Darmstadt, during her tour of the continent, she prefers not to have tea with her party but waits for supper at the table d'hôte "among whiskered Germans and Prussians" (2:61). Yet her statement that she felt at ease although she was "the only female at table" is belied by both its insistence and her behavior in this situation. She pretends to be unable to speak German or French, cutting off the possibility of communication to distance herself safely from the men. She and the other women of her party are frequently seen as oddities. Near Simplon two shopkeepers remark how strange it is that anyone would spend so much time and money just to see a strange country, but that women would do so is "altogether inexplicable" (2:267). As if to validate the appropriateness of woman as traveler, Dorothy's journal includes the anecdote of a seventy-year-old woman who had recently walked through the treacherous Col de Baume. Further emphasizing that "English Women (in quest of pleasure, at least) are certainly more adventurous than those of any other European Nation," she tells the story of an English girl whose horse had fallen down one of the precipices but who had remained unharmed, although her horse was killed (2:282). A Frenchman they encounter in the Alps distinguishes between these women and ladies, who, according to this Frenchman, do not go climbing around the mountains with a guide. In this instance, Dorothy and Mary Wordsworth have set out on their own; the later journals show Dorothy traveling with other women for all or part of the journey rather than staying mainly in her brother's company.

At the beginning of *Journal of a Tour on the Continent* Dorothy enumerates her goals for the journey and emphasizes her own pleasure in walking and physical exertion by drawing a humorous comparison between herself and two young ladies. Since both girls cannot fit inside the coach, one must sit outside with the coachman. Unwilling to be seen on top of a coach, however, the young woman decides to walk into town. Her friend, whom Dorothy points to as "superfine in delicacy," taunts her with the probability of "a sad long dreary walk!" (2:7). Dorothy finds these young women "ludicrous," especially in the context of her own ambition: "to cross the Alps on foot." Here the older woman contrasts her own responses with those typical of a "country-town-bred young Lady," whom she finds immature, spoiled, unaware. The girls described here are foils for Dorothy's own sense of how her life has allowed her to develop a certain competency and philosophical awareness from what others can only respond to with pettiness and stupidity.

Even as an older woman touring the Isle of Man, Dorothy can recount the pleasure of hearing people say of her "that woman steps so light she's made for walking" (2:410). In *Journal of a Tour in the Isle of Man*, Joanna Hutchinson again serves as a foil. When she first leaves for the tour, Dorothy is lonely and depressed but becomes active and cheerful when she meets up with "dear Joanna" (2:402). In contrast to Joanna, who has become too frail to go far from home, Dorothy makes a walking tour of the island with Joanna's brother.

Her account of this tour may be read as a series of calls on different women whom Dorothy describes in terms of various traditional feminine characteristics and concerns: "Mrs. Garstand luscious with 'Loves,' and 'Dears', 'sweet Mona' and 'sweet Fanny,' and the 'darling cow' that gave 8 lbs. butter" (2:408); "Mrs. Brew and her friend Miss Trivett, the one faded and sickly, yet bright, and elegantly formed—the other a lively little shrimp toothless in the under jaw, hard-worked hands and arms, telling of all day labour in her little garden" (2:412). She tells of how Mrs. Stepney, who lived with her lover until discovered by her real husband and family, was finally able to divorce, remarry, and move to a different cottage (2:414). She visits the "tall, thin gentlewoman" Miss Forbes and her nieces who live "in the dullest corner of a dull street" that smells "of herrings in every crevice" (2:414). Mrs. Gubbins is now a widow, her husband having recently died at eighty-three years of age. The filthy but cheerful kitchen of Mrs. Dukes and her two daughters is a frequent stop. Having tea at Mrs. Putnam's, Dorothy also visits Mrs. Pinnace, who at only thirty-four years of age, has had fourteen children and buried ten of them. It is doubtful that William would have been interested in going on these visits; Dorothy does so when she travels without him, making the everyday lives of ordinary women fit material for a travel journal.

Her discussions of these women contain a practical apprehension of their difficult, sometimes wasted lives. Near the end of *Journal of a Tour in the Isle of Man* she writes of entering a squalid hut with her "companion, a young Methodist, who exclaimed to the poor inmate 'How happy you are—here you have every thing—health and contentment'" (2:416). Unable to see why the Methodist should think the woman happy or healthy, Dorothy is quite impatient with this sanctimonious conclusion. She sees the woman's pathetic, wasted condition and in a gesture of practical sympathy, offers her money, which, she observes, "certainly seemed to give her more comfort than my friend's felicitations on her blessed condition" (2:416). All around her Dorothy sees women crushed, their potential wasted, and she reacts bitterly. On the Isle of Man she visits Island Castle and mentions the incarceration of Lady Stanley and of Fenella, the heroine of Scott's *Peveril of the Peak,* but she revises the stories, changing them into examples of a wife jailed and driven mad by her husband and a young girl forced to pass her life in imprisonment. Childbearing, running a kitchen, the death of children one has borne, widowhood, adultery are the common expectations of women's lives that Dorothy depicts and that contrast with her own mode of existence as traveler and writer. A woman, however, cannot have it all. The image in the last entry of her *Excursion on the Banks of Ullswater* affirms the rightness of her own choice to be the one who travels, who goes out, while it shows what she has given up. Outside in the world, stars, "chearfulness," life are in the night sky. Inside the cottage, "Mary and the children in bed—no fire—" (1:422).

Dorothy's concern with herself in relation to other women may enable the fuller responses she has to such feminine presences as the fish women of Calais. These women, "the very lowest of the people," impress everyone because they are so ugly. Dorothy is the only one to find "something of liveliness, of mental activity, interesting," in these women (2:10). She is aware, in fact, that her view of them may be only fanciful projection, for she knows she tends to respond to any signs of intelligence in the women she encounters. Her doubts are perhaps reinforced by William's poem on the same encounter, "Fishwomen.—On Landing at Calais," which speculates about how horrifying it would be if underwater nymphs were as hideous as the fish women—a possibility, since it is said that the ocean "enfolds" what is seen on land. Reassuringly, however, he concludes that the sea nymphs are really lovely. Because they are the opposite of some ideal of sea beauty, the fish women exist in William's poem only as models of ugliness. He simply does not consider what Dorothy perceives. Dorothy's description might also be viewed as a protest against her brother's circumscribed literary standards of beauty, and his inability to respond to these human women.

The women Dorothy encounters and so carefully describes as she travels evoke an extraordinarily complex response from the woman writer who so constantly sets herself among and against them. The women she writes of on the continental tour are often described in terms of pain, sickness, and disease. In Cologne she sees plants put out on "decaying walls and windows," and sustains "something of the melancholy which I have felt on seeing a human being gaily-dressed—a female tricked out with ornaments, while disease and death were on her countenance" (2:43). This observation, encompassing a view of a city as well as of a woman, complements Dorothy's growing concern in the later journals with decay and death, especially her own. On the way back from the continent, in fact, the ship strikes a sandbar and her death seems certain. Her terse comment on the incident reveals the mixture so common in Dorothy's writing of resignation and hostility. "My Brother, thinking it would be impossible to save his wife and me, had stripped off his coat to be ready to swim" (2:333). During the continental tour Dorothy frequently mentions being unwell and presents herself as frailer than in earlier journals. Traveling here becomes a conquering of obstacles; she maintains a certain suspense in the journal, since it seems so unlikely that her "ambition" of crossing the Alps can be satisfied. The phrase "sick and weary" appears frequently; she is sometimes too weak to stay with the rest of the party.

Her concern with the passage of time, death, and decay in the later journals results in images of future destruction as well as past presences. Sitting in a central square of Ghent, she sees multitudes of swallows on the roof of the cathedral. "The restless motions and plaintive call of those little creatures seemed to impart a stillness to every other object, and had the power to lead the imagination gently on to the period when that once superb but now decaying structure shall be 'lorded over and possessed by nature'" (2:22). In this observation, Dorothy herself must be one of the objects stilled by the swallows, and she thus intimates her own death. At the same time, however, as she and the rest of the world are rendered still by natural process, she reasserts the primacy of language, of her own particular "calling." Death and destruction as natural process here must give way to death and destruction as linguistic process, as they are understood and controlled by metaphor. Her revision of William's line from Book 6 of *The Prelude* emphasizes this disjunction of the world as language and the world as object. Her borrowing from the "Immortality Ode" helps further recall William's version in which man's artifacts both dominate and complement the "aboriginal vale." Dorothy makes the line describe man's eradication. Finally what will be left is the saying of what will be left, an epitaph of language become what remains. Coming up against the primacy of writing, she falls here into the locus of a linguistic double bind: the disjunction of the world as language vs. the world as object.

Her focus on death is also handled literally in *Journal of a Tour on the Continent*. The Wordsworths meet a young American who later drowns in the Lake of Zurich and whose death casts a pall over their trip and her narrative. And he is only one of nature's victims. Wolves come from the higher Alps to kill sheep and human beings: "Only a few months ago, a child had been devoured—eaten up, all but the skull" (2:222). Three weeks before their visit, two travelers and three guides had died on Mont Blanc "by the snow giving way" (2:283). In the later journals, Dorothy's views of the natural world are informed by her concern with death. She perceives Mont Blanc, the Arve, and the Vale of Chamouny—those locations central to romantic writing—largely in terms of death, desolation, terror, and "everlasting snow."

Dorothy also recognizes in the "summer loveliness" of these locations the way death and destruction in nature generate their opposites. Her narrative progresses in part by drawing these oppositions together, although she is not as assertive as the men of romanticism about the symbiosis of the mind and of nature, and the power of aggressive imagination to act on a world that it both creates and perceives. As they climb on the Col de Baume, Mont Blanc to their left, the river Arve and village of Chamouny below, Dorothy looks back to describe the mountains in phrases of desolation: "blackness," "barrenness," "a multitude of wasting precipices." They speak of going to the Mer de Glace the next day, the Sea of Ice, a place of continuous winter. Descending towards the vale, William and Dorothy lie down beside a stream "not delightful to the eye, for it was grey and muddy, but travelling with a voice as chearful as the brightest. We shut our eyes to listen, and to feel the pleasure of the sunshine in perfect rest." Here, pleasure is described partly in terms of the unpleasant, the "not delightful" stream, the absence of beauty. One sense must even be shut down if the world's "pleasure" is to be felt. And the phrase "in perfect rest" refers not only to the peaceful, tranquil moment but also to the perfect rest of death (2:282–283).

Dorothy goes on to say that she was the only member of the party not disappointed with Chamouny. It is not as she imagined, but in certain ways, again having to do with desolation, it more than fulfills her expectations. The oppositions are there; "summer loveliness" does coexist with "the cold of the Glaciers." The vale is much larger than she had expected, "the central ravages more dreary—the spaces of barren ground more extensive." Here the deathlike, negative principles in nature bring her to a positive response, an awareness of completion and fulfillment, a scene she finds compelling (2:283).

Her visit to the Mer de Glace receives the next extended description in *Journal of a Tour on the Continent*. In contrast to her frequent concern with discontinuities, this episode works by attempting the identification and organization of extreme oppositions into organic coherency and continuity. The scene is "wonderfully grand, and harmoniously composed—yet fantastic and curious." Dorothy's first response to the Mer de Glace is one of a civilized, literary consciousness: looking at the snow makes her recall "images of castles, spires, towers, ancient cities, and fragments in the desarts of the East" (2:285). These images, which might be conditioned by popular nineteenth-century poems and travel books about the East, are for her, inadequate and "*transient*." Ultimately, she must think about "lonely Nature, and the first mysterious Cause of whatever we behold." Finally, then, her mind turns to origins, to beginnings, in this scene of "everlasting winter," of deathlike finality. The name Mer de Glace brings together the idea of origins—"mer," "mère," "mother"—and death—"glace," absence of heat and life. Continuing the interplay of oppositions, Dorothy describes how the sun is extremely hot, but she becomes chilled and withdraws to watch the rest of her party go out onto the ice. Upon their return, she decides to venture out and, despite the protestations of one of her friends, actually goes farther out than anyone else. Self-assertion finally replaces withdrawal and frailty. Still, the possibility of death, absorption into the glacier is ever present. On the glacier she looks into hollows filled with clear, green water that obscures the depths. "If a foot were to slip you might be lost for ever!" (2:286). They descend for a better view of the Arve and the power of the scene releases a statement about the structure of both the world and the human psyche.

> It is very curious, perhaps more curious than beautiful, yet no one can behold without admiration the exquisite hues and gem-like clearness of the edges of the arch, and of the fearful green chasm beneath it, whence the River rushes with terrible commotion and a thundering sound. I could have sate the day through to look only and listen, and dream of the underground workings, the obscure passages—to be concealed for ever from human eye. No spectacle that I ever beheld—not even the ocean itself—has had an equal power over my mind in bringing together thoughts connected with duration and decay—eternity, and perpetual wasting—the visible and *in*visible power of God and Nature. (2:286)

The view of nature here combines William's view in *The Prelude* and Coleridge's in "Kubla Khan," but Dorothy is most interested in what lies "underground," in phenomena approached partly through the senses but also through the dream—and finally concealed from sight. Even in what is partially a description of the unconscious, however, she works from a natural description at the same time as she emphasizes that these recesses cannot be brought into view.

The oppositions thus held in place—duration, decay, perpetual wasting, the visible and invisible—figure in her next description of their visit to the Glacier de Boisson. She begins her account at five o'clock in the morning as she wakes up. "The sky was clear, promising another delightful day" (2:287). The scene is set in terms of "delight," "light," and "illumination," but the stream of ice that they first must cross is long, desolate, and a constant reminder of death. William is the last across and Dorothy watches him, thinking, "If a foot had failed, death was inevitable" (2:288). Nature is both murderous—a huge "gulph," a field of "never-wasted snow, and rocks"—and fertile—"a green, mossy, flower-besprinkled forest." Advancing through the forest, they encounter grandeur and destruction.

They view the pyramids of ice, "a glittering vision" of "dazzling and fantastic shapes," wasting "rapidly in the summer heat" (2:288–289).

Significantly, Dorothy's view of the glacier is quite different from Mary's. Mary has all her expectations fulfilled about what a glacier should be. Dorothy, on the other hand, does not even wish to be satisfied, finding the glacier far more "enchantingly beautiful" than anything she has the power to imagine (2:289). Dorothy calls into question the power of abstract imaginings. "The mind," she maintains elsewhere, "is not satisfied with its own imaginings" (2:297). She reasserts the need to be faced with data, with reality, and plays down the force of imaginative projections. Here she addresses one aspect of her brother's statements in *The Prelude* about the power of his imagination. At first sight of Mont Blanc, he "grieved / To have a soulless image on the eye / Which had usurped upon a living thought / That never more could be" (6:453–456). One reading of this passage is that reality somehow intrudes on William's own projections. The idea becomes part of the complex network of relationships among nature, imagination, and poetic discourse that William develops in *The Prelude*. Showing the mind's dependence on nature, he traces its independence from the natural world. Dorothy will not make the same claim for what she projects; she would rather emphasize the reality that stimulates her imagination, that is essential to her mode of seeing.

Still, preconceptions, what one imagines something will be like, are especially important in *Journal of a Tour on the Continent*, since Dorothy deals with so many landscapes and experiences previously described by her brother. The narrative is in part her version of Book 6 of *The Prelude*. She asserts the power and validity of her own way of seeing, while displaying her brother's information about the same journey and incorporating his memories into the text. Dorothy sets William's version of past events, as well as what she thought would be there, against what she sees and feels when she arrives on a scene. At least four time lines move through this journal: William's past, his past as he has related it to Dorothy, Dorothy's past, and her present. The juxtaposition of verb tenses reflects these time schemes. When they visit Lake Como, Dorothy writes in the present: "the town of

Como is spread before us. It is like another lake—so different from the former—being narrow, and shut up between green mountains." Recalling William's description of the place, she traces "that path which my brother had formerly paced." She also brings her own past fantasies to the scene, for she has thought about "pursuing the track of his youthful steps" (2:225). Some of what she sees on the trip is interesting to her, in fact, simply because William's tales have made her like "the traveller who has been dreaming of Switzerland from the days of his youth" (2:83). Neither William's stories nor her own past interpretations of them, however, can match present reality. Of the ravine of Ticino, for instance—"However high might have been our expectations they were far short of the reality" (2:196). That William's words do not equal her vision is clear in her description of Lake Como, "whose very name since the days of my youth had conjured up more delightful visions than any spot on earth. How different the reality at that moment and in that place!" (2:215).

Copying and reading *The Prelude* simply do not measure up to crossing the Alps oneself. Dorothy's account of her own journey combines her joy at finally accomplishing such a feat with the awareness that it is somehow too late, that her youth has passed and that death approaches. What was for William a prelude is for Dorothy a finale. Yet although she characterizes herself as sickly through much of the journey, the actual crossing of the Alps brings with it rejuvenation.

> And here let me express my thankfulness for the strength and chearful spirits with which I was enabled to undertake a journey on foot across the Alps, having but a few weeks before suffered so much from oppression and sickness that I had little hope of being able to accomplish the journey in any way. The change was marvellous, for when I began to climb the mountains at Lauterbrunnen, the full possession of health and even youthful vigour seemed to have returned;—and never again did I suffer a moment from pain or weakness—hardly from fatigue. In our walk to Altdorf, along a wide level, enclosed by hills, the heat was extreme. (2:174)

Not only is she healthy again, but she is the strongest of her group. Her vigor allows her to become the leader, to walk ahead of the others. "I was alone—the first in the ascent" (2:184). She emphasizes her independence by portraying herself as often outdistancing her party. Solitude here is assertive and strong, as reflected in the verbs she chooses. "I pushed forward" (2:76), "—passed alone above the unfenced precipice—and wondered to find myself in such a place, fearless and in safety. I plunged into the forest" (2:148). Being away from her family is a kind of release. She experiences the raw material that can be shaped into her own work on "crossing the Alps." At night, after "happy days spent in crossing the Alps," the material will not let her sleep. Images present themselves to her not as *"dreams"* but as "realities" (2:188). She now possesses her own reality, an acquisition perhaps responsible for her energy, and is no longer dependent on her brother's words.

Yet the journal that celebrates Dorothy's journey on the Alpine trail also memorializes her lost youth and revises her brother's memories. The scenes she recounts in most detail are those in which her brother has experienced disappointment or pain, and her brother's images and memories are very much present in her material. Sitting at the top of the ascent at St. Gothard, she describes "Entering into my Brother's youthful feelings of sadness and disappointment when he was told unexpectedly that the Alps were crossed—the effort accomplished—I tardily descended towards the Hospital" (2:190). Dorothy must have been more aware than any other reader of *The Prelude* what William felt when he didn't even realize that he and his friend Jones had crossed the Alps. Having imagined that it would be some kind of earth-shaking experience, William was disappointed when reality failed to match his imaginative predictions. Perhaps because her imagination is more able to work on account of what is actually occurring before her, Dorothy experiences no such problem. Nonetheless, she "enters into" her brother's depression. She is not at this point in William's situation of descending because she has been "Unwilling to turn the mountain." She has not in effect crossed the Alps, so the feeling is manufactured from William's experience. Furthermore, she describes this process as an "effort." Why then would she do it? She may be performing a gesture of love, acting as a sort of scapegoat who is taking on some of his pain. Or entering into his feelings may be something she is conditioned to affect; so she makes a perfunctory effort to do so. Or she may be dealing with his experience one more time to move it to a subsidiary place, since she has her own Alpine material to develop.

Of course she never dismisses William's memories, and they are often bound up with her own recalled anxieties. Crossing from Switzerland to Germany she notes, "This first sight of that country so dear to the imagination, though then of no particular grandeur, affected me with various emotions. I remembered the shapeless wishes of my youth—wishes without hope—my brother's wanderings thirty years ago, and the tales brought to me the following Christmas holidays at Forncett; and often repeated while we paced together on the gravel walk in the parsonage garden, by moon or star light" (2:86). Her time spent in Germany with her brother undoubtedly provides some of these dear remembrances, but until this time it is her brother who has had most of the experiences to repeat. Her own youthful wishes, shapeless perhaps because they were both unorthodox and uncharacteristically self-related, may have had to do with her desire to have "tales" of her own to relate. Now, no longer restricted to the parsonage garden, she can bring back the narrative of the travel journal. Yet even now she characterizes her wishes as being "without hope," describing both the improbability of realizing them that she assumed at the time and the hopelessness of desires fulfilled so late as to be meaningless. Wishes granted thirty years later must bring with them bitterness at what might have been and sad memories of what she once was. Her choice of life both empties and fulfills her.

In another instance, her walk through Simplon Pass, Dorothy again sets her present against her past and that of her brother. She begins by rising at dawn, having determined to cross Simplon on foot, since she has proven to herself that she still retains the vigor to do so. She sets off alone and has so much energy that she somehow passes Mary, who has left before her. William, Dorothy, and Mary finally meet, and Dorothy details the landscape as they ascend. Her emphasis on past travelers and their routes, her recurring use of the word "trace," help establish the images of her own journal as signs of missing presences. Her discussion of Napoleon, who once dominated the region as a political power, also emphasizes a landscape of absences. The three pass a huge granite column, intended for Napoleon's triumphal arch at Milan, which Dorothy now sees as the most impressive record possible of "disappointed vanity and ambition" (2:257). Whatever man tries to impose on this region, be it government, monument, memory or description, is somehow overpowered by time and nature. Moisture has destroyed the painting on a ruined convent. They proceed through terrain that seems wilder and wilder, as if to emphasize nature's dominance. Traces of an old road mark the way to a large spittal that William identifies as "the very same where he and his Companion had passed an awful night" (2:259). In *The Prelude,* William's description of this building follows the passage on imagination and the discussion of natural phenomena as "Characters of the great apocalypse." It is a key place in his life and because she has been hearing about it for thirty years, Dorothy wishes to enter. William, however, refuses, and she lacks "the courage to pass the threshold alone," a decision she later much regrets (2:259).

Dorothy's request, however, might not be as simple as my recounting indicates. She here uncharacteristically asks William to do something that he is both unable and unwilling to do. To accommodate her might destroy him. For William, the house is haunted. The "tremendous torrent" that came "thundering down a chasm of the mountains" when he was there as a young man, the tremendous torrent so like the power of his own imagination, is "now, upon this sunny clear day, a brisk rivulet, that chearfully bounded down to the Vedro" (2:259). William cannot enter the scene of his great confrontation with the power of his own mind any more than he can return to the past and recapture the poetic power that once was his. Dorothy is also asking for the substitution of a literal, historical fact—to see "what was going on within doors"—for a timeless, imaginative fact—"the tales of thirty years gone by." Her desire to take an ideal and match it to fact both misses the point of William's design in *The Prelude*—a mistake that Dorothy was unlikely to have made unintentionally—and attempts to place William in an almost impossible situation as she asserts her own categories of imagination against his. At this spittal, thirty years before, William experienced the trauma of discovering that physical reality did not deliver; imagination did. This frightening possibility for a poet who invests so much in the world of nature is underscored by the further realization that the natural world may be only a sign or trace of "Characters of the great apocalypse." Dorothy's version of the crossing of Simplon insists again on the primacy of physical detail, on the representation of a world reported by the senses. She tours, as the title of her work emphasizes. A tourist stops at various places of note to see the scenery, to match a physical response to what she has heard about the place. William, on the other hand, simply cannot become a tourist. To reenter the spittal would invite a devastating confrontation not only with his past but also with his favored mode of imagination.

Dorothy's reactions in the rest of the entry combine awareness of and sympathy for her brother's plight with self-castigation, aggression, and finally the assertion of her own imaginative view. She does not push William and does not herself enter but is annoyed and considers herself a coward for not being more independent and for not asserting herself against her brother. She has, after all, entered into his vision for years. His refusal to be a tourist with her is an act of self-preservation that she nevertheless would be justified in regarding as a selfish repudiation of her. Yet she also remains sympathetic and understanding. She voices a dilemma Carol Gilligan has found to be typical of women, who frequently find themselves "suspended between an ideal of selflessness and the truth of their own agency and needs." Feminine development, so centered on interconnections and relationships, engenders a certain self-effacing response to family members that finally must go against a woman's personal needs. Women often describe the conflict Dorothy sets out here: "the tension they feel between responsibilities to others and self-development" (138).

Even as Dorothy here reveals the incompatibility of her needs and William's, she does not exhibit any overt anger against him, criticizing herself instead. As they leave the area, she even attempts to build up her brother's past experience. In a statement requiring both literal and figurative interpretation, she speculates how much more treacherous the precipices must have been when he crossed them, especially without the "broad road" of their journey that "smoothes every difficulty." William had to undergo much more than she. She soon, however, mentions her own vigor once again, and seeing a carriage full of gentlemen, "could not but congratulate myself on our being on foot" (2:259).

Perhaps because he is somewhat overcome by his past, William separates himself from his wife and sister. Dorothy and Mary "being before W., sate and pondered" (2:260). Seeing a footpath that would be a shortcut but that proceeds directly upwards, Dorothy admits they fear to take it because they are no longer young, unlike the youth they see climbing on it. They "could not summon the courage to follow him, and took the circuit of Buonaparte's road" (2:260). Still, she finds the narrow passes through which she is actually proceeding more impressive and "interesting to the imagination" than the surrounding mountains. Her vision turns a woman crossing a bridge into a conveyor of life, spirit, and grandeur. The path and the bridge take on a new dimension when Dorothy discovers that they were "the same we had so often heard of, which misled my Brother and Robert Jones in their way from Switzerland to Italy." She again recounts William's reactions, emphasizing this time how "The ambition of youth was disappointed." William, who is waiting to point out the track, rejoins them, and Dorothy states the impossibility of her saying "how much it had moved him, when he discovered it was the very same which had tempted him in his youth" (2:260). She cannot fully articulate his reactions, perhaps because she can now write her own version of the path and the bridge and has expressed her own responses to them. She nonetheless writes, "The feelings of that time came back with the freshness of yesterday, accompanied with a dim vision of thirty years of life between." It must be his feelings that are returning, but they are important enough for her to include, especially since she sees them in the context of thirty years of memory, or thirty years of absorbing his version of the Alps. She generously joins his view of things again. "We traced the path together, with our eyes, till hidden among the cottages, where they had first been warned of their mistake" (2:261). In William's way, the physical detail becomes unimportant—the path is finally hidden—but the spot of time, the event in this case, is paramount.

As they proceed to the town of Simplon, however, Dorothy's story more aggressively takes over. She celebrates her crossing of Simplon with a large, merry dinner party. In keeping with this emphasis on civilized organization, they go out "to look at a living Chamois, kept in the stable" (2:261). William and Mary go to bed, but Dorothy continues her own celebration and walks "with some of the Gentlemen about 1/2 a mile." She is "not at all fatigued" (2:261) after the difficult walk. She is also able to sleep soundly, in contrast to William's anxiety-ridden insomnia in the spittal the night of his crossing.

Dorothy's description of her crossing of the Alps, then, differs markedly from her brother's version. Her method here is characteristic of her approach in the later journals. Through insistent recounting of physical detail, she demonstrates both her delight at her good physical condition and the realization that the kind of vigor she once had is gone, her hostility to and her adoration of her brother, her problems with asserting herself in his presence, her awareness that although she can now present her own version of what has been William's material, much of her potential has been wasted. The problems of re-creating this particular kind of experience through language and the place of both natural sublimity and communal life in a woman's existence also help shape her travel journals. The supremacy of physical reality and the way her mind operates in concert with natural phenomena once again order her statement about the structures of her own imagination.

IV.

Poems

✤ ✤ ✤ ✤ ✤ MEMORY AND ABSENCE, TWO CON-
trolling impulses of the travel journals, work in Dorothy's poetry as well. Memory allows the writing of what has been, but
the Dorothy of both travelogue and poem desperately seeks to
preserve not the absence but the presence of what she describes.
In many of the poems, as in the travel journals, the absence that
makes the work possible exists in opposition to the speaker's desire for that absence to end so that she can be part of a communal, domestic scene. The poems show her need for the Grasmere
community and her contrasting need to distinguish herself
from it.

Uneven in quality, Dorothy's poetry sometimes has the effect
of making us more appreciative of her talents as a prose writer.
But it would have been surprising if any writer living in the
Wordsworth household did not attempt to compose poems, and
so she wrote at least those collected here. Some of their occa-
sional formal awkwardness may result from a struggle in her
writing life as the prose stylist breaks through the poetic attempt. In her later journals, Dorothy experiments with what in
the hands of writers like Baudelaire and Rimbaud would become the sophisticated form of the prose poem. She arranges
extended passages in verse form, as in these lines describing her
departure from Cambridge to Whitwick:

Saturday 1st May 1830
On new Terrace—Sun bursts out
before setting—unearthly and
brilliant—calls to mind the
change to another world—Every
leaf a golden lamp—every twig
bedropped with a diamond. The
splendour departs us rapidly—

Such passages make obvious the latent poetry of the Grasmere and Alfoxden journals, in the pieces that describe Dorothy's personal life with her family. It is doubtful, however, that their author would have acknowledged this composition as a poem, for it is so different from the poetry of the Grasmere community.

Dorothy's poetry, even more than her prose, is bound up with the form and language of the writers around her. At times it seems that the rhymes, ballad forms, and words of romantic verse, especially William's, provide an enabling structure for telling of the felicity and pain of her life choice. The woman who has no children writes of caring for babies and of the ambivalence of being a mother substitute. The woman who lost her father and mother writes of the importance of having a paternal roof attended by maternal care. The woman who was supposed to be eternally a part of nature writes of being imprisoned on a couch of pain. Her poems do not refuse the "I"; they are as interested in self as William's, as they carry on the self-definition of her other work.

Many of Dorothy's poems are written in the voice of a woman who considers her life and her past in relation to the children or younger women around her. In her earliest poems, specifically addressed to very young children, the speaker is a presence who can mediate the sometimes terrifying forces of the natural world or who can deal with concerns about disrupted parental presence. The importance of a coherent family life, preferably supported by a strong patriarchal presence, is also the focus of several poems.

Nature's "fostering" presence, for both children and adults, appears in various ways—as an encouraging, loving guide but also as a substitute for the real thing, a stepparent. Beautiful and fertile, as well as destructive, nature in Dorothy's poetry is consistently orderly. It generates delight, love, and peace and, unlike nature in William's poems, does not terrorize the observer. The component of fear is absent. Nature can be dealt with by the poem's controlling voice and is at worst an amoral, inexorable force. Dorothy takes up possibilities William raises about the restorative function of the natural world, turning frequently to the words of "Tintern Abbey," perhaps because it is there he entertains his most specific and dramatic predictions for her. Especially in the later poems, she engages the Wordsworthian myths of nature, time, and memory.

During the last years of her life her poetry was paramount. She copied and recopied her verses; she recited them continually. In the Commonplace Book, several poems come after a sort of title page inscribed "Sick-Bed Consolations." They are poems of sickness graphically described, of her "feverish strife," of a "fearful rush of pain." Frequently turning to phrases of Christian solace, the speakers seek explanations and assurances in a religious faith that is vaguely problematic and undercut by poetic syntax.

Dorothy also writes poems that analyze her life as a woman in the Lake District, that set her past fantasies against present realities—her own and those of other women. In certain of her poems, an older, sickly, "enfeebled" speaker addresses a young woman who serves as both her contrast and complement. The writing of the poems establishes a series of oppositions such as youth/age, health/sickness, freedom in nature/sickroom as prison. Setting out these oppositions in composing the poem, the narrator encounters her own youthful energies mirrored in the young women she addresses.

Frequently commenting on their own composition, the poems also consider poetry writing in general. Dorothy seeks simplicity, wishing to avoid elaborate poetic artifice. In a fragment that echoes the poem to Julia Marshall, she writes of "Simplicity our steadfast theme, / No works of Art adorned our scheme." The simple life is fantasized in simple language. In "Lines Intended for Edith Southey's Album," she contrasts her own "unadorned record" with the "praise in transport high" offered Edith by the "Bard," (presumably William) and views his approbation as a "needless task." The same poem also deprecates her own poetry, which "issues from a lowly Fount" in contrast to the scintillating sources of other poems—Edith's father, the laureate Robert Southey, or Bard William. The narrator of "Lines to Dora H." writes out of "fancy" rather than the higher faculty of imagination. The problems with writing poetry that have plagued her since youth are outlined in the poem to Julia Marshall. Although she "*reverenced*" the poet's skill, she feared that her poems would evoke derision from her playmates (perhaps William) and especially from her mother. Her poetry denigrates itself as well as its author. While possessed of a certain bravado, the note to "A Holiday at Gwerndovennant" that pleads for "accommodating ears," "good humour," and forgiveness for "bad metre, bad rhymes—no rhymes—identical rhymes & all that is lawless" outlines her concerns about the form of her poetry. Her pieces do not fit the standards of other poems, Dorothy is sure, and so she sometimes uses the word *irregular* in their titles. The title "Fragment" may indicate a typically romantic fascination with the poetic fragment or it may indicate that Dorothy considered the poem incomplete. Her choice of subject matter in its frequent concentration on the domestic scene and the practicalities of daily life also distinguishes her from other romantic writers and their concerns with what are traditionally considered "larger issues."

Yet her independence is symbiotic. Her poems participate in the norms of romantic poetry even while they deviate from them. Like so many other romantic poets, Dorothy writes of nature and the self in nature. Her emphasis on birds as songsters, on that which makes the music of nature, complements the way her own poems seek to echo and celebrate this music. She is also concerned with individual existence in time and space, with the growth of the individual ego. The fascination of the romantics with things medieval evidences itself in her poetry though such references as "The laurelled knight," the "holy shield," "the steed," nature's "baronial Hall." Most obviously, her poems exist intertextually with those of her brother, at times speaking within his vocabulary as they revise his perceptions.

The poetic presence of her brother made it difficult for Dorothy to write poetry. Her habitual self-denigration is everywhere evident as she sets her poems against his. Margaret Homans argues that the very presence of William and "The Masculine Tradition," a tradition that especially during the romantic period reinforced woman's otherness by so feminizing nature, made it almost impossible for women to have the kind of subjectivity necessary to poetic discourse (12–40). Yet Dorothy Wordsworth writes poems and feels they are of value. Mary reports in a letter that desiring to send a woman friend something "that would be valuable when she was gone," Dorothy copies out a book of her poems (181). In one version of the poem "Miss B. Southey," she signs herself the "poetess." While there may be a touch of irony involved in so autographing an eight-line ditty, Dorothy Wordsworth stands as a woman writing the poetry of English romanticism.

Three of Dorothy's early poems—"To my Niece Dorothy, a sleepless Baby," "An address to a Child in a high wind," and "The Mother's Return"—were probably written between 1805 and 1807 and were published with William's poems of 1815, signed in some editions "A Female Friend" and in others "By My Sister." They received this favorable notice in a letter from Charles Lamb: "We were glad to see the poems by a female friend. The one of the wind is masterly, but not new to us. Being only three, perhaps you might have clapt a *D.* at the corner and let it have past as a print[e]rs mark to the uninitiated, as a delightful hint to the better-instructed. As it is, **Expect a formal criticism on the Poems of your female friend** and she must expect it" (3:141). Given Dorothy's lack of faith in her ability to write poetry, the prospect of being designated publicly as the poems' author must have produced some anxiety. Yet, she did allow herself to be published, so she must have felt she had something of worth to say.

In these poems, a nurturing, probably female speaker addresses young children to provide comfort or correction while attempting to reintegrate the child into a natural or familial pattern through her talk. (Although a man could be the speaker, cultural biases and biographical data suggest a feminine presence.) In the original version, the children are obviously William's, raising the subject of Dorothy's relationship to her brother's children and her place in his household. When he published the poems, William changed the names and titles, thereby distancing the pieces from their specific domestic situation. "To my Niece" becomes "A Cottager to her Infant;" Johnny becomes Edward in "An address," and his name is cut from "The Mother's Return," where he becomes "the eldest."

Dorothy's namesake, her niece called Dora, the "sleepless Baby" of her original title, figures often in her poems as a younger female with whom the speaker interacts. Although William removed Dora herself from the poem when he published it, the Fenwick note quotes his report that the poem was "Suggested to her [Dorothy] while beside my sleeping children" (*PW* 2:477). This statement contradicts the sense of the poem: the woman experiences that frequently exasperating situation in which an infant simply cannot stay asleep. Seeming to drop off, the baby pops up suddenly—"starts." In contrast to William's epigraph, Dorothy's speaker assumes an active relationship with the child, offering the baby her breast to sleep on. Thus the speaker demonstrates the necessary and often unceasing actions involved in child care. In parallel syntax that reverses the sense of "Then sing" in the "Immortality Ode," the speaker makes that common plea of mothers: "Then hush," "Then . . . sleep." Listing a set of circumstances, she inquires, "Then why so busy thou?" William's assertive plea for song is revised to a question that seeks silence.

At the same time as the speaker urges the child to rest as everything else in the house seems to rest, the poem describes movement and wakefulness. While seeking cessation, the speaker concludes with a stanza of sparkling light and waking "when it is Day." The wind "sings"; a mouse nibbles; the moon sparkles and shines; the rain hits the window. The child is "busy" and "starting." Each stanza ends with a shortened line that sets off the child as awake and active. The phrasing of the second stanza equates the child and the mouse, a baby too, busy at this moment because the kitten, another baby, is asleep. That they are babies both mitigates the hunter-prey relationship of cat and

mouse and makes it more sinister, adding a degree of uneasiness
to the quiet of the cottage. Contrary to expectation, the wet,
cold, dark outer world is not countered by an interior suffused
with warmth and coziness. The windowpane may physically
keep out the rain, but the internal line rhyme of "pane" and
"rain" allows pane/pain into the room.

In structure and setting, Dorothy's poem resembles Coleridge's
"Frost at Midnight." In both poems a narrator deals with a cottage asleep and an infant in that cottage; in both the inside is
framed by what is going on outside. Coleridge begins and
ends with the frost on the window; the first and last stanzas of
Dorothy's poem deal with the world around the cottage interior
depicted in the middle stanza, thus literally surrounding the interior description. In Coleridge's poem, however, the mind at
work in the cottage appears joined to the frost performing its
artistry. Dorothy's poem attempts no such resolution. Rather,
there remain the distinct presences of the child, the narrator, and
the surrounding world, discontinuous in a scene that seeks nurturing wholeness, and her poem makes obvious the qualifica-
tions contained in Coleridge's depiction of continuity.

In his tendency to generalize, William turns the situation into
a commentary on social class by adding two stanzas to the poem
that Dorothy vigorously crosses out in the Rydal notebook.

> Ah! if I were a Lady gay
> I should not grieve with thee to play
> Right gladly would I lie awake
> Thy lively spirits to partake,
>   And ask no better chear.

> But, Babe! there's none to work for me,
> And I must rise to industry;
> Soon as the Cock begins to crow
> Thy Mother to the fold must go
>   To tend the sheep & kine.

Dorothy's care giver, perhaps reflecting her own situation, is not
necessarily the child's mother. In placing this poem with those
"Founded on the Affections" William further situates it as a
piece about the relationship between a mother and her child,

emphasizing the point by separating the poem from the other two, which he places in "Poems Referring to the Period of Childhood." Dorothy, however, is concerned with one detail of her relationship with the child, not with the larger issue of the pressures a lower-class peasant woman might feel.

Here, as elsewhere, Dorothy refuses to generalize, in common with many women writers, whose work is frequently demeaned for this refusal. Such particularity is seen as evidence of limited scope, of failure to take a global view. Dorothy's poem comes from a life spent in what Carol Gilligan characterizes as "intimate and generative relationships," but the tendency has been to value those literary works, usually written by and about men, that concern themselves with larger issues—the Poet and his growth, Prometheus and his unbinding. Dorothy's poems, like her journals, provide part of what Gilligan calls "the missing text," the record of a woman's concerns with individuals closest to her (156).

The speaker of "An address to a Child in a high wind" concerns herself with one particular child in one particular house as she establishes a more comforting environment for both herself and the child she addresses. In this poem, the speaker attempts to deal with the power of a force of nature by personifying it and by bringing the invisible into visible examples. Establishing in the title that both the child and the words of the poem are concurrently involved in a "high wind," the narrator poses a question which she soon says cannot be answered.

> What way does the wind come? what way does he go?
> He rides over the water and over the snow,
> Through the valley, and over the hill
> And roars as loud as a thundering Mill.
> He tosses about in every bare tree,
> As, if you look up you plainly may see
> But how he will come, and whither he goes
> There's never a Scholar in England knows.

The speaker will provide explanations and consolation through physical evidence. Telling the child to look at what the wind does and to listen to the way it sounds, she describes the effects

in terms of familiar household objects: a cushion, a pillow, milk,
a bed. Moving from the darkness that makes things more frightening, she looks ahead to daylight when she promises further
explanation. The scene described is one of nature violated—"a
great rout," "cracked branches" "strew'd about." But the child
will go view the scene "with" the speaker, who will be a comforting presence then, even as she is when she finishes her tale of
what he will see in the orchard with a description of an upright
tree covered with apples in summer.

Returning to the present, the speaker points to the wind, now
possessed of claws and a growl, as an animal presence on the
roof. This typical childhood fear—the wolf that can come down
the chimney—is assuaged by the narrator's description of a protected, protecting interior. Defense against the possible abuses
of nature lies in the domestic structure that provides for a glazier
to seal the windows, an old woman to bring coals, and a caring
adult to share "a canny warm house" with the child. The word
"canny" appears in the north of England but is primarily a
Scottish term. It works in several ways in the poem, allowing the house to be cunning in the sense of artful, endowed
with supernatural powers (thus a better defense against the
wind's supernatural powers), gentle and soft, and snug, comfortable, warm, and cozy.

> Come, now we'll to bed, and when we are there
> He may work his own will, & what shall we care.
> He may knock at the door—we'll not let him in
> May drive at the windows—we'll laugh at his din
> Let him seek his own home wherever it be
> Here's a canny warm house for Johnny and me.

In this poem a warm, snug interior and finally the even smaller
enclosure of a bed counter the harshness of the outside world for
both the child and the speaker, who ends the poem with a final
reference to her protected self.

Johnny's parents are never mentioned in "An address to a
Child in a high wind," perhaps because other factors allow the
child to be cared for. In "The Mother's Return," the narrator
again appears as a surrogate mother in charge of a household of

three children. Through talk, she controls the time of their real mother's absence. Speaking of "The bonds of our humanity" as "the mystery / Of time and distance, night, and day," the speaker also brings up the subject of maternal bonds, the bonding of mother and child. The ties that bind and the bonds that restrain have been set against one another by the mother's absence. "The Mother's Return," marking the close of her time away, will effect something of a resolution; the writing of the return and discourse contained in the poem itself also help resolve the conflict. The poem is a work about time and discourse.

The narrator relies on vocabulary that defines the "bonds of time": "month," "tomorrow," "time," "night," "winter gone," "the clock that gives the law," "moments," "five minutes passed." Time in the poem has to do not only with the mother's absence but with the development of each child, for it differentiates their stages of growth. The eldest, John, can react to implement his desire to see his mother. Still at the instinctual stage, the younger girl responds emotionally and without focus. The infant cannot respond at all by himself but is acted on by the other two. The speaker would like to join the children's glee but cannot because her stage of life is removed from theirs. Her time has passed, and its passing is given slightly negative cast by the words *infected* and *wanton*.

Because of her time of life, however, the speaker can and must tell the boy what is inappropriate about his response. As much as the poem is about time, it concerns the talk or language that both allows and seeks to control time. Along with the vocabulary of time, words of talk order the poem: "tidings," "speak," "shouted," "hear," "told," "listens," "chatters," "discourse," "talk'd," "sing," "tales," "repeat." Stages of life are defined partly in terms of talk. The boy reacts with a simple sentence of command, the girl with chatter, undifferentiated babble. The baby is an "infant," one in the state of being "without words." His response must be projected by the speaker. Language is seen in the poem as the one possible control of time. In the young boy's case, the words remain ineffectual in regulating the time of the mother's absence. The narrator, however, corrects him and leads the children "into fond discourse" that provides a record of the time the mother is away. The "tales" the children will repeat to their mother will further organize the time of her absence. In a larger sense, the poem itself defines "The Mother's Return." In one way, however, her presence will bring about another kind of absence. The narrator's final description of the sleeping children closes the poem with words that can signify a final emptiness.

> Five minutes passed—and Oh the change!
> Asleep upon their beds they lie.
> Their busy limbs in perfect rest.
> And closed the sparkling eye.

The phrases "limbs in perfect rest," and "closed the sparkling eye" conventionally describe death. The children will in a certain sense be dead to the speaker once their real mother comes home. Her language thus points to the necessary ambivalence of the substitute mother.

Dorothy's interest in young children and her perceptive observations of them are the basis of a later poem, "Loving & Liking," in its expanded version, "Irregular Verses Addressed to a Child." The poem first appeared as a sonnet in the Commonplace Book. It finally becomes a piece of sixty-eight lines written in couplets, a kind of eighteenth-century poem of instruction in which an older narrator attempts to teach a child something about language usage, specifically the difference between the words *loving* and *liking*. The additions to the sonnet largely have to do with relations between people—the narrator and the child, the child and his family.

The poem seeks to demystify words, to bring them into a child's context.

> There's more in words than I can teach,
> But listen Child!—I would not preach;
> Yet would I give some plain directions,
> To guide your speech and your affections.

Paralleling William's statement about writing in the language of common man, the speaker emphasizes the necessity of talking plainly and avoiding preachiness, of using words children can understand. The speaker puts her examples in line with a child's main focus: food. Typically when children cite something that they love or hate, the object in question has to do with what they eat. This usage, the poem shows, is incorrect; they should be talking instead about liking or disliking food. (Children actually have their own version of this concern. "Do you love chocolate cake?" one will ask. After the inevitable "yes," comes: "If you love it, why don't you marry it?"). In Dorothy's poem, the roasted fowl, the fricasseed frog, the strawberry as food are contrasted with living counterparts that are the possible foci of love. In each instance, the living creature is presented in an extended description that enhances it. We need not go into the differences between a frog and a toad, but they are probably chosen as traditional samples of slimy ugliness that can nonetheless be beautiful in their naturalness. The stewed frog exists in the negative context of a Frenchman's bog and cooking pot. (This culinary jingoism complements the anti-French jokes Dorothy copied into the Commonplace Book and is about as overtly political as her poems become.) Alive and in his pool, however, the frog radiates sparkling grace.

In defining categories of feelings and how they should be applied, the poem finally suggests reliance on what it terms the "law of nature." If a living entity follows its own law of nature or its instinct, then it may be loved. Again the examples provided—the bird or mouse that a child might chase from the house, the cat that a child might find disgusting as she toys with her prey—represent typical responses of young children. The child addressed here is exposed to the notion of relative modes of value, to the idea that there are different kinds of good, a necessary lesson for children, who are basically intolerant.

"The Address to a Child" turns to human relations, putting together a familial structure for the child. His family, like others in Dorothy's poems, is complete—father, mother, two brothers, and a sister. It is held up as something to be cherished. Family life generates "the first affections," in William's "Immortality Ode" "the fountain light of all our day." Dorothy's poem begins by offering itself as a guide for "affections," and taking advan-

tage of the pun involved, establishes "these right affections" as
the properly applied terms of loving and liking as well as the
force that "leads" a child through life. The examples centered
on food from the first part of the poem are also reworked into a
metaphor reminiscent of those in "Tintern Abbey."

> You love your Father and your Mother,
> Your grown-up, and your baby Brother,
> You love your Sisters and your friends
> And countless blessings which God sends,
> And while these right affections play
> You *live* each moment of your day;
> They lead you on to full content
> And Likings fresh and innocent.
>
> That store the mind, the memory feed,
> And prompt to many a gentle deed.

These "affections" will "feed" the memory and will also
"prompt to many a gentle deed," setting out early familial relations, rather than a scene viewed from the banks of the Wye, as
the basis for "acts / Of kindness and of love." Or if we accept
Richard Onorato's argument about the extent to which in writing of nature William also writes of the mother, then Dorothy
in her poem emphasizes and expands the intimate personal relationships underlying William's reactions as he composes above
Tintern Abbey.

Two other poems, "A Holiday at Gwerndovennant" and
"Christmas day" also explore the power of the family group.
"A Holiday at Gwerndovennant" suggests that for a child the
best part of going away may be returning to his father's house.
The speaker in the poem is again a nurturing female presence
who must remain separated from the children visiting her, first
because of her age, then because they return to their parents.
"Christmas day" describes an extended family as it returns to its
patriarchal center.

For Dorothy Wordsworth, Christmas Day had special significance. As she wrote to Lady Beaumont, "in my inner heart it is
never a day of jollity" (2:122). It was her birthday, a day of self-

examination, and it was a repeated reminder that as a girl she did not have an immediate family to be with at Christmas.

The first two lines of "Christmas day" establish what the holiday is supposed to be like, what people are supposed to do on it. "This is the day when kindred meet / Round one accustomed social fire." This is not only a time of community, but of community with a past: the fire is not only "social" but "accustomed." The viability of the opening statement, however, depends on two conditions, set up in the poem by two "if" clauses. The first has to do with the survival of the "hoary Sire / In patriarchal age." In him the family has generational and masculine continuity. The second conditional clause introduces the possibility of a grandmother, her presence an additional piece of happiness. If they are both alive, they can experience complete joy in their home by gathering their family into it and thus effecting the desired unity of the opening description.

It is the grandfather's power that really draws in the family. The house is primarily his—"the Grandsire's reverenced roof." In the Commonplace Book there is a couplet that establishes the grandfather's power and importance even more firmly: "The lowliest is the proudest seat, / The foot-stool at the Grandsire's feet," lines also scribbled into a late journal. These words, which demonstrate such submission to masculine authority and such a longing for both that power and that submission, are not included in the final version but are shadowed by lines that place the "appropriate seat" "beside his honour'd feet." The relationships are thus not so rigidly hierarchical, the grandfather's power not quite so absolute. The text indicates other ambivalence about an all-powerful father figure. First the wife is his "supporter"; then she is more his equal, having "shared" everything. This relationship is further examined at the end of the poem.

> She who all joy, all grief has shared
> Now is their happiness complete:
> Their Children & their Children's Children meet
> Beneath the Grandsire's reverenced roof,
> Where faithful love through trying years has stood all proof.

The last line is difficult. Does *proof* refer to trial or testing? Or is faithful love being held up as proof? If so, as proof of what? The possibility exists that living a life for the family is not the most fulfulling of all existence, although it allows a perfect Christmas day for some.

The importance of a parental center, as well as the presence of a speaker who is a nurturing force but is still cut off from that center, figures in the poem "A Holiday at Gwerndovennant." The poem begins as the narrator addresses a group of children visiting this small farm, owned by Thomas Hutchinson. Although the children are to have "three days' mirth and revelry," the poem includes only the two days in which language illuminates the time of the speaker's life. What starts out as a celebration of holiday and going away becomes a celebration of home and family in yet another poem about absence and the possibility of domestic reunion.

Forms of female power organize the first part of the poem. The first two stanzas set out certain conditions of the visit. The speaker, although some forty years older than the children, hopes to join them in play. The place of springtime festivity is not a hall in the usual sense but a chamber built by nature. Leading the group to "this placid, secret nook," the "I" of the poem catalogues sights and sounds to establish the place as decorated, song filled, and lent to them by an accommodating, generous nature. Phrases more usual to interior descriptions compose this view of the outer world. Nature functions as a self-generating female presence, responsible for the creation of "perfect harmony," the concluding words of the description.

Arriving at this "chosen place," the speaker describes a momentary pause and then disjunction as the children stop in the center, look around, and finally race away from their mothers, now characterized as "grave & slow-paced dams." Left to consider what she now realizes was an unrealistic hope of being united with the children, as in "The Mother's Return," the speaker realizes she is simply too old to "travel in one stream" with them. The two groups of adults and children, now established and described, allow the contrast of youth and old age so frequently found in Dorothy's poetry as well as a setting out of a series of other oppositions: childhood/adulthood, shouting/ stillness, present/past, society/isolation.

Along with such oppositions however, other unities emerge. The women's withdrawal to the "stillest nook" allows them to read a book, but one of memory rather than of conventional pages. The children's actions provide a mirror that reflects the narrator's own past. While she slips in and out of William's vocabulary of recollection in solitude, this speaker's memory functions in the context of community.

> But now, recall'd to consciousness
> With weight of years of changed estate,
> Thought is not needed to repress
> Those shapeless fancies of delight
> That flash'd before my dazzled sight
>   Upon this joy-devoted morn.

> Gladly we seek the stillest nook
> Whence we may read as in a book
> A history of years gone by,
> Recall'd to faded memory's eye
> By bright reflexion from the mirth
> Of youthful hearts, a transient second birth
>   Of our own childish days.

The first-person pronoun becomes plural; the narrator sits and recalls with a group of women. The phrases "fancies of delight / That flash'd before my dazzled sight" may recall the daffodils that "flash upon that inward eye," but Dorothy's narrator is not in a "vacant," "pensive" mood enjoying the "bliss of solitude." In her poem it is the immediate, noisy presence of the children that triggers the imagination.

It is community that characterizes the joy of the children, not the magnificent isolation frequently at work in William's descriptions of childhood, a revision with which Dorothy seems not completely at ease. These children stay in a group devoted to "social play." They organize themselves into structured activities, depending on one another for sought-after interaction. The course is termed "unbridled," suggesting that the author might wish it to retain some of the wildness of her brother's descriptions of early years. But the day is more completely described as totally structured, especially when play is interrupted by the "noon-tide meal," here a formal, communal ritual. All obey orders and seat themselves in "a Round," the appropriate unifying form for a controlled occasion.

The "long vernal day" continues until twilight, silence, and tiredness replace sunshine, noise, and energy. The children, again participating in an organized ritual, say their prayers, and the day of the holiday passes into a night of long sleep. Once more emphasizing that the children are part of a group, the speaker describes them all awakening together. As one who knows children, Dorothy must realize the impossibility of such an occurrence. She is dealing here with one aspect of an idealized childhood—the security of being part of a group and of being cared for in an established place. When the children wake up, they realize that the time of expectation is over, but they are happy because they are returning to the most important structure of all—"the dear paternal roof." The speaker experiences another separation as they leave.

The most important option the children in this poem possess is not necessarily that of going on holiday but of having a home with a father and mother in it to return to. This familial structure is far more crucial, according to the poem, than the others in which they have participated. Significantly, it is this last part of the poem that Dorothy copies over and over again into her late journals.

And of all the possible incidents involved in coming home, the poem selects for emphasis that of telling about the vacation.

> They reach the dear paternal roof,
> Nor dread a cold or stern reproof
> While they pour forth the history
> Of three days' mirth and revelry.

The speaker sees this chance of reportage as an ultimate happiness enhanced by the willingness of the parents to listen. The children need not "dread a cold or stern reproof" as they "pour forth" the story. (The other use of "reproof" in Dorothy's poems, also has to do with possible chastisement for articulation. In her poem to Julia Marshall, speaking of why she didn't write poetry as a young girl, the narrator says she feared reproof and ridicule.)

Freedom from this negative reaction to their talk is a main component of the "happy lot" the speaker defines in the rest of the poem. As in "The Mother's Return" the age that separated her from the children's activities enables her to instruct them on childhood, time, and memory. Like the speaker of the poem on loving and liking, she believes that familial ties underpin childhood happiness.

> Ah Children! happy is your lot,
> Still bound together in one knot
> Beneath your tender Mother's eye!
> —Too soon these blessed days shall fly
> And Brothers shall from Sisters part.

A double jointure characterizes the line "still bound together in one knot." Watching over them is their "tender Mother's eye." The care of both parents allows childhood to be free from sorrow and from strife. But disruption, a falling out of the unities of childhood, is inevitable. Here, it is described as brothers parting from sisters, a reference which in the context of Dorothy's biography need not be elaborated. The "punctual pleasures" of childhood's home, however, will always serve as a source of strength through memory. In this phrasing a point (punctual) of pleasure, a "spot in time" that is connected with the home rather than with a landscape provides continuity and renovation.

Finally, the poem becomes a consideration of the workings of time and memory. The past is greatly valued as unique for each person and as the determinant of what a person is. Dorothy amends "the child is father of the man" to "the child and his familial relations . . ." Holidays are important because they mark off the flux of childhood, giving the memory points of reference around which to organize the past.

The poem also proposes language as another possible organizer of time. The children "pour forth the history / Of three days' mirth and revelry," thus defining the time with words. Their history has enabled the "history" of the narrator, their activities having allowed her to "read as in a book / A history of years gone by." The text of "A Holiday at Gwerndovennant" defines not only the past, present, and future of children and speaker but the festive day itself.

In "A Holiday at Gwerndovennant" the speaker finds her "scheme" for the day "idle" and undoable. The attempt at organization does not work out, although within the poem's larger context some control over the time of the day is effected. A different kind of attempt to order the world through language occurs in the way Dorothy's poems deal with nature. The masses of detailed description that characterize her journals cannot fit within the space of her poems, but nature's presence is certainly felt within them. In the poem on loving and liking one basis for evaluation is the "law of Nature," a phrase implying an orderly universe that can be discerned and, in the context of the poem, can be written about in plain terms.

Another poem that outlines a "scheme" of nature is "Floating Island at Hawkshead, An Incident in the schemes of Nature." The speaker in this poem is an observing presence who sets out certain possibilities in the way the world works, of which the reader should be aware. The phenomenon described is the appearance and disappearance of an island visible to anyone who takes the trouble to look. Implied throughout this poem, which presents nature not necessarily as explicable but as observable, is the notion that too many people gaze vacantly at nature and so remain unaware of its complexity.

The mode of description makes nature into a feminine presence that can be self-destructive or that "may cease to give." Although nature's destructive possibilities are always present, whatever ruin occurs is part of forces continually operating in the world. They are complex—*schemes* is plural—but always organized. Asserting an amoral evolution in nature, the poem contains detached, objective description that says "That's the way things go."

The island is presented as a throbbing, warbling, living presence containing all the elements necessary to animal life: "Food, shelter, safety." When the island disappears, these amenities are gone and nature causes the collapse of an entire world. The poem begins by emphasizing harmony, but after the opening lines, each stanza turns on words of rupture: "undermined," "loosed," "dissevered," "die," "take away," "passed away," "lost fragments." The reader is addressed as one of those who may be wandering absentmindedly through nature, and the possible vacantness of his day may parallel the vacantness of the spot where the island was before it "passed away," or died. This fragmentation and disunity, however, exist within nature's harmony, and there is always the possibility of renewal and regeneration. "Yet the lost fragments shall remain, / To fertilize some other ground."

Both destructive and generative in this poem, nature appears in other of Dorothy's poems as a "warder," "guard," "sustainer," "giver of gifts," "attuner," "at rest," "faithful," "true," "wise," "pursuing her daily task." In "Lines intended for my Niece's Album," nature is made like the book in which the poem will be written; both are green; both sustain elements of life. Nature, the book, "The works of God's Almighty power," and writing—as the poet's creations—are made equal to those of God.

In Dorothy's poems, as in William's, nature is sometimes presented in the context of God and conventional religion. Natural piety, the religion of nature, and standard Christianity both complement and oppose one another in her work. One drawing together of natural religion and Christianity occurs in "Lines written (rather say *begun*) on the morning of Sunday April 6th, the third approach of Spring-time since my illness began. It was a morning of surpassing beauty." This extended title, which recalls "Lines Composed a Few Miles above Tintern Abbey, on Revisiting the Banks of the Wye during a Tour. July 13, 1798," dates the poem among those connected to the last part of Dorothy's life, and the verse of this period frequently intersects with "Tintern Abbey." The speaker herself is emphasized as a fixed point of endurance, which issues the poem. Immobile on her couch, she cannot join the Sunday morning procession to church, but her mind is "free to roam," and so what she does is interpret the sabbath. Having rightly understood the sound of the bells, the serious of all ages "give to pious thought a tongue." The speaker of the poem attempts a similar act, articulating a system of correspondences between the holy world of nature and the holy world of man, between bodily decay and eternal sureties, between suffering on earth and resurrection in heaven.

In the first stanza of the poem, the construct of man's sabbath is applied to the singing of birds, which becomes in this system a "full choral hymn." The narrator's imagination thus brings about a confusion of the human and natural. The text keeps before the reader its awareness that the speaker's personal perceptions are being imposed on the world and that the descriptions are constructs of imagination and language as well as observable data. "My eye beholds," "I hardly hear," "seems sanctified," "I could believe." The notion that through its example nature is involved in getting people ready for prayer on Sunday morning is introduced as "a fancy, a fond thought." Equally fanciful might be the interchange between man and nature so crucial to William's thought. Religion and nature cannot really be interfused. The poem points, for example, to the tension between human religion and mankind's use of nature in the relationship with animals. The sabbath seems a time of truce between them when the horse is no longer "goaded" and the ewes feel "safe." One must ask, safe from what? Sabbath harmony and peace exist only because they are differentiated from the toil and blood of the other days of the week.

When she interprets nature's holiness as a "Fit prelude" to man's "holy task," the speaker begins a consideration of Christian piety and prayer, of humbleness, faith, and trust in Jesus. No longer physically able to join in the mechanisms of organized worship, she is left to imagine what is going on and to seek consolation in the promises of religion. They do not completely work for her. The failing body, the inability to be in nature, should push her to absorption in a conventional Christian God, but Dorothy crosses out the last stanza of the poem, which preaches further piety and ends with a question that challenges what has been asserted about the compensations religion offers.

> Such gifts are mine: then why deplore
> The body's gentle slow decay,
> A warning mercifully sent
> To fix my hopes upon a surer stay?

So Dorothy finally concludes the long poem and the many four-stanza versions of it that she sends to friends. Why deplore the body's decay? The question may be answered two ways. The immediately surrounding lines indicate a response to the effect that the illness should not be deplored. The possibility of another reply is made obvious, however. The body's decay should be deplored precisely because it cuts her off not only from religious rituals but also from physical participation in the holiness of nature.

The frequency with which the phrases and sentiments of Christianity appear in Dorothy's later poetry suggests that as she grew older she may have wished to convince herself of what would both make up for past disappointments and ensure a blissful eternal future. As in "Lines written . . . ," however, these pieties are frequently undercut. Sometimes, as in the poem on loving and liking, they are tacked on in a homilitic fashion and appear out of context with the rest of the piece. Sometimes the syntax contradicts what would be simplistic religiosity. In "To Sarah Foxcroft's Infant," for instance, the older speaker seems to be a religious, trusting person accepting whatever happens in God's ordered universe.

> I will not seek to fathom God's decrees
> Nor look beyond that present happy time,
> Trusting that, careless as the summer breeze
> A hand divine will lead thee through thy prime.

But maybe this speaker is not so convinced about the rightness of the way things are. At least one clause can be ambiguous.

What exactly is "careless as the summer breeze"? Whereas one might think that the infant is careless, and happily so, the syntax can suggest that the divine hand is careless. A narrator who posits a God with a careless hand cannot be totally committed to the universe of conventional religious piety.

Four other poems, each about death, preach with Christian resignation that life is but a sorry prelude to eternal beatitude at the same time as they question such faith. In "To Christopher Rennison," the way in which the two stanzas contradict one another calls into question the promise of a better life awaiting one after death. The subjects of the first stanza are a life and the tales of that life, an existence that is scarcely the "daily task of duty" of the second, which is the one that may be peacefully surrendered. The life that will be "told" is of roaming the hills and coming home to talk to adoring children, an idyllic mode of living that has little to do with a daily grind. The clichés of stanza two—"race is run," "daily task of duty done," "peacefully resign"—fit with the pious, somewhat clichéd sentiments this stanza preaches but not with the vital terms of the first. In the beginning the poem seems to be a celebration of life and language that should not necessarily conclude with resignation and death.

In "A Tribute to the Memory of the Revd John Curwen," not only Christian piety and acceptance but also writing about a man somehow mitigates death. Here the subject is remembered and praised for his humble naturalness. To emphasize his spontaneity and his freedom "from worldly art," the word *heart* appears in each of the first four stanzas. The importance of the heart in his tribute also complements "his great design"—"the spread of Christian love." As the poem constructs a tribute to Curwen by building up a picture of his virtues and good deeds, it operates through a process of subtraction, imitating its subject, the ultimate subtraction of death. Families appear fractured: "the widow," "the orphan." Curwen strips himself of his family by counting as "naught" his ancestry. While the text places him in memory as an individual defined by his virtues, it also mentions his detractors. The last stanza inserts a dissonant view—"a carping few" who have little use for the man and his works. Perhaps these doubts about the man are brought in at this point to lend a note of realism that will make the undiluted praise more convincing. Or it may indicate that Christian virtues are not universally accepted.

"Innocent were the lives they led . . ." is another epitaph centered around Christian virtues in which the total goodness of the subjects is rendered questionable. The poem describes two dead women in terms of their narrowly circumscribed feminine roles as daughters and sisters. They were "Innocent," "gentle," "duteous," "kind," and "full of love," done in by the world's sorrows not necessarily because they are too good to live in this "world of care" but perhaps because they are too weak.

> Too weak afflictions rod to bear
> By accident & by sorrow were
> In early noon of life
>
> Removed from this world of care
> In heavenly blessings sweet to share
> From trouble free & strife

In this final version of the poem, "weak" can be either a physical or a spiritual quality. In a rejected stanza, Dorothy makes "weak"a purely physical term.

> Too weak afflictions to bear
> Sickness & sorrow—not despair
> Blighted them in the noon of life

The poem then finally is left ambiguous, perhaps to refuse the Christian view that God gives no more than can be borne and to dilute the virtues of the two women with their lack of fortitude. They are acted upon "By accident & by sorrow," suggesting a passive giving up. Furthermore, they died young and were "Removèd," which may indicate a certain lack of joy at entering the supposedly blessed state of death.

The world of care and possible blessed removal from it also figure in "No more the Pastor with his flock . . ." Viewing a deserted church, no longer the scene of religious ritual, the speaker describes the death of organized religion, replaced in the second part of the poem by nature's ministry. As "pious feelings" settle in her breast, she receives from nature the elements formerly contained in "these sacred walls." The five-stanza poem is divided into two parts of three and two stanzas. The first two stanzas of the poem and the last two stanzas, describing a certain cessation of earthly life, surround the third stanza, which has to do with a lively, blessed, carefree, love-filled, heavenly world. But the second part of the poem revises the first to make the natural world seem somehow more holy than the religious world of the first part.

The repetition of "No more" in the first lines introduces a poem of negation, a kind of telling that inverts the former sweet sound of the "chapel bell or chimes." Desolation, described in terms of sounds that have ceased, is broken only by a whisper that suggests the possibility of a promised land in heaven. The "mansion for all lovely forms," his sister's "memory . . . as a dwelling-place / For all sweet sounds and harmonies," which William proposes in "Tintern Abbey," becomes in this poem "A blessed Mansion in the skies," a building of structured belief.

In a telling by progressive subtractions through absences, the second part of the poem describes still more cessation. Pensiveness is transferred to the day even as the thoughtful, observing presence becomes the center of the description. Each line contains words of rest that are brought to bear on the "I" of the poem as she unhurriedly passes through the scene: "pensive," "quiet," "slowly," "soothed," "calm," "rest," "profound," "settle." But rather than the desolation of the first stanzas, the effect here is one of positive assurance, a control brought about by the nature of the day. Dorothy's consciousness responds to nature's piety even as she explores the characteristics of organized piety that remain continually problematic.

The vocabulary and concerns of organized religion are not so pervasive in the poems that deal most powerfully and directly with Dorothy's state of being in the last years of her life. It is her relationship with the worlds of nature and writing that mainly concerns her. Her poems become her most fulfilling mode of expression. In a letter of 1837 she writes, "I will give you some of the many verses which have slipped from me I know not how—since I cannot now so well express my thoughts and feelings to you" (6:455). Yet the texts indicate that the refuge she finds in this highly controlled language is essentially a removal to a realm of absence and difference, a condition she must necessarily contrast with the world of objects in nature that help define her early life.

"Thoughts on my sick-bed" (while lying on my sickbed, about my sickbed) takes up some of the contradictions of her state.

> And has the remnant of my life
> Been pilfered of this sunny Spring?
> And have its own prelusive sounds
> Touched in my heart no echoing string?

The two questions of the opening stanza are answered negatively with a response that establishes the contrast of youth and old age at the same time as it asserts the presence of the first in the second. The word "pierced" links the two ages. She describes her active youth: "With busy eyes I pierced the lane." Years later, bliss comes "piercing to my couch of rest." Within her present passivity, the narrator remembers the active life of her youth in an experience recalling that of the narrator in "I wandered lonely as a cloud" as he lies on his couch. Apparently feeble and powerless, she maintains the feeling of more power than ever before. In sick old age, she claims more control, perhaps because now everything is done for her, perhaps because now so much can be made manifest. In the lines "But joy it brought to my *hidden* life, / To consciousness no longer hidden," the word *it* may refer to "the work" or perhaps the bringing to her of bouquets described in the previous stanza. Hidden away from society and nature because of her sickness, she joyfully receives these offerings. But the line may also assert the bringing forth of long hidden awareness and feelings. With old age comes the power to act, say, and think much that youth is forced to suppress. This is a line she copies again and again in her late journals and is perhaps the most concise description of Dorothy Wordsworth's own later life.

The poem turns back on itself. The bouquet of "The first flowers of the year," now brought to her, may contain "the earliest Celandine" that she so eagerly welcomed "With joyful heart in youthful days."

> With joyful heart in youthful days
> When fresh each season in its Round
> I welcomed the earliest Celandine
> Glittering upon the mossy ground;
>
> With busy eyes I pierced the lane
> In quest of known and *un*known things,
> —The primrose a lamp on its fortress rock,
> The silent butterfly spreading its wings,
>
> The violet betrayed by its noiseless breath,
> The daffodil dancing in the breeze,
> The carolling thrush, on his naked perch,
> Towering above the budding trees.

The flowers she recalls in describing this youth are those of William's poetry: "the celandine," "the primrose," "the violet," "the daffodil." The poem is an ambiguous dialogue with the poems of William's great decade, celebrating the old interdependence while shaping the words to fit her own struggle, her "consciousness no longer hidden." Not only William's flowers but his thrush and butterfly also appear. Finally, the words and predictions of "Tintern Abbey" conflate with the language of the Lucy poems to organize much of Dorothy's text. The violet, hidden like Lucy, is "betrayed," the word of "Tintern Abbey," but here betrayed by absence almost tangible—"noiseless breath." Remembrance is generally of things isolated: the violet, the daffodil, the thrush "on his naked perch" set away from "the budding trees." To name these objects of youth in isolation is not a surprising reaction from the invalid so long separated from nature. The renovation the poem describes, however, comes from trust in nature signified through the language of

Lucy. Dorothy's repetition of "hidden" turns with a slight revision, to the "Half hidden" violet of "She dwelt among the untrodden ways." The phrase "With some sad thoughts the work was done" puts into her context "Thus Nature spake—The work was done—" of William's "Three years she grew in sun and shower." Even as she revises his poems for her own purposes, Dorothy may wish her use of them to reassure her brother that she still remembers his vision and finds it worthy of her consideration. Memory serves continuity here, a reinforcement of William's hope in "Tintern Abbey." In a revision by subtracting from William's seemingly irreducible "No motion has she now, no force," the line "No need of motion, or of strength, / Or even the breathing air" asserts both her independence from and the possible reality of her brother's "prophetic words."

It is, however, partly the absence of health and nature that makes this nature of memory possible, that enables the fulfillment of William's prophecy. What can be had is the language of nature. The poem considers words, writing, and the various relationships that have characterized Dorothy's community of writing. Speech and silence are two organizing oppositions of the poem, which seeks to deny silence, to be evidence of the "echoing string" set vibrating by the sounds of spring. Because of the narrator's condition, words, with all the absence their presence signifies, must replace all else. While this state may be fine for recalling William's words of prophecy, the person who must exist in it cannot be completely unambivalent about it. And yet it may be a state of power, precisely because of the words she now possesses. From infancy, the time without words, William has been a "friend," "brother," but first the "Bard," the one who writes. In the poem, the narrator not only controls the world through language but also controls the language of William's poems. The word "pilfered" calls attention to itself, especially as placed in Dorothy's poem with "prelusive" and "piercing," words connected by sound, but also by their possible relationship to the language of William's and Dorothy's poetry. Her observations were taken little by little (pilfered) by other writers years ago. Her sounds, first prelusive to her brother's, now "pierce" his in the variegated sense of that word:

"see thoroughly into," "puncture," "penetrate with pain," "discern," "pass a sharp instrument into." Again a question placed in the poem brings an answer different from the response she would seem most likely to propose. Her being has indeed been "pilfered." The "echoing string" does not exist in her heart because her sound was there first for others to echo.

The short poem "When shall I tread your garden path . . ." also proceeds through a series of questions, the answers to which may well be negative because of the speaker's "feebleness."

> When shall I tread your garden path?
> Or climb your sheltering hill?
> When shall I wander, free as air,
> And track the foaming rill?

The speaker envisions outward expansion—movement from garden path to sheltering hill to foaming rill—but the poem contracts to the couch where she has lain "Five years in feebleness," revealing a figure existing in stationary opposition to the verbs of the first stanza, all of which have to do with the ability to use one's legs: "tread," "climb," "wander," "track." The final lines of the poem generalize the movements of the first stanza to travel in the hills, this time with "vigorous step."

> A prisoner on my pillowed couch
> Five years in feebleness I've lain,
> Oh! shall I e'er with vigorous step
> Travel the hills again?

In this poem Dorothy writes the terrifying negatives inherent in William's "Nature never did betray the heart that loved her." The five years of this poem have brought none of the rejuvenating gifts nature appears to give to the speaker of "Tintern Abbey" after his five-year absence from the scene. Dorothy's speaker must go back into nature if she is not to be separated from it. The poem remembers not only William's view but "Thoughts on my sick-bed" as well. There the narrator was "No prisoner;" here she is "A prisoner." No "Power" or "Memory" relieves her condition. The desire to escape enclosure, however, is militated against by the very terms in which it is phrased. The probable answer to her questions is a devastating "never."

The narrator of "When shall I tread your garden path . . ." wants to counter her five years of immobility with movement. The poem "To Thomas Carr, My Medical Attendant," however, describes finally coming to rest after a five-year journey of pain. A sea of pain, a "perilous path," a voyage almost taken off the earth make up these years. Finally rest returns her to life. The opposition of motion and rest helps organize the telling of these five years as they do those of "Tintern Abbey." Dorothy's repose, however, is that of the survivor who defies the phrases of religious resignation found in the poem through hints that her "Medical Attendant" was not so judicious and not such a "faithful Friend." He did, after all, depart, certain that she would die. His "holy trust" obviously ought not to have been trusted and has been something of a desertion of her being.

Imprisonment because of "failing strength" and "tottering limbs" and the restorative function of the poetic act are main concerns of "Lines to Dora H." This text, like many of Dorothy's other poems, speaks to a young woman and is written specifically to go into her album, her book of poetic keepsakes. "Lines to Dora H.," "To Rotha Quillinan," "Lines intended for my Niece's Album," and "Lines intended for Edith Southey's Album" are all of a mode that might be called "album verse," and Dorothy's album poetry fulfills the formal expectations of the genre at the same time as it diverges from them. Most such poetry is light banter, often having to do with some characteristic of the person to whom it is addressed. Dorothy, on the other hand, addresses the young woman in order to explore her own situation, often in an intensely personal way. Again she juxtaposes her pain-wracked, confined present to her youthful time in nature, emphasizing those characteristics of the young woman that release her own awarenesses.

"Lines to Dora H." begins as the speaker describes herself in relation to Dora's "tiny spotless book." Her emphasis is on writing, on the confrontation of the artist with her material, although the characterization of the book as unmarked and delicate may be transferred to the figure of innocent young girl dealt with at the end of the poem.

> No fairy poem wherewith to write
> No fairy prompter to indite
> Waits Dora upon me

Though she lacks appropriately supernatural materials and inspiration, the speaker is nonetheless illuminated by the potential for poetry—the "spotless" book awaiting her poem. This description, however, carries with it the idea of the poem as a stain and also the negative homonym "indite/indict." The speaker may indeed be found criminal for "venturing" this poem, for sullying the book, especially if "tremulous fingers feeble hands" refuse in this instance, as they so often do, to be directed by the mind, which in any case "full oft is misty dul & blind."

> How venture then to draw a line
> Over this delicate book of thine

The catalogue of her inadequacies as writer ends with a characteristic question, which might evoke an answer of, "It would be better if you did stay away from this book; you are really not fit to write in it."

The question, however, brings up only a possibility of negativism. In the action actually undertaken, the poem continues with a consideration of the kind of album poetry being composed. Here, as in other of Dorothy's texts, album poetry is seen in relation to the painting that young ladies traditionally engaged in, an art of delicate "cunning" but free from the "wildness" characteristic of the speaker's youth. References to this craft of feminine drawing appear in several of the album poems as they consider various ways of signing youth, old age, the passage of time. In "Lines intended for my Niece's Album" the content of the book allows permanence for the young girl's thoughts, her "hopes," and "visionary scheme," which exist in "vivid hues," a phrase that makes painting part of the expression undertaken. In "To Rotha Quillinan" the narrator refers to "The Rosebud drawn by James's skill." A biographical interpretation would allow this reference to be a pressed flower, drawn from the soil by James Dixon, the Wordsworths' gardener. But the "never-fading" flower may also be a rosebud "drawn" in the sense of sketched into the album. In any case, the flower can serve as a sign of past happiness.

In "Lines to Dora H." the speaker has refused to participate in the accepted feminine occupation. Drawing is contrasted with the mode of signification the poem employs. This rejection of a traditionally feminine skill questions the whole emphasis placed on the importance of "her album" in a young woman's life. This womanly occupation can, after all, be considered essentially trivial. Dorothy herself never kept an album; rather, like her brother, she kept a commonplace book. Refusal to understand these feminine pursuits becomes linked in "Lines to Dora H." with the narrator's chronic inhibitions about writing. "Nor in my early years the line / Eer flowed in fancy's theme" comments on the lines of drawing and of poetry. If she did write, she sought "simple truth," emphasizing the plainness and forthrightness usually absent from album poetry, which she denigrates in her poem for Edith Southey's album as often containing "The studied phrase of flattery."

The speaker of "Lines to Dora H." also speaks of her writing as containing and being contained in "The wild growth of a happy youth." The present, the "now" of the poem, contrasts with that time as it projects an aged, half-blind, "tottering" figure, caught in a room that becomes even more of a prison as she describes how it is not "A cell of sorrow or of gloom." Although her condition is similar to that described in "Thoughts on my sick-bed" and "The worship of this sabbath morn . . . ," in this poem her senses allow "Free entrance" for nature's beauties. Only after considering her poetic art, her past, her painful old age, here mitigated by nature's beauty, does the narrator turn to consider the young lady addressed. Even then, the girl appears in the context of the speaker's remembrances of herself as affectionate adult presence. Her "faithful recollections" contrast with the "shadowy recollections" of the "Intimations Ode" to construct a clear definition of how she used to be. Dorothy's album poems are about the woman speaking much more than about the girl addressed.

"To Rotha Quillinan" is likewise a poem about the speaker and her illness. Here the young girl addressed is a counterpart of Dorothy herself in that Rotha too was a motherless child. A letter further links her to Dorothy.

> Here is a Blank space (left for Dora I suppose) but I cannot help saying one word—that your little Daughter is writing beside me—copying a poem for her own pleasure—that I *delight* in having her beside me; for she is the best and pleasantest and happiest Child I ever knew—In this judgment of her we all agree—adieu my dear Friend—Yours ever D. W. Senr (5:386)

In the poem to Rotha, the speaker tells of how she can face the past, perhaps wishing to reassure the girl whose life might parallel her own, although in her youth and innocence Rotha only recalls "Bright days of mirth & innocent glee."

> Though helpless, feeble are my limbs
> My heart is firm, my head is clear,
> And I can look upon the past without a
> > pang, without a fear.

The narrator's viewpoint is of one who having passed through a great trial, can now contrast her mental and emotional strength with her wasted body. Yet the poem brings up the possibility of fearing and regretting one's past even as this possibility is denied. Perhaps though, through various modes of organization—here writing and drawing as evidenced by the written lines and the drawn rose—the past can be open to some control.

At the same time as the rosebud is a preserving record, it is also arrested, like the lovers on Keats's urn, forever about to enjoy the kiss. This paradox is further considered in "Lines intended for my Niece's Album." The poem characterizes the album as the "tiny Book" for preserving memories of people, ideas, and emotions, allowing them to retain "endless youth," to "unchanged . . . stand" through "changeful years." Stasis, however, is not a totally positive condition in the poem; it is opposed by the notion of life-giving "quickening breath." The artists contributing to the album, as well as the girl who in a biblical echo "gavest the word" for its creation, all bring about development and maturation. The older, wiser speaker of the poem explains this opposition of product and process to the girl whose "youthful mind" may not have understood the implications of her act.

The greenness of the book's cover might be an emblem sad or gay, a sign of possible despair or joy. In an extended comparison of the book's greenness to Nature's "favored hue," the speaker points to nature's green beauty, her "faithfulness" and "trueness," the "gay" factor. The other side of the emblem may have to do with the book's "Perennial green" enfolding leaves (pages) which must lose their spotlessness to "live" or to receive a poem. The book is finally one of death, unchanging in its greenness, unlike the variousness of nature, and containing "Memorials," "something that keeps remembrance alive," though its object has died. Indeed, many of the contributors to Dora's album—Scott, Lamb, Coleridge, and Dorothy—wrote of death and aging as inevitable process, perhaps because they themselves felt death imminent.

F. V. Morley describes Dora's album as a green leather book to which some sixty different people contributed over twenty years. It was an object of some concern in the Wordsworth household. In a letter to Edward Quillinan, William writes, "You kindly propose certain Autographs for Dora's book, and every person you name on the score of genius is worthy of being there" (5:537). Poets, including Arnold and Tennyson, wrote in the album even after Dora's death. William's own contribution, the sonnet "Nuns fret not at their convent's narrow room," should be mentioned here in relation to Dorothy's text. His poem emphasizes various kinds of restraints, among them feminine confinements and the happiness that is possible within them, as well as the pleasure and worth contained in the metric confines of sonnet writing. Dorothy writes of Dora's power to effect poetry. Feminine restraints are not a means to happiness. Rather, the speaker is caught in an unhappy identity of an "aged Friend" who doubts that any value lies in her poetic undertaking.

The self-doubt expressed in this particular poem is partly attributable to its context among the contributions of famous poets. Uneasily aware of these authorial presences, these "true Brothers of the Lyre," the speaker questions her place among them. "No poet I," she asserts. She is excluded from patriarchal power; it is Dora's "gifted Sire" who provides the impetus behind the "real poetry" of the album, the poetry composed by men. Other women, such as Felicia Hemans and Maria Jane Jewsbury, contributed to Dora's book, but the poets worthy of consideration in "Lines intended for my Niece's Album" are distinctly masculine.

The speaker questions not only her own poetic ability, but the whole enterprise of leaving poetry for remembrance. Any benefit to her may be negligible, since she is old, will soon die, and will be unable to hear any praise for her efforts—no Christian consolations here; death is final. The concluding stanza, however, raises another possibility.

> Yet still a lurking wish prevails
> That, when from Life we all have passed
> The Friends who love thy Parents' name
> On her's a thought may cast.

Addressing the relationship of absence, memory, and writing, the speaker's desire to be saved from obscurity prompts her to "inscribe [her] name." Yet even here, her own name, her inscription, works in terms of another's. Interpreted biographically, the poem's conclusion makes Dorothy Wordsworth's future identity dependent on Dora's "Parents' name," specifically in the second version of the poem, on William's, as "Parents'" becomes "Father's."

Despite feelings of dependency and poetic inadequacy, Dorothy creates a speaker in "Lines intended for Edith Southey's Album" who attempts a poem that might be a "record . . . Of tender love which may not die." Dorothy once again writes in the voice of an older, sickly woman, preparing for death by taking an affectionate farewell of the young woman who has asked for a poem. This longest of the album poems takes on the texts of other authors as it emphasizes Edith's poetic presence as the "Laureate's Child," the daughter of Robert Southey. In the background must also lie the first Edith, Southey's wife, in all her terrifying insanity.

The opening line, "Fair Edith of the Classic Hill," relates Dorothy's text to William's poem "The Triad," in which the "noblest Youth," perhaps "Some God or Hero, from the Olympian clime," is presented with three possible spouses: figures representing Edith Southey, Dora Wordsworth, and Sara Coleridge (*PW* 2:292–298). Holding up Edith as a perfect consort, able through her goodness and care to make a man happy under any circumstances, the speaker of William's poem demands, "What living man could fear / The worst of Fortune's malice, wert Thou near" (ll. 56–57). While Dorothy might understandably have felt uneasy with the poem because she responds to other factors of Edith's life, the objections voiced in her own poem have to do with what she considers the highly stylized, classically adorned hoopla of this poem and of others written to young women. She finds it somehow inauthentic. "To sound her praise in transport high," as "the *Bard*" would do, is "a needless task."

Setting her poetic concerns against William's—albeit tentatively—Dorothy Wordsworth finds his wanting. Her poem seeks to create a record of bonding between two women. Her "page" describes itself as telling "Of tender love," of "Friendship" between "Old and Young." At the same time, however, as she literalizes the bond—"A strong cord draws me to the Maid"—she is "Uttering the pensive word, farewell."

> Edith, farewell: and trust me, friend,
> All anxious hopes are now at rest;
> The evening sun shines on my bed;
> As bright the Calm within my breast.

Characteristically, unification and rupture define each other. Through this connection of her sickness with the sunset, the speaker turns the poem of bonding to one of leave-taking, and her personal, specific farewell becomes a general farewell to the world and a discussion about the ways in which God prepares a person for death.

Once again, Dorothy brings the forces of conventional Christianity to bear on the situation, and once again, she hints that they cannot be totally accepted. Speculating that pain such as she has experienced is given to make one appreciate the "one blest end, eternal life" that comes with death, the speaker asserts it "senseless" to struggle with God's arrangements. "Order prevails." But the narrator cannot resign herself to being without "sense" and must finally insist on the importance of what is seen. The poem of conventional resignation reverses into a statement of Dorothy's more habitual manner of vision. Objects that we "*see*" retain the most power. The speaker cannot bring herself to take that leap to faith in "the *unseen*," the supposedly "permanent," the heavenly immutable. Caught as she is in the attractions of the physical world, she can only hope for some coherence when the final moment comes.

Health and vigor bring "joy" that both "dazzles" and "bedims," for it causes such brightness that sight is lost. Given Coleridge's use of *joy* in "Dejection: An Ode," the word must have been a charged one in Dorothy's imagination. For Coleridge, joy may counter dejection, bringing "the spirit and the power," "the sweet voice," "the luminous cloud" all of which come from the "light" and "glory" that "issue forth" from the soul as it confronts the natural world. Without this projection, the world is dead: "in our life alone does Nature live." After hearing Coleridge recite "Dejection," Dorothy describes in the Grasmere journals how she found herself "in miserable spirits" (113). As tenuous as Coleridge's assertion finally shows itself to be, it would have been particularly disturbing to one so in tune with and so dependent upon the world of natural objects. In "Lines intended for Edith Southey's Album" the aging, housebound woman seeks to reject the joy so completely tied to what she calls the transitory "wonders of this beauteous world." Her attempt is unconvincing.

In addition to the album verse, Dorothy wrote other poetry for the women with whom she felt special affinity. Her relationships with Dora Wordsworth, Julia Marshall, and Joanna Hutchinson form the basis for three poems: "To D.," "Irregular Verses" (first called "To Julia Marshall—A Fragment"), and "Lines Addressed to Joanna H. from Gwerndovennant June 1826." Composing to and for these women allows her to range widely through such personal concerns as anxiety about writing, her relationship to the world of nature, her debilitating illness, and even the possible failure of the kind of life she has led. Paramount in these poems is the consideration of various possible and untenable relationships between women.

Although the speaker of "To D." should be differentiated from the girl she addresses because of age, they are linked to one another both by their relationship to the surrounding world and by love. The "cord" of the poem to Edith Southey is here a "thousand delicate fibres." Dorothy utilizes the form of the sonnet to help effect this unification and to consider the relationship of an older and a younger woman. Each contrast the sonnet suggests comes in the context of a preceding similarity.

> A thousand delicate fibres link
> My heart in love to thee dear Maid
> Though thine be youth's rejoicing prime
> My lively vigour long decayed

Setting out the opposition between the two, the first quatrain also allows the infusion through those fibers of "youth's rejoicing prime" into the speaker's heart. The description of her condition as "lively vigour long decayed" brings at least the language of youth into age. The middle part of the sonnet draws the two women together even as it continues to contrast them.

> Thou art a native of these hills
> And their prized nursling still hast been

And thou repay'st their fostering love
As testify thy happy looks, thy graceful joyous mien.

This mountain land delights us both
We love each rocky hill;
I hither came in age mature
With thoughtful choice and placid Will.

Their common response to their surroundings equates them; their arrival in this nature at different points in their lives is again a variation depending on time. The summarizing two lines, equating and differing, describe the similar characters of the two women, a kind of "wise passiveness" arrived at differently, again because of temporal points in their lives.

And I have found the peace I sought
Which thou *un*sought hast found

The comparisons and contrasts centering around various stages of life are more fully worked on in the poem to Julia Marshall, finally called simply "Irregular Verses." The speaker again addresses the daughter of an old friend, in this case Julia, the child of Jane Pollard to whom Dorothy wrote so many of the self-revelatory letters of her early years. In keeping with Dorothy's view of the holiday, this "Christmas rhyme" is a gift that analyzes the "hopes," "fears," possibilities, and actual occurrences in the life of a woman closely connected, again through the heart, with the young woman addressed. The three feminine presences in the poem—Julia, her mother, and the speaker—affect and are affected by the consideration of time and its passage that the poem explores. Although the poem may appear unnecessarily somber and although it concludes by claiming itself supererogatory, the speaker hopes that Julia, as a serious, young woman, can accept its importance.

In this poem about women in time, the speaker works through the stages of her life, beginning with her young womanhood, when she constructed her "girlish vision" of future happiness. The "bliss" of the picture thus painted hangs out of time, a revision of William's "bliss" at being alive in *The Prelude,* which is connected to the revolutionary moment. Hers is a bliss of imagination and of language; it can never come to pass, perhaps because it is simply not a possible choice of life. The existence projected in the vision centers around two women living in an idyllic country setting, a dream of feminine harmony and self-sufficiency that, the poem reports, did not materialize. Although the "visions" retained a sustaining power in "riper years," each woman "pursued a different way." The conventional life the friend accepts surely does not match the speaker's fantasy. Motivated by "duty," her life of wife and mother may be "dignified" and "useful"; it is scarcely an exhilarating existence. Near the end of the poem, slipping into the vocabulary of death, the speaker warns of the possible effect that "this poor memorial strain" about the death of their dream, the extinction of their hopes, might have on Julia's mother. The stanza is a sad comment on the way of life open to such a woman. The explanation of and attempted consolation for her tears is muted by its possible echo of William's line from "Resolution and Independence." Dorothy writes: "—The happiest heart is given to sadness; / The saddest heart feels deepest gladness." William writes: "We Poets in our youth begin in gladness; / But thereof come in the end despondency and madness" (ll. 48–49). The grief of Julia's mother for what might have been can only worsen as age brings increasing realization of lost potential and the wasting of a woman's one life.

Set off as it is, Dorothy's couplet is generally applicable to women and, through William's lines, to herself as poet, a topic of some discussion in this poem. Rather than detailing her own life after the two women parted, the speaker goes back to a much earlier stage of her existence, her childhood, which she describes in terms of thwarted poetic aspirations. Returning to her present, the speaker further justifies her tale "Of hopes extinct, of childish fears," by again referring to time, emphasizing the importance of not wasting one's days in cheerful inanities of the present moment.

The characterization of Julia as "mirthful" but "placid—staid" and not "giddy"—establishes for her a kind of normalcy.

The imagination working in the poem, however, moves between oppositions that exist as divergences from this female steadiness. When she was a girl, the speaker says, hers was "an active busy brain / That needed neither spur nor rein." The goading energy of the spur and the restraint of the rein are two opposing forces that help structure the poem. The cottage fantasy contrasts the freedom of the "foaming stream" and the confinement of the "crystall Well," the "wanderings to the topmost height" and the "belt of hills" that "wrap it round." The spot "fondly framed" when hope was "untamed" further carries out the opposition as does the discussion of rhyme and prose in which rhyme is seen as a controlling inhibition of the more expansive imaginative expression that prose allows. Finally, the feelings of Julia's mother will not be "checked," reined in; rather the content of the poem will spur on the "tear" and "rising sigh" at the reining in of her hopes.

Like the "Irregular Verses" addressed to Julia, "Lines Addressed to Joanna H. from Gwerndovennant June 1826" describes a relationship between women that was broken by the exigencies of life. The woman addressed had to leave the place of shared happiness "to roam / Far off, and seek another home." Visiting the spot some years later, the speaker recalls their past experience and once again says "farewell" to the "deep verdant, woody Dell." The emotions caused by rupture and necessity play equally on both, so that the speaker tells her own story in writing of the other woman's absence. Joanna's life in this spot is a time of personal freedom not subject to control of fashion, a time during which she could follow her own impulses. Such freedom is not permitted the two doomed women of the poem.

Even as she remembers their past together, the speaker feels the sorrow of their parting, recalling that she had "heav'd a bitter sigh" and that Joanna had wept silently. The anticipation and fact of their time together exists in the awareness that they have no chance of maintaining any such relationship with each other or with the natural world and maybe even that "'tis best" that Joanna leave. It is an alliance that demands isolation; even to consider it, the narrator places herself in "the deepest, darkest shade / Within the covert of that glade." The relationship causes internal, imaginative awareness to overwhelm the senses, the perceptions of the "bodily ear."

The remembrance constructs a time of feminine nurture. The house is made to belong to the woman: "thou hadst hous'd me in thy home." The hostess leads her friend through a song-filled scene of maternal care, "through the dingle deep." The obtrusive word "dingle" here emphasizes both terrain and sound in its meaning both as a cleft between the hills and a tinkling, jingling sound. They come to the place "where the snow-white lambs / Sported beside their quiet dams."

The sounds of nature act as a connection to the past. The thrush the speaker hears sings in the "self-same lofty Tree" where she and Joanna heard a thrush singing. Describing the bird of their youth as "Unshrouded," the narrator raises the topic of death and loss that she remains to explore. Moving from present to past to present again here involves a recital of the oppositions of youth and maturity, rejoicing and mourning, heat and shade, light and dark that then and now help define the short-lived relationship of two women.

The life open to Dorothy Wordsworth did not include the existence in a community of women about which "Lines Addressed to Joanna H." and other poems fantasize. Rather she passed her womanhood in a community of writing that was centered around her brother. The poem "a Sketch," her twelve-line description of their arrival in the chosen vale to begin that life becomes a twenty-two stanza poem, "Grasmere—A Fragment," that expands to deal with the ambiguities in Dorothy's choice.

Commencing from a perspective that allows an overview of the valley, the poem celebrates the beauty of Grasmere. Within the unity of the vale, however, the poem focuses on individual cottages. In a text that seeks to image community, the very title of "Fragment" counteracts the notion of wholeness. The natural objects of the poem are those of the Grasmere journals. The "stately rock" recalls "Sara's rock," the "Rock of Names" carved with the initials W.W., M.H., D.W., S.T.C., J.W., S.H. (74). The journal mentions Coleridge's love of rose hips, fruit of the roses that cover the rock. The speaker stands under a monument of the community, but she has "wandered out alone." She remains that "creature by its own self among them" (61).

The joys and sorrows of the choice described in "Grasmere—A Fragment" become more obvious if Dorothy's final version of her arrival at Grasmere with William, her first view of "that dear abode" is contrasted with William's version in "Home at Grasmere" (*PW* 5:319–320). Their similar vocabularies include "wanderers," a "shed," and "inmates"; rivers question them both. But his description corresponds more closely to letters written to Coleridge (1:273–281) and is probably a more faithful account. William includes mention of several days of delightful sightseeing in his description; Dorothy speaks of a "perilous storm" of the preceding night, emphasizing by contrast the beauty and rest found in Grasmere. Although it is winter, she hints at spring and its attendant notions of joy, resurrection, and new beginnings. According to William in the letters and "Home at Grasmere," they arrived in the village during the early evening, "and round us gently fell / Composing darkness, with a quiet load / Of full contentment, in a little Shed" (ll. 174–176). In Dorothy's poem they arrive early enough for her to take a walk, a seemingly independent action that in her poem's telling actually indicates dependence and passivity.

"Grasmere—A Fragment" opens with a scene of harmony that sets off the solitariness of the cottage as attracting the speaker's heart.

> Peaceful our valley, fair and green,
> And beautiful her cottages,
> Each in its nook, its sheltered hold,
> Or underneath its tuft of trees
>
> Many and beautiful they are;
> But there is *one* that I love best,
> A lowly shed, in truth, it is,
> A brother of the rest.
>
> Yet when I sit on rock or hill,
> Down looking on the valley fair,
> That Cottage with its clustering trees
> Summons my heart; it settles there.

Suggesting the continual reenactment of her move to Grasmere, the poem states how her heart perpetually "settles" there. This particular cottage is made masculine by the phrase "a brother of the rest," which perhaps relates to the importance of Dorothy's brother in the domestic scene she so passionately desired. The cottage is also "The very Mountains' child," and this phrase, too, connotes familial structure. The other cottages are feminine and "seduce" the masculine "wanderer's mind."

> Others there are whose small domain
> Of fertile fields and hedgerows green
> Might more seduce a wanderer's mind
> To wish that *there* his home had been.

Everything conspires to draw people to Grasmere, to build community. The human and the natural worlds join to provide shelter, safety, and security in this vision. The "mossy walls" keep out the storm; the "shelter of those trees" screens the cottage.

Nature also entices the speaker into Grasmere. Arriving there, the speaker leaves her only friend to walk by herself. In another reference to the seductive quality of the cottages, she is "Lured" from the "public road," a general statement about her unconventional choice as well as a specific indication of her activity. "Led" by "This pathway" "Eastward, toward the lofty hills" (perhaps an indication of future aspirations), she finds friendship, festivity, and "revelry," compensations for past deprivations. She draws a message from the landscape as her eyes, fixed downward as she begins her walk, gaze up and out.

During this walk she affirms her choice of life: "My youthful wishes all fulfill'd, / Wishes matured by thoughtful choice." Yet she is acted upon even during this short walk, even when she is alone.

> —Beside that gay and lovely Rock
> There came with merry voice
> A foaming streamlet glancing by;
> It seemed to say "Rejoice!"

My youthful wishes all fulfill'd
Wishes matured by thoughtful choice,
I stood an Inmate of this vale
How *could* I but rejoice?

That the streamlet urges her to "Rejoice!" implies the need for such encouragement, implies feelings that are not joyful, especially given the ambiguity *rejoice* takes on at the end of the poem. The poem details her passage from "Stranger"—"All faces then to me unknown"—to "Inmate of this vale." Perhaps in a benevolent sense, the word inmate engages William's phrases "her Inmate Man" and "inmate of this active universe," but the word has negative connotations, too. In nineteenth-century usage the word was not applied to prisoners, but it was used to indicate a patient in an insane asylum or a person not properly belonging to the place he inhabits. Describing the movement to at-homeness in the vale in "Home at Grasmere," William allows the term its uncomfortable connotation as he views the birds showing "pleasure," "inmates though they be / Of Winter's household" (ll. 194–195). And the last line of Dorothy's poem, though it may echo "A poet could not but be gay" in William's "Daffodils," does so ambivalently, with a characteristic question. The structure of the sentence—"How *could* I but rejoice?"—brings up the possibility that the speaker in fact does not rejoice, that the life described is sad and unfulfilled. Moving to Grasmere, she determines what her life will be; she makes a covenant. While the stately rock of the poem suggests the solidity and steadfastness of that commitment, it also works with other echoes of William's "Michael" to recall the stone of Luke and Michael's broken covenant. William's narrator begins by telling what happens "If from the public way you turn your steps" and concludes by pointing to the rocks of the "unfinished Sheep-fold . . . Beside the boisterous brook of Green-head Ghyll" (*PW* 2:80–94). Dorothy's voice speaks to his with her "public road," her "foaming streamlet," her path by sheep and shepherds trod, and her revisions of William's words allow the sharpening of the possible contradictions in the life she describes.

Another source of ambiguity in the poem comes from the speaker's attitude to winter. Telling of how her view of the seasons has changed, the narrator says she formerly "griev'd" at summer's passing but now no longer does so because of the beauty of winter in Grasmere. The passage from summer to winter, however, is not merely a seasonal shift in this poem. Taking up life in Grasmere becomes part of the speaker's movement from youth to maturity, from summer to winter. The summer of her youth has passed and that must be troublesome, no matter how excited she is about the life she is to begin.

While settling down in Grasmere fulfilled Dorothy's long-held dream, it brought with it the knowledge of missed past and future opportunities. Life at Grasmere both encouraged and inhibited a woman trying to find an identity as a writer among men of genius. By the time of the composition of "Grasmere—A Fragment," Dorothy's "sole companion-friend" is no longer hers alone; she has written some of her most extraordinary poetry and prose in her attempt to deal with her situation.

V.

Dorothy Wordsworth and the Women of Romanticism

❖ ❖ ❖ ❖ ❖ IT IS TO DOROTHY WORDSWORTH'S relationships with the men around her, especially her brother, that her preference for prose can perhaps be traced. William Wordsworth's attitude towards the many women poets who sought him out was ultimately one of amused tolerance. He was somewhat put out that Felicia Hemans devoted herself to poetry, to the neglect of proper womanly endeavors. Isabella Fenwick reports his observation that "her education had been most unfortunate. She was totally ignorant of housewifery, and could as easily have managed the spear of Minerva as her needle" (*PW* 4:461). For her part, Hemans, whose poetry enabled her to support a number of children and who was something of a nineteenth-century cultural heroine, felt obliged to play the flirt with William, simpering, "Mr. Wordsworth, how *could* you be so giddy?" (Morley 40).

William's attitude towards women poets, combined with his poetic genius, must have intimidated Dorothy and inhibited her efforts at poetry. No doubt William's view also influenced her own attitudes towards the many women poets with whom she, as a member of the Grasmere community, came into contact. Her encounters with other women writers were important to her. She insisted on getting down the exact details of a visit to Anna Seward, although William was positive a visit never even occurred.[1] Maria Jane Jewsbury was a figure of great significance to Dorothy, who frequently referred to her in letters and later copied a number of Jewsbury's poems into the journals. But Dorothy does not admire her for her writing alone. A letter of 1826 describes a visit during which Dorothy "halted a few days at Manchester with Miss Jewsbury, the Authoress of Phantasmagoria etc—and was even more pleased with her at home than abroad. Her talents are extraordinary; and she is admirable as a Daughter and Sister" (4:427). Dorothy's sentence puts "home" and the fulfillment of Jewsbury's two familial roles on a par with her writing of poetry. The usual balance of art and domesticity forced on women was, for Dorothy, as for most women, a source of both strength and irritation. "I think," Jewsbury wrote, "I could make a decent paper descriptive of the miseries of combining literary tastes with domestic duties" (Gillett xviii). Perhaps in keeping with William's view, perhaps as a reflection of her own situation, Dorothy in her letters praises Joanna Baillie for being a homebody, not just a "literary Lady" (3:596).

William once contemplated writing a piece to be entitled "An Account of the Deceased Poetesses of Great Britain—with an Estimate of their Works," but he decided that the topic was not "sufficiently interesting for a separate subject" (*Letters* 5:4). In his correspondence with Dionysius Lardner about the matter, William suggested that a better plan might be to begin with Sappho and provide a comparative study of women poets in ancient and modern Spain, Germany, France, and England. Such a project would have discovered a number of contemporary subjects.

A great many more women—authors of prose and poetry alike—were involved in the romantic movement of the early nineteenth century than even some feminist critics allow. The *Norton Anthology of Literature by Women,* for instance, cites Charlotte Smith, Mary Tighe, Dorothy Wordsworth, Mary Shelley, and Jane Austen but locates "the most vivid traces of Romanticism as it was defined by male poets" in such writers as

---

1. For a complete discussion of what Dorothy calls the "Seward Dispute" see the letters of May 1825, 5:356–357 and 366–368.

the Brontës, Elizabeth Barrett Browning, and Emily Dickinson, all of whom worked later in the century (183). But unquestionably many women were writing during the romantic period. In her *Age of Books,* Jewsbury comments: "Your youngest daughter may unknown to you, write all the poetry for a magazine, besides having a volume of 'Fragments in prose and verse' almost ready for publication. You may have a talented washerwoman quite clever at composition" (Gillett 57). Aware both of the dreadfulness of the stuff so many scribbling ladies were producing and of the importance of what they were doing, Jewsbury shows how women writers revised and threatened the canon of the male literary establishment, itself an object of her hilarious satire. *The Young Author* proclaims it "perfectly infamous for a woman to write and write well; they ought to be satisfied with reading what men write. I shall make a point of abusing every clever book written by a woman" (Gillett 57).

The women who wrote were aware of the differences between themselves and the men, but wrote nevertheless within the powerful tradition of romanticism not to produce "vivid traces of Romanticism as it was defined by male poets" but to develop a woman's version of that tradition, to explore certain "feminine" possibilities within the general phenomenon of romanticism. A brief look at works by certain women of the period (my choice is admittedly arbitrary) provides a context for Dorothy Wordsworth's writing and reveals characteristics of this women's romanticism.

The Grasmere circle out of which Dorothy worked was only one such group of authors. Romantic writers in England and in America consciously formed themselves into communities that often enabled their art. The Grasmere-Keswick fellowship, the Hedge Club, the Transcendental Club, the Byron and Shelley households are perhaps the best known of the romantic groups. In each community, a writing woman member actively challenged central notions that have achieved canonical status in our standard accounts of romanticism, while she proceeded from and depended on these notions. Thus, women created a romantic literature of their own.

This process that we have been looking at in Dorothy Wordsworth's work also helped generate perhaps the most famous romantic work of all, Mary Shelley's *Frankenstein,* a book that grew out of a communal situation—the contest between Percy Shelley, Byron, and Mary to see who could produce the best ghost story. With her entry, Mary Shelley not only won the contest but also, as Mary Poovey has shown, feminized parts of Percy's romantic aesthetic to create a story that raises feminine ambivalence about the act of writing to mythic proportions. In *Frankenstein,* Mary Shelley questions romantic imaginative assertion. Victor Frankenstein, like the narrator of *Alastor,* seeks to know "what we are" (1. 29). Mary makes Percy's concern with the alienation from nature and people entailed in this quest the central agony of *Frankenstein* as Victor's search culminates not in the story of the poet but in the life of a monster that bears out the meaning of his appellation—monster, from *monstrum, moneo* to warn, to admonish. Frankenstein's creature exists as a horrible warning against the power of creative genius, as a warning about what can happen when someone really does find out "what we are."

In *Frankenstein,* Mary Shelley considers Lord Byron's and Percy Shelley's views of nature. In Byron's *Manfred* the spirit of Mont Blanc—an important location for both the men and women of English romanticism, who wonder and worry at its seemingly amoral inhumanity—finally may be seen as one more external structure that the hero confronts. In Percy Shelley's "Mont Blanc," as in *Frankenstein,* imaginative power is necessary to natural power; consciousness creates meaning, whatever it may be. In the novel not only does the glacier bring destruction, but the entire Alpine topos exalts Victor Frankenstein above the murder and desolation his creature signifies. After each low point in his life, Victor finds himself in a landscape typical of Percy's poetry. Often this natural scene provides a kind of reviving sustenance for him, such as when, after the execution of Justine, he visits the valley of Chamounix and Mont Blanc. "These sublime and magnificent scenes afforded me the greatest consolation that I was capable of receiving. They elevated me from all littleness of feeling, and although they did not remove my grief, they subdued and tranquillized it" (92). The meaning Victor's consciousness creates as it confronts Mont Blanc allows nature to diminish his guilt at his role in William's and Justine's deaths. In both poem and novel imagination standing before the abyss creates significance. But the "Power in likeness of the Arve com[ing] down" is remote and disconnected from human values. This position may be socially unacceptable. Given the basic amorality of this power, the individual imagination can make anything of it, including, Mary Shelley shows us, monsters, and can seem to elevate through aerial perspective any human endeavor—even murder. In Victor's case, the confrontation with the Mont Blanc of Percy's poem allows him to deny the conventional morality that would entail responsibility for Justine. Here the flow of things vacates human solidarity as sublimity replaces William and Justine.

Disruption, discontinuity, and destruction characterize both human relationships in *Frankenstein* and the face of the mountain in "Mont Blanc." Poem and novel record "the sound of the river raging among the rocks," the "caverns echoing to the Arve's commotion," the "shattered" "vast pines" "strewing" the river's path (*F* 90, *MB* l. 30). The movements of the glaciers the poem describes destroy the civilizations man has constructed and "the dwelling-place of insects, beasts and birds" (ll. 109–115). Yet in the poem, the destruction on the mountain is resolved into the fructifying river of life. Catastrophic change, the geological shifts caused by the ice, is, in keeping with scientific theories like those of Cuvier, part of the ongoing history of the earth. Creation and destruction are cyclical. *Frankenstein,* however, does not portray these possibilities of continuity. The novel shifts from the sea of ice at Mont Blanc to the polar sea of ice, disintegration, and destruction.

The scenery of Mont Blanc, which can invigorate Victor, can also depress him or can seem ambiguous. When he returns home to mourn William, he observes that the fact of nature can be read in different ways. "Dear mountains! My own beautiful lake! How do you welcome your wanderer? Your summits are clear; the sky and lake are blue and placid. Is this to prognosticate peace or to mock at my unhappiness?" (72). As Percy asserts in the *Defence,* "All things exist as they are perceived; at least in relation to the percipient" (7:137). This statement helps explain Victor's reactions to the natural world and also provides a commentary on his creature, who, because those around him perceive him as hideous, becomes a monster. Blind De Lacey thinks he is a good fellow. The man–nature interrelationships that Percy Bysshe Shelley envisions are shown in *Frankenstein* to contain the possibilities of antisocial responses.

Having felt only man's revulsion, the monster is educated in human language, history, and psychology by listening to Felix read Volney's *Ruins of Empire* to Safie. Volney's narration of the rise and fall of empires and of the French Revolution and Felix's explanation of the book reveal man to the creature as "at one time a mere scion of the evil principle and at another as all that can be conceived of noble and godlike" (114). Percy's *Revolt of Islam* takes Volney as one source for its positive, revolutionary ideals.[2] The creature's experience, however, is a horrifying inversion of the universal harmony and brotherhood Volney predicts for the human race. Man, Volney asserts, will become free of prejudice and stop destroying himself and others "parce qu'il est dans son intérêt de l'être [because it is in his interest to do it]" (134). Furthermore, rationality and law will triumph because men can agree on a basic structuring principle for society: "*qu'il faut tracer une ligne de démarcation entre les objets véritables* et ceux qui ne peuvent être vérifiés [that a demarcation line must be drawn between verifiable objects and those that cannot be verified]" (292). At the end of *Ruins* a perfect state is about to come into being. "Alors, le législateur ayant répris la recherche et l'examen des attributs physiques et constitutifs de l'homme, des mouvements et des affections qui le régissent dans l'état *individuel et social,* développa en ces mots les lois sur lesquelles la nature elle-même a fondé son bonheur [And so, the lawgiver, having researched and studied man's physical and constitutional characteristics, the impulses and inclinations governing him as an individual and as a social being, developed in these words the laws upon which nature herself based his happiness]" (293). The

2. For a discussion of Volney's influence on Percy Shelley's *Revolt of Islam,* see Kenneth Neill Cameron's *Shelley: The Golden Years.*

monster can never fit in. It is universally verifiable that he is hideous, and therefore all who see him brutalize him. Peace can be achieved on earth now, says Volney, because men can communicate with each other, especially through printing, but the written record the creature provides serves only to authenticate his horrible and unnatural origins.

From the first, Victor refuses to accept responsibility for these origins. The creature's pitiful narration of being abandoned and then trying to make his way in a hostile world makes the reader think, "If only Victor had not misperceived and deserted his creation." Frankenstein's tragedy, Harold Bloom writes in an afterword to the Signet edition, stems "from his own moral error, his failure to love" (217). Mary Shelley does not in this novel accept the idea of universal, all-embracing love outlined in *Prometheus Unbound* but rather shows specifically what happens when a progeny is just too hideous to love. Following Ellen Moers, Sandra Gilbert and Susan Gubar work out the reader's sense that in producing the creature Victor "has a baby" (*Madwoman* 232–234). Mary Shelley considers the existence, or in this case the nonexistence, of some kind of natural, maternal love.

The various disruptions of human relationships explored in *Frankenstein* are literalized in *The Last Man,* another novel by Mary Shelley directly related to her life in a community of writing. After a terrible plague sweeps the earth, the "solitude and silence" of Percy's "Mont Blanc," "co-heirs of her kingdom," become "vacancy." The plague vanishes from the earth when Lionel Verney arrives at Mont Blanc, and he is left as "some Oedipus to solve the riddle of the cruel Sphinx" (311). His narration provides the opposite answer to Oedipus' solution of "man." The novel shows how man disappears from the earth, how it becomes a place of "no man."

The work is most often treated as a roman à clef: Adrian is Percy; Raymond, Byron; Ryland, Cobbett; Lionel, Mary herself. As the last man, Lionel Verney tells the story of his group. As the last of her group, Mary Shelley does the same, telling the story of one of the communities of English romanticism. If we read the novel as roman à clef, we can see it as a way for Mary Shelley to seize power, to revenge herself by killing off everyone else in her group. Or, we can say that she expresses the guilt and loneliness of the survivor for having outlived the members of her literary community. Perhaps the novel is Mary's means of expiating her guilt through the repeated dramatization of loneliness, of being deserted by the entire world. Lionel does contract the plague, but he alone recovers. Perhaps the book should be read as the thoughts of the last survivor of a cultural event—the plague of overreaching male romanticism. Certainly, even in a basic geographic sense, the novel's settings map the history of the two generations of English romanticism. For Lionel begins "among the valleys and fells of Cumberland" (8), where Dorothy Wordsworth walked, and moves through the cultural and political center of London, across Western Europe to Switzerland, Greece, and Italy, coming ultimately to fulfill Percy Shelley's elegiac injunction, "Go thou to Rome." This situating of the narrative obviously intends more than a simple repetition of the writer's own eastward passage. *The Last Man,* to borrow F. L. Lucas's terms, is an allegory of the rise and fall of the romantic ideal.

In *The Last Man,* Mary Shelley, finally, engages the writing of her former companions to reject their most cherished metaphysical assumptions as the ever-renewable historical cycle of *Prometheus Unbound* is terminated. "Poets are the unacknowledged legislators of the world," concludes Percy's *Defence,* but Adrian, Lionel, and Raymond can in no way govern. The dramatic possibility of "Ode to the West Wind"—"If Winter comes, can Spring be far behind?"—takes on a terrifying irony in plague-stricken England, where winter brings relief and "plague is the companion of spring, of sunshine, and plenty" (230). Emphasizing the negative possibilities in the assertion that "nature never did betray the heart that loved her," Mary shows spring in its beauty mocking man's misery. Nature is alive and gorgeous; man is dying and hideous. All interchange between man and the world breaks down when the mind is seen as the passive recipient of natural malevolence.

In her Author's Introduction, Mary Shelley presents the story as being pieced together from writing discovered on "frail and attenuated Leaves of the Sibyl" (4). Whereas the "withered leaves" of "Ode to the West Wind" are linked with power "to quicken a new birth," the Sibylline leaves tell only of death. Although it invokes the Shelleyan sense of "imagination and power" and "that ideality, which takes the mortal sting from pain," the Introduction clearly states that her fiction of death necessarily misrepresents its own unknowable origin. For the Sibyl's verses, "obscure and chaotic as they are . . . owe their present form to me, their decipherer." And though they have "suffered distortion and diminution of interest and excellence in my hands," they were "unintelligible in their pristine condition" (4). This decipherment, which inevitably distorts and diminishes the original unintelligibility can be read as a kind of open avowal of linguistic opacity or nonreferentiality that points up romantic distrust of the positive powers of language.

But exactly to whom are these texts "unintelligible in their pristine condition" Obviously not to the "decipherer" who presents the story. She must, however, rework them to make them more generally accessible. "Scattered and unconnected as they were, I have been obliged to add links, and model the work into a consistent form" (3). The linguistic structures into which she forces the text, those of the dominant male culture, must necessarily distort the language of the primal feminine, the Sibyl. Both Mary Shelley and Dorothy Wordsworth find the forms of conventional, male language somehow at odds with the realities their writing presents. Living as they did in communities so involved with linguistic theory, it is not surprising that the women of romanticism concerned themselves with problems of language.

The story of the Sibyl's leaves, like the experiments in prose and the rejections of language that Dorothy Wordsworth undertakes, confirms some of the observations on women and language made by such contemporary theorists as Julia Kristeva, Hélène Cixous, and Luce Irigaray. Kristeva defines the "semiotic discourse" used by such authors as Joyce, Mallarmé, and Artaud as writing that goes against the conventions of standard language. "Semiotic discourse" bespeaks an infantile fusion with the mother, a refusal to separate from her, become a man, and accept the language of the father. Because of this maternal connection, Kristeva characterizes "semiotic discourse" as particularly feminine. In *The Last Man* semiotic discourse surrounds that primal feminine figure, the Sibyl, whose cave within the earth, entered through a hidden, dark, narrow passage, is clearly womanspace. Thus this source is made distinct from the typical muse of male poetic inspiration, nor is this the Sybil of Coleridge's *Sibylline Leaves*.

Regardless of the origins of the work, however, most writers, Mary Shelley included, force their material into standard forms, here a novel. Dorothy Wordsworth, however, approximates this "semiotic discourse" in the oddly shaped structures of her journals and poems, so reminiscent of Mallarmé's poetry. Her structures allow a relationship with the mother that complements the models of feminine development set out by Chodorow and Miller that so connect to Dorothy's work. The language for writing the feminine, which Cixous and Irigaray describe as fluid, open, without discernable contours, also characterizes Dorothy Wordsworth's texts.

As we have seen, Dorothy Wordsworth's writing often goes like this:

> *Thursday, 24th.*—Brilliant day. Passed the afternoon on the lake. The views were very beautiful. Downy seeds of various kinds, thistle, dandelion &c.,&c., were thickly strewed over the bosom of the lake; we had never before observed such numbers of them lying on the water.

This passage, however, was not written by Dorothy Wordsworth but by Susan Fenimore Cooper (*Rural Hours* 269). As the daughter of James Fenimore Cooper, Susan Cooper writes from the context of a familial group rather than the kinds of larger communities we have been discussing, but she deserves brief consideration here for several reasons. Her responses to the natural world as well as to the literature being produced around her are notably close to Dorothy Wordsworth's. It is really quite striking, in fact, how much alike these two women sound. Such similarities between the writings of women on different sides of the Atlantic in the early nineteenth century make explicit some of the connections between British and American romanticism, often seen as problematic. And here is yet another instance of a woman writer involved in the romantic tradition that we have usually read as a masculine one.

Writing of the self and the self in nature, Susan Cooper, like Dorothy Wordsworth, often defines herself in part by massing details of natural description in elliptical, fragmenting phrases. Compelling too is the sharp distinction between her visions of nature and those of James Fenimore Cooper. In contrast to the physical and psychological wilderness that must be conquered in *The Leatherstocking Tales,* Susan Cooper's nature is almost pacifically self-controlled. Her book *Rural Hours* translates the drama of her father's martial universe to an ordered world of natural continuities and social relationships. Describing the very location seen panoramically at the opening of J. F. Cooper's *The Pioneers,* where it is used to establish the utility of the land, she chooses, instead, to pile up natural detail, locating value in minutiae. Her interest is in definition of the land rather than in its exploitation. The narrator of *Rural Hours* works at a level that seems literally and conceptually mundane, concentrating on simple details that pass before her eyes. Through cataloguing what is immediately around it, the imagination at work gains its own definition. It is the same process so often found in Dorothy Wordsworth's journals, a method Hélène Cixous praises in *Vivre l'Orange* of representing the external objective world in a nondominating nurturing way. It is a process that respects both self and other in the creation of a romantic self.

The "I" of the text of *Rural Hours* refuses aggression into the public world. Dedicated to "The Author of 'The Deerslayer,'" *Rural Hours* was published anonymously, the author identified only "as a lady." Although she denigrates the merits of the book, Cooper is able through language and nature to create and control relationships otherwise denied her life of dedication to her father's writing.

Rural Hours is not of a common form. When Cooper does move into her father's genre of the novel, she presents the book under his name as editor. The author of her *Elinor Wyllys; or, The young folk of Longbridge* is identified as Amabel Penfeather, who expresses her fears about her "first appearance in print—a first appearance too, of one, who even now that the formidable step is taken, feels little disposed to envy the honors of authorship" (v). Yet the very name "Amabel Penfeather" undercuts her hesitation with its connotations of "I am able to write," or "I love to write," or "I am a beautiful feathered pen." As she revises well-known tropes of her father's natural world in *Rural Hours,* Cooper revises the narrative structure of his novels in *Elinor Wyllys.* Often in J. F. Cooper's novels, young women are traveling to join their fathers or to regain the protection of an older, patriarchal figure. In *The Pathfinder,* for instance, Mabel journeys to meet Sergeant Dunham; in *The Last of the Mohicans* the sisters attempt to reach their father. Elinor seeks no such paternal protection; her father is dead, and he is more than ably replaced by the financial and moral support of the women who surround Elinor, women possessing the "fortitude and perseverance" to cope with almost any social or personal crisis (1:115). Unlike the heroines her father creates, Susan Cooper's Elinor is independent and extraordinarily ugly. Moreover, she does not have the European finishing that her father found so essential to ideal women like his Eve Effingham in *Home as Found.* Elinor's character is formed by the support and models provided by other American women. As her father emphasized the importance of male bonding, so Susan Cooper demonstrates the power of female alliances and the American domestic scene.

The same uneasiness with the ideal of woman as serene, beautiful, and unassertive characterizes the writing of Margaret Fuller. The circle to which she belonged with Thoreau and Emerson was surely one of the most productive in the history of American romanticism. Seeking "a friend who would enable me better to comprehend myself," Fuller fixed upon Emerson (*Memoirs* 1:154). She could not, however, exist as adoring disciple, and her very profession became criticism and revision. As editor of *The Dial* from 1840 to 1842 she had literary power over the members of her group. Although she, like other contemporary editors, rejected several of Thoreau's essays, Fuller began publishing his material, pieces that set out much of what is used in *Walden* and in *A Week on the Concord and Merrimack Rivers.* It is not surprising, therefore, that Fuller's own nature travel book, *Summer on the Lakes,* published in 1844, should speak to the work of both Thoreau and Emerson.

Fuller tells us, "What I got from the journey was the poetic impression of the country at large" (50). Her poetic renderings, however, are combined with a certain pragmatism that shows impatience with the theorizing and generalizing of the men of her group. In a dialogue in *Summer on the Lakes,* Fuller as Free Hope is perhaps taking on Emersonian philosophizing personified as Self-poise. It is almost as if she cannot permit herself the time for and luxury of philosophical liberalism. "What is done interests me more than what is thought and supposed" (74). Fuller's ambivalence about life in the Transcendental group is resolved only when she can remove herself from that community in favor of Byronic expatriate action in revolutionary Italy.

Before leaving the country, however, Fuller published *Woman in the Nineteenth Century,* a work that turns transcendental thought to feminist concerns.[3] In her extensive work on Fuller, Marie Urbanski notes the many Emersonian ideas and phrases Fuller incorporates into her book: confidence in democracy, a mystical belief that intuition leads to a comprehension of God's truth, the importance of individual character, and the concepts of "correspondence" and "undulation." Fuller took, Urbanski writes, "the arguments that Emerson promulgated about the individual and applied them to women" (109). Emerson's well-known concept of self-reliance, which takes many different forms in his work and which can describe the spiritual independence of a Thoreau as well as the free enterprise of a Cornelius Vanderbilt, takes on a different character in *Woman in the Nineteenth Century.* Fuller employs the term to make a statement about feminine independence in the context of America's male-oriented familial, marital, and educational systems. She tells the stories of women who develop themselves alone, of Catharine Maria Sedgwick

---

3. The book has been seen as relating to the group in opposite ways. To Vernon Parrington, an early twentieth-century scholar, it seems "her parting shot at a world that had done its best to stifle her" (432). In David Robinson's more recent criticism it is a "fulfillment rather than a repudiation of transcendentalism" (95).

and of Miranda, the squaw who sets her wigwam apart, who leaves the group to live out her assurance that she was "betrothed to the sun" (101).

Particularizing Emersonian generalities to illuminate the connections between men and women, Fuller exhibits a certain distrust of transcendental idealizing in favor of a focus on more common societal relationships. Ann Douglas notes how Fuller always referred to the Transcendentalists in the third person (338). Similarly, Dorothy Wordsworth frequently referred to William as "The Poet." Writing the story of the feminine self, the women of romanticism could never be totally integrated into communities of writing where men concerned themselves with what have generally been seen as the Great Romantic Issues: depictions of the self-made Promethean and Byronic hero and the power and agony self-fashioning engenders, the demonstration of man's mind as "A thousand times more beautiful than the earth / On which he dwells," the vision of poets as the "unacknowledged legislators of the world." Examining women's alternatives from within familial and social structures, from inside the space usually allotted women, Dorothy Wordsworth, Jane Austen, Maria Jewsbury, Mary Shelley, Margaret Fuller, Susan Cooper, Felicia Hemans, Joanna Baillie, Laetitia Barbauld, Jane Taylor, Mary Russell Mitford, and a number of other women writing in the early nineteenth century find in the traditional concerns of feminine discourse the positive power of seeming feminine stasis. Raising children, baking gingerbread, doing laundry, waiting for men, getting married, not getting married—these may be animating points of existence.

The anxiety romantic women exhibit about writing as well as the subjects on which they focus are typical of women writing in many periods of literary history. My extended treatment of Dorothy Wordsworth's work has shown it to be almost a compendium of various observations women have made about their own writing and the writing of other women. Dorothy's subject matter corresponds to "the little bit (two Inches wide of Ivory)" on which Jane Austen in a letter describes herself working (189). Within the Wordsworth household, Dorothy sought "a room of her own" and moved into the "female space" set out by Mari

McCarty. Finding the characteristics of postmodernism to be the traits of women's writing, Rachel DuPlessis in "For the Etruscans" illuminates Dorothy Wordsworth's writing and the writing of other romantic women as well: "inwardness, illumination in the here and now (Levertov); use of the continuous present (Stein); the foregrounding of consciousness (Woolf); the muted, multiple, or absent *telos;* a fascination with process; a horizontal world; a decentered universe where 'man' (indeed) is no longer privileged."

"Women reject this position," DuPlessis continues, "as soon as it becomes politically quietistic or shows ancient gender values. For when the phenomenological exploration of self-in-world turns up a world that devalues the female self, when the exploration moves along the tacit boundaries of a social status quo, she cannot just 'let it be,' but must transform values, rewrite culture, subvert structures" (286–287). It is in their particular literary context, the counterforce they provide to male romanticism, that Dorothy Wordsworth and her contemporaries exhibit their particular romanticisms. In the context of their typical anxieties, the women of romanticism established uniquely similar social and intertextual relationships that allowed, in Harold Bloom's terms, the production of similar significant misreadings. Given the general principle of male literary dominance, the particular uses of language we have been looking at, as well as their lived experience, mark these women as part of the romanticisms in which they find and define themselves.

Texts by romantic women writers explore the powers of domestic, passive, natural continuities in the context of the powerful, assertive male revolutionary consciousness that we characterize as the High Romantic Vision. In word and deed, men are spinning off in all directions, not fully taking into account the structures offered by a more pragmatic domestic imagination. We have seen how Dorothy Wordsworth returns continually to the smallest details of life in "A Cottage in Grasmere Vale." In discussing her writing Alan Liu analyzes "the story of laundry that occurs in the *Journals* literally in housework and figuratively in textual labor and Nature" (123), a focus very different from her brother's.

Both Shelleys express uneasiness with the life of the wandering outcast, but Mary Shelley elevated this anxiety to a consistent theme of her novels. *Valperga, Perkin Warbuck, Lodore, Falkner, Frankenstein, The Last Man*—all demonstrate the destruction that results when domestic continuities are rejected for glory, wealth, and even certain kinds of imaginative assertion. In the figure of Raymond in *The Last Man,* an individual who abdicates familial responsibilities to lead a Greek revolution, Mary Shelley emphasizes the effect of Byronic overreaching on one's own household. The personal and domestic relationships Susan Cooper sees in the natural world, as well as the power of Longbridge, Elinor's home, speak to the same kind of domestic concern.

The very possibility of an assertive male ego may depend, according to Felicia Hemans, on the solid, feminine presence in a domestic scene. In her extraordinary collection, "Records of Woman," Hemans shows what women are doing during great historical moments. The madonnalike Switzer's wife, for example, holds her baby and presses her husband to revolution: "—this, thy son, / The babe whom I have borne thee, must be free! / And the sweet memory of our pleasant hearth / May well give strength—if aught be strong on earth" (172). In the poem "Joan of Arc in Rheims," the heroine's familial ties seem far more important than the empty pomp of the coronation.

More vital than Wordsworthian nature is the tranquil, nurturing domestic scene that is usually a part of even the bloodiest account. Nature's presence—"reed and spray, and leaf, the living / strings of earth's Eolian lyre"—is not enough to sustain the heroine of "Edith," who dies because she is deprived of her family (175). Hemans rewrites the Byronic Turkish tale into such stories as the "Bride of the Greek Isles" and "Madeline, a Domestic Tale." In these poems about women who leave their mothers to marry, Hemans explores mother–daughter relationships in the context of swashbuckling pirates and the excruciating pain they cause. Her account of Lake District scenery focuses on "The Memorial Pillar," a roadside monument near Penrith that marks the spot where Ann, Countess Dowager of Pembroke, parted from her mother Margaret, Countess Dowager of Cumberland.

Forms of art establish themselves in Hemans's daughters, wives, and mothers. In Hemans's telling, Prosperzia Rossi, the talented sculptress, shows her work to a knight who looks at it and at her with indifference. Her art, might have been even greater, "But I have been / Too much alone" (173). The speaker standing at "The Grave of a Poetess" first sadly contrasts—in an echo of "Resolution and Independence"—the joy of "All happy things that love the sun" with the nonexistence of the woman lying "parted from all the song and bloom." Her song, however, has been one of a sorrow perhaps only death can assuage (185).

Although Hemans made more money from her writing than any of them, her male contemporaries did not read her work particularly seriously. Yet despite frequent condescension from the men—even when they tried to help—she and other women state the absolute necessity to their own work of the men of romanticism and of the male romantic visions. Hemans moved her family to the Lake District to participate in the Grasmere community. In her dedication of *Phantasmagoria* to William Wordsworth, Maria Jewsbury established him as her poetic mentor. After her husband's death, Mary Shelley lost her inspiration and wrote in her journal how she felt "fallen and degraded! My imagination is dead, my genius lost, my energies sleep. Why am I not beneath that weed-grown tower?" (192). Dorothy Wordsworth made the unconventional decision of living with her brother and writing, incurring, de Selincourt notes in his biography of Dorothy this disapproval from Aunt Rawson: "Dorothy and Wm. have now a scheme of living together in London, and maintaining themselves by their literary talents, writing and translating. . . . We think it a very bad wild scheme" (58).

The ambiguities and tensions resulting from this life choice are detailed in Dorothy's work. They also informed her physical presence as De Quincey shows us in contrasting Dorothy's appearance with Mary Wordsworth's.

Immediately behind her moved a lady, shorter, slighter, and perhaps, in all other respects, as different from her in personal characteristics as could have been wished for the most effective contrast. "Her face was of Egyptian brown"; rarely, in a woman of English birth, had I seen a more determinate gipsy tan. Her eyes were not soft, as Mrs. Wordsworth's, nor were they fierce or bold; but they were wild and startling, and hurried in their motion. Her manner was warm and even ardent; her sensibility seemed constitutionally deep; and some subtle fire of impassioned intellect apparently burned within her, which, being alternately pushed forward into a conspicuous expression by the irrepressible instincts of her temperament, and then immediately checked, in obedience to the decorum of her sex and age, and her maidenly condition, gave to her whole demeanour, and to her conversation, an air of embarrassment, and even of self-conflict, that was most distressing to witness. (2:238)

The self-conflict De Quincey describes evidences itself in Dorothy as woman and Dorothy as writer. Surely we must question the assertion with which de Selincourt begins his biography: "Alike by what she wrote and what she was, Dorothy Wordsworth illumined her brother's life and poetry. She would have desired no fuller tribute" (1). Her journals chronicle constant physical complaints—headaches and cramps—perhaps not just physical symptoms but manifestations of those frustrations De Quincey notes. In fact, De Quincey speculates that her final illness might have been mitigated had she actively engaged in a literary career.

But, of course, Dorothy Wordsworth did have a "literary career," although not of the kind we may be accustomed to valuing as such. Staying in her brother's house allowed her to participate in the artistic world in a way few women could. Her journals provided raw material for at least thirty-five of William Wordsworth's poems. Indeed, William Heath sees evidence in certain poems that at times in 1802 William's sensibility was subordinate to Dorothy's (113–120). So part of her career was helping to create some of the grandest poetry of the century. More important, Dorothy's own writing comes out of her relationship with her brother. The country walks, the reading and discussions, the emotional tensions of her life with William formed the subjects of her own art. The life of a woman in nature, the life of intimate relationships and domestic concerns, the process of writing that life—these form the elements of her own career as well as the "literary careers" of many women writers of the early nineteenth century.

The accomplishment of these women is to show what a great stake the culture has in the moral, political, and intellectual visions they present. Within the ambiguities of their lived situations, these women make a claim for themselves as equal but opposing forces. It is a claim in line with Mary Wollstonecraft's ideal of becoming equal to but not more powerful than. It is a rejection of the male suggestion that "women should be free to be like us."

Theirs is a romanticism that celebrates the interests of home, family, and children, a writing of the domestic that deals with the grandeurs and griefs of women as care givers and keepers of community. These suggestions about the structure of the female romantic imagination can be construed as a cliché of passive, feminine dependence, but Dorothy Wordsworth and other romantic women writers are often radical in their very conservatism. Their focus on individual relationships, their refusal to appropriate the world, their homebound determinism allow the telling of the story of the feminine self, the drawing together of a powerful literature of the choices women could make, wanted to make, had to make.

APPENDIX ONE

The Collected Poems Of Dorothy Wordsworth

The poems of Dorothy Wordsworth have received sporadic publication both during her life and after but have never before been collected. I print here all the poems that could be located through an extensive search, but there may be others. Dorothy copied, recopied, and sent her verse to friends and correspondents, creating in the process many versions of every poem. Moreover, as she aged, she turned increasingly to poetic expression. The way she writes out her poems, especially in the late journals, provides a fascinating record of her mind's wanderings/deterioration/development.

These conditions create special problems for the editor. Variants and fragments are important. Occasionally, in what appears to be an incoherent assemblage of lines, a point evolves with painful clarity. Thus penciling "Thoughts on my sick-bed" up and down and sideways on a page brings her to a statement about "my inner self no longer hidden," "consciousness no longer hidden." Yet later versions of the poems can make establishing a base text problematic, since often a poem as it is last penned has degenerated into incoherence. In each case, therefore, I have chosen as base text, designated (1), the most fully developed, most conventionally coherent, finished version, not necessarily the latest version. Sometimes the choice of base text is purely arbitrary. Variant readings show discrepancies among the manuscripts, except those having to do with punctuation and minor spelling changes, such as "publick" for "public." William included versions of a few poems in his collections, and William Knight printed more in *The Poetical Works of William Wordsworth* (1896). I include William's published texts as variants, since he may have been working from manuscripts of which I am unaware. Texts of four lines or fewer are included as fragments rather than variant versions. I have reproduced Dorothy's punctuation and spelling. [ ] indicates a gap in the manuscript; [?] indicates an illegible world; [?word] indicates a conjectural reading.

The handwriting varies. Most of the time it is legible, but as Dorothy apparently could snap in and out of sanity, so her writing goes from perfect neatness to a strange scrawl. As late as 1849 she provided a fair copy of a four-stanza version of "Lines written (rather say *begun* . . .)." The difficulties often lie more in the way she overwrites or writes up and down a page than in the handwriting itself. I discuss particular editing problems in the notes to each poem.

My main source for the poems has been Dorothy's Commonplace Book, preserved at Dove Cottage. The book is approximately eight inches by eleven inches and contains eighty-seven leaves. Dorothy used it primarily from 1826 to 1832, copying into it letters, recipes, home remedies, news items, as well as her own poetry. She sometimes worked on a poem right in the Commonplace Book before providing a fair copy, which she also recorded there.

Another source of fair copies is the Coleorton Commonplace Book preserved in the Pierpont Morgan Library in New York. This book, watermarked 1800, is about six inches by six inches. It contains fair copies of William's poems as well as versions of five of Dorothy's poems: "To my Niece Dorothy, a sleepless Baby," "An address to a Child in a high wind," "The Mother's Return," "a Sketch," and "Grasmere—A Fragment." These poems also appear in Dorothy's Rydal Notebook, described in Appendix Two, and at the end of a copy that Catherine Clarkson made of *Recollections of a Tour made in Scotland*. Both manuscripts are perserved at Dove Cottage. Fair copies of seven poems are in the Coleridge Collection of Toronto's Victoria University Library. Five are versions of poems in the Commonplace Book, so I have dated the other two—"To Christopher Rennison" and "To Rotha Quillinan"—accordingly.

Dove Cottage also holds the Mary Jones Album, a slim volume, watermarked 1821, containing three poems as well as a version of "Mary Jones and her Pet-lamb." The Mary Barker Album preserved in Oxford's Bodleian Library contains fair copies, probably in Mary Barker's hand, of poems by various authors, among them four by Dorothy. These occur about halfway through the album and follow a copy in Dorothy's hand of "The year 1814." This album of 118 sheets of paper is approximately seven inches by nine inches and is watermarked J Whatman 1794. The Wordsworth Collection at Cornell University contains manuscripts of Dorothy's poems, as do the Ashley Collection in the British Museum, the Bristol Central Library in England, the Lilly Library at Indiana University in Bloomington, the Brown University Library, and the Swarthmore College Library.

Dating the poems is often problematic, complicated by the way Dorothy would work with lines, sometimes for years, before placing them into an extended version of a poem. Occasionally, she would extract stanzas to put together a short version. Some of the fair copies contain no indication of dates; dates on others must refer to the time of copying rather than of composition. I present the poems chronologically here, according to the following dates:

To my Niece Dorothy, a sleepless Baby.

The days are cold; the nights are long
The north wind sings a doleful song
Then hush again upon my breast;
All *merry* things are now at rest
  Save thee my pretty love!   5

The kitten sleeps upon the hearth;
The crickets long have ceased their mirth
There's nothing stirring in the house
Save one wee hungry nibbling mouse
  Then why so busy thou?   10

Nay, start not at that sparkling light
'Tis but the moon that shines so bright
On the window-pane bedropp'd with rain
Then, little Darling, sleep again
  And wake when it is Day.   15
       By Miss Wordsworth

NOTE: Dorothy's niece, Dorothy, later called Dora to avoid confusion, lived from 1804 to 1847. In the Rydal notebook, Dorothy crosses out the following two stanzas and the title, The address to my Niece/ Altered by my Brother.

Ah! if I were a Lady gay
I should not grieve with thee to play
Right gladly would I lie awake
Thy lively spirits to partake,
  And ask no better chear.

But, Babe! there's none to work for me,
And I must rise to industry;
Soon as the Cock begins to crow
Thy Mother to the fold must go
  To tend the sheep & kine.

Catherine Clarkson includes the stanzas with this note: "N.B. The third & fourth stanza's are by W.W." They were published with the poem in 1896.

VERSIONS: (1) fair copy in Dorothy's hand in Coleorton Commonplace Book; (2) fair copy in the Mary Barker Album; (3) William's published version of 1815; (4) fair copy in Clarkson *Recollections*; (5) copy in Dorothy's hand in Rydal notebook

title To Dorothy Wordsworth, a sleepless Baby by her Aunt— Dorothy Wordsworth (2); The Cottager to her Infant (3) (5); To my Niece Dorothy, a sleepless Baby. / The Cottager to her Infant (4)

An address to a Child in a high wind

What way does the wind come? what way does he go?
He rides over the water and over the snow,
Through the valley, and over the hill
And roars as loud as a thundering Mill.
He tosses about in every bare tree,   5
As, if you look up you plainly may see
But how he will come, and whither he goes
There's never a Scholar in England knows.

He will suddenly stop in a cunning nook
And rings a sharp larum:—but if you should look   10
There's nothing to see but a cushion of snow,
Round as a pillow and whiter than milk
And softer than if it were cover'd with silk.

Sometimes he'll hide in the cave of a rock;
Then whistle as shrill as a buzzard cock;   15
—But seek him and what shall you find in his place
Nothing but silence and empty space
Save in a corner a heap of dry leaves
That he's left for a bed for beggars or thieves.

As soon as 'tis daylight tomorrow with me   20
You shall go to the orchard & there you will see
That he has been there, & made a great rout,
And cracked the branches, & strew'd them about:
Heaven grant that he spare but that one upright twig
That look'd up at the sky so proud & so big   25
All last summer, as well you know
Studded with apples, a beautiful shew!

Hark! over the roof he makes a pause
And growls as if he would fix his claws

Right in the slates, and with a great rattle   30
Drive them down like men in a battle.
—But let him range round; he does us no harm
We build up the fire; we're snug and warm,
Old Madam has brought us plenty of coals
And the Glazier has closed up all the holes   35
In every window that Johnny broke
And the walls are tighter than Molly's new cloak.

Come, now we'll to bed, and when we are there
He may work his own will, & what shall we care.
He may knock at the door—we'll not let him in   40
May drive at the windows—we'll laugh at his din
Let him seek his own home wherever it be
Here's a canny warm house for Johnny and me.

VERSIONS: (1) fair copy in Dorothy's hand in Coleorton Commonplace Book; (2) fair copy in Mary Barker Album initialed DW. at end;
(3) William's published version of 1815, in which the poem is dated 1806;
(4) fair copy in Clarkson *Recollections*; (5) copy in Dorothy's hand in
Rydal notebook

   title   Address to a Child, During a boisterous Winter Evening (3)
   1–19 omitted (5)
   1   what] which (2)
   3–4   Through woods & through vales and o'er each rocky height /
Which the goat cannot climb takes his sounding flight (2); Through
wood, and through vale; and o'er rocky height / Which the goat cannot climb takes his sounding flight. (3)
   15   a] the (2) (3)
   16   But] Yet (2) (3)   his] the (2) (3) (4)
   21   there] then (2) (3) (4)
   25   so] *omit* (2)
   30   great] huge (2) (3)
   34–37   Untouched by his breath see the candle shines bright / And
burns with a clear and steady light / Books have we to read, we have
stories to tell / And tales to repeat. (2); Untouch'd by his breath see the
candle shines bright, / And burns with a clear and steady light; / Books
have we to read,—hush! that half-stifled knell, / Methinks 'tis the sound
of the eight o'clock bell. (3)
   43   canny] cozie (3)   Johnny] Edward (3)

The Mother's Return

Sweet Babes a month is past and gone
Since your dear Mother went away,
And she is coming home again;
Tomorrow is the happy day.

O blessed tidings! thought of joy!   5
John heard me speak with steady glee;
He silent stood; then laugh'd amain,
And shouted, "Mother, come to me!"

Louder & louder did he shout
With childish hope to bring her near   10
"Nay, patience! patience! little Boy
Your tender Mother cannot hear."

I told of hills, and far-off Towns,
And long, long Vales to travel through
He listens, puzzled, sore perplex'd,   15
But he submits; what can he do?

No strife disturbs his sister's breast;
She wars not with the mystery
Of time and distance, night, and day,
The bonds of our humanity.   20

Her joy is like an instinct, joy
Of Kitten, bird, or summer's fly;
She dances; runs, without an aim
She chatters in her ecstacy.

Now John takes up the giddy note,   25
And echoes back his sister's glee;
They hug the infant in my arms,
As if to force his sympathy

Then settling into fond discourse,
We rested in the garden Bower;   30
While sweetly shone the evening Sun
In his departing hour.

We told o'er all that we had done—
Our rambles by the running stream

'Mong pebbles fair, through beds of flowers,   35
Sights fresher than the brightest dream.

We talk'd of change, of winter gone
Of green leaves on the hawthorne spray,
Of birds that build their nests & sing;
And all since Mother went away!   40

To her these tales they will repeat,
To her our new-born tribes will shew,
The goslings green, the ass's colt,
The lambs that in the meadow go.

—Now strikes the clock that gives the Law   45
To bed the children must depart;
A moments heaviness they feel,
A sadness at the heart.

'Tis gone—and in a merry fit
They run up stairs in gamesome race,   50
I, too, infected by their mood,
I could have joined the wanton chace.

Five minutes passed—and Oh the change!
Asleep upon their beds they lie,
Their busy limbs in perfect rest,   55
  And closed the sparkling eye.

NOTE: In his published version, William dates the poem 1807. In
April of that year, William and Mary visited London for a month,
leaving Dorothy in charge of the children, John (almost four years old),
Dorothy (two and a half), and Thomas (ten months), at Coleorton.

VERSIONS: (1) fair copy in Dorothy's hand in the Coleorton Commonplace Book; (2) fair copy in Dorothy's hand and signed by her in
the British Museum (Ashley): eight quarto pages of white paper 7-1/4
x 8-1/16 inches, watermarked RW & H Nichols 1828, three of them
blank, inscribed on the last page by Lady Monteagle, to whom Dorothy gave the manuscript, "Lines written by Dorothy Wordsworth
when her brothers Children had been left in her care—on their parents'
expected return."; (3) fair copy initialed DW in the Mary Barker Album; (4) William's published version in his poems of 1815; (5) fair copy
in Clarkson *Recollections*; (6) working copy in Dorothy's hand in Rydal
notebook

title omitted (2)

1 A month, sweet little ones is passed (2); A month sweet little ones is passed and gone (3); A month, sweet Little-ones is passed (4); A month sweet little ones is gone passed (6)

3 And she tomorrow will return (3) (4) (6)

6 John heard me speak] The eldest heard (3) (4) (6)

7 He silent] Silent he (3) (4)

10 childish] witless (4)

17 breast] joy (2)

22 summer's] summer (2) (3) (4) (5)

25 Now John takes up the merry note (2); Her brother now takes up the note (3) (4)

stanzas 8 and 9

> So passed away the first glad hour;
> Then settling into fond discourse
> We rested in the garden bower
> While sweetly shone the evening star in his departing hour.
>
> We told o'er all that we had done,
> Our rambles by the swift brook's side
> Far as the willow-skirted pool
> Where two fair swans together glide (2)

34 running stream] swift brook's side (4)

35–36 Far as the willow-skirted pool / Where two fair swans together glide. (4)

36 brightest] fairest (3)

37 talk'd] told (2)

45 But see the evening star (3); —But, see, the evening Star comes forth! (4)

50–53 *omitted* (3)

a Sketch

> There is one Cottage in our Dale,
> In naught distinguish'd from the rest
> Save by a tuft of flourishing trees,
> The shelter of that little nest
>
> The publick road through Grasmere Vale   5

Winds close beside that Cottage small;
And there 'tis hidden by the trees
That overhang the orchard wall.

You lose it there—its serpent line
Is lost in that close household grove—   10
—A moment lost—and then it mounts
The craggy hills above.

NOTE: Although this sketch was worked into "Grasmere—A Fragment," it is distinct enough to warrant separate publication.

VERSIONS: (1) fair copy in Dorothy's hand in the Commonplace Book; (2) fair copy in Dorothy's hand in the Mary Jones Album; (3) fair copy in Dorothy's hand in the Coleorton Commonplace Book; (4) fair copy in Clarkson *Recollections*; (5) fair copy in Dorothy's hand in Rydal notebook

title omitted (2); A Fragment (3) (4) (5)
1   one] a (4)
3   tuft] grove (2) (3) (4) (5)
4   The shelter of] That shelter well (3) (4) (5)

Grasmere—A Fragment

Peaceful our valley, fair and green,
And beautiful her cottages,
Each in its nook, its sheltered hold,
Or underneath its tuft of trees

Many and beautiful they are;   5
But there is *one* that I love best,
A lowly shed, in truth, it is,
A brother of the rest.

Yet when I sit on rock or hill,
Down looking on the valley fair,   10
That Cottage with its clustering trees
Summons my heart; it settles there.

Others there are whose small domain

Of fertile fields and hedgerows green
Might more seduce a wanderer's mind   15
To wish that *there* his home had been.

Such wish be his! I blame him not,
My fancies they perchance are wild
—I love that house because it is
The very Mountains' child.   20

Fields hath it of its own, green fields,
But they are rocky steep and bare;
Their fence is of the mountain stone,
And moss and lichen flourish there.

And when the storm comes from the North   25
It lingers near that pastoral spot,
And, piping through the mossy walls,
It seems delighted with its lot.

And let it take its own delight;
And let it range the pastures bare;   30
Until it reach that group of trees,
—It may not enter there!

A green unfading grove it is,
Skirted with many a lesser tree,
Hazel & holly, beech and oak,   35
A bright and flourishing company.

Precious the shelter of those trees;
They screen the cottage that I love;
The sunshine pierces to the roof,
And the tall pine-trees tower above.   40

When first I saw that dear abode,
It was a lovely winter's day:
After a night of perilous storm
The west wind ruled with gentle sway;

A day so mild, it might have been   45
The first day of the gladsome spring;
The robins warbled, and I heard
One solitary throstle sing.

A Stranger, Grasmere, in thy Vale,
All faces then to me unknown,   50

I left my sole companion-friend
To wander out alone.

Lured by a little winding path,
I quitted soon the public road,
A smooth and tempting path it was,   55
By sheep and shepherds trod.

Eastward, toward the lofty hills,
This pathway led me on
Until I reached a stately Rock,
With velvet moss o'ergrown.   60

With russet oak and tufts of fern
Its top was richly garlanded;
Its sides adorned with eglantine
Bedropp'd with hips of glossy red.

There, too, in many a sheltered chink   65
The foxglove's broad leaves flourished fair,
And silver birch whose purple twigs
Bend to the softest breathing air.

Beneath that Rock my course I stayed,
And, looking to its summit high,   70
"Thou wear'st," said I, "a splendid garb,
Here winter keeps his revelry."

"Full long a dweller on the Plains,
I griev'd when summer days were gone;
No more I'll grieve; for Winter here   75
Hath pleasure gardens of his own.

What need of flowers? The splendid moss
Is gayer than an April mead;
More rich its hues of various green,
Orange, and gold, & glittering red."   80

—Beside that gay and lovely Rock
There came with merry voice
A foaming streamlet glancing by,
It seemed to say "Rejoice!"

My youthful wishes all fulfill'd,   85

Wishes matured by thoughtful choice,
I stood an Inmate of this vale
How *could* I but rejoice?

D Wordsworth Senr
Rydal Mount Sept. 26th
1829

NOTE: The dating of this poem is uncertain, although its position in the Coleorton Commonplace Book indicates an early composition. Knight prints a version of the long poem with this epigraph: "This is extracted from a copy of an appendix to *Recollections of a Tour in Scotland* by Dorothy Wordsworth, written by Mrs. Clarkson, September–November 1805. It was composed by the poet's sister. In February 1892 it was published in *The Monthly Packet* under the title 'Grasmere: A Fragment,' and with the signature 'Rydal Mount, September 26, 1829.' It is now printed from the MS. of 1805.—Ed."

VERSIONS: (1) fair copy in Dorothy's hand, signed and dated September 26, 1829, in Trevenen Album, Wordsworth Collection, Cornell University—a small, dark-green, gilt-edged volume with "Emily Trevenen, 1829" written on the inside of the front cover, containing poems from her acquaintances, including Robert Southey and Maria Jane Jewsbury, as well as Dorothy; (2) fair copy in Dorothy's hand in Commonplace Book (ten-stanza version); (3) fair copy in Dorothy's hand in Commonplace Book (two-stanza version); (4) fair copy in Dorothy's hand in Commonplace Book (ten-stanza version); (5) fair copy in Dorothy's hand in Mary Jones Album; (6) fair copy in Mary Barker Album; (7) fair copy in Dorothy's hand in Coleorton Commonplace Book; (8) fair copy in Clarkson *Recollections*; (9) fair copy in Dorothy's hand in Rydal notebook

title   A Cottage in Grasmere Vale (2); After-recollections at sight of the same Cottage (3); A Winter's Ramble in Grasmere Vale (4); A Fragment (5) (7) (8); A Fragment by Dorothy Wordsworth (6)

  1–40   *omitted* (3); 1–49 *omitted* (4)
  4   underneath] guarded by (2)
  7   shed] roof (6) (7)
  11   clustering] grove of (6) (7) (8)
  14   and] with (6) (7) (9)

15   seduce] intice (2)   a wanderer's] the Traveller's (6) (7) (8) (9)

18   My fancies, they perchance are] My fancy is unfettered— (2)

22   rocky] craggy (2) (5) (6) (7) (8) (9)

27   the] those (6)

31   group] Grove (6) (7) (9)

36   bright] fair (6) (7) (9)

41–48   *omitted* (4)

41–88   *omitted* (2)

48   One] The (5); A (6)

49–88   *omitted* (3)

49   Grasmere, in thy Vale] in the neighbourhood (5) (6) (7) (8) (9)

54   I quitted soon] Quickly I left (4)

57   toward] towards (4) (5) (6) (9)   lofty] mighty (6) (7) (8)

59   stately] lofty (6) (7)

before stanza 17   And lodged in many a *penciled in* (4)

after stanza 17   And lodged in many a sheltered chink *penciled in* (4)

70   its] that (6)

73   Full long] I've been (7) (8)

74   I griev'd] I sighed (6); Have sighed (7) (8)   summer] summers (7)

75   I'll grieve] will sigh (6); I'll sigh (7) (8)

76   pleasure] gladsome (6) (7) (8) (9)

80   glittering] glowing (5) (6) (7) (8)

> A twofold harmony is here,
> I listen with the bodily ear
> But dull and cheerless is the sound
> Contrasted with the heart's rebound.

Lines Addressed to Joanna H. from Gwerndovennant June 1826

> Now at the close of fervid June   5
> Upon this breathless hazy noon
> I seek the deepest, darkest shade
> Within the covert of that glade
>
> Which you and I first named our own

When primroses were fully blown,   10
Oaks just were budding, and the grove
Rang with the gladdest songs of love.

Then did the Leader of the Band,
A gallant Thrush, maintain his stand
Unshrouded from the eye of day   15
Upon yon beech's topmost spray.

Within the self-same lofty Tree
A Thrush sings *now*—perchance tis He—
The lusty, joyous, gallant Bird,
Which on that April morn we heard.   20

Yet Oh! how different that voice,
Which bade the very hills rejoice!
—Through languid air, through leafy boughs
It falls, and can no echo rouze.

But in the workings of my heart   25
Doth memory act a busy part;
That jocund April morn lives there,
Its cheering sounds, its hues so fair.

Why mixes with remembrance blithe
Which nothing but the restless scythe   30
Of death can utterly destroy,
A heaviness a dull alloy?

Ah Friend! thy heart can answer why,
—Even then I heav'd a bitter sigh,
No word of sorrow didst thou speak   35
But tears stole down thy tremulous cheek.

The wish'd-for hour at length was come,
And thou hadst hous'd me in thy home
On fair Werndunvan's billowy hill,
Hadst led me to its crystal rill,   40

And led me through the dingle deep
Up to the highest grassy steep,
The sheep-walk where the snow-white lambs
Sported beside their quiet dams.

But thou wert destin'd to remove   45

From all these objects of thy love,
In this thy later day to roam
Far off, and seek another home.

Now thou art gone—belike 'tis best—
And I remain, a passing guest,   50
Yet, for thy sake, beloved Friend,
When from this spot my way shall tend,

Mournfully shall I say farewell
To this deep verdant, woody Dell.
And to that neighboring sunny Cot   55
Where thou so oft hast bless'd thy lot.

And, if my timid soul might dare
To shape the future in its prayer,
Then fervently would I entreat
Our gracious God to guide thy feet   60
Back to the peaceful sunny cot
Where thou so oft hast bless'd thy lot
Where lonely Nature led thy soul
To brood on Heaven—where no controul
Of fashion check'd thy steadfast aim   65
To satisfy whatever claim
A tender conscience might suggest
Of faithful cares leading to pious rest.

NOTE: Thomas Hutchinson, the brother of Mary and Joanna (1780–1843), owned a small farm near Hindwell, Gwerndyffnant (or Gwern-dovennant or Werndunvan—Dorothy used various spellings). According to a note in the *Letters* 4:481, Dorothy visited the farm on May 10, 1826.

VERSIONS: (1) fair copy in Dorothy's hand in journal, September 25–November 1, 1826; (2) fair copy in Dorothy's hand in Commonplace Book; (3) copy in Dorothy's hand in journal, June 29–September 24, 1826

title omitted (3)   H.] Hutchinson (2)   Gwerndovennant]
Gwerndovennant * *at bottom of page* * pronounced Wondunvan (2)
  3   dull] weak (3)

7   deepest, darkest] darkest deepest (3)
20   we] I (2)
22   Which] That (2)
47   In thy declining days to roam (2)
57–62   *omitted* (2)
63–68   *omitted* (3)

A Holiday at Gwerndovennant

IRREGULAR STANZAS

You're here for one long vernal day,
We'll give it all to social play,
Though forty years have roll'd away
    Since we were young as you.

Then welcome to our spacious Hall!   5
Tom, Bessy, Mary, welcome all!
Though remov'd from busy men,
Yea lonesome as the fox's den
'Tis a place for joyance fit,
For frolic games & inborn wit.   10

'Twas Nature built this Hall of ours,
She shap'd the banks, she framed the bowers
    That close it all around;
From her we hold our precious right;
And here through live-long day & night,   15
    She rules with mildest sway.

Our carpet is her verdant sod;
A richer one was never trod
In prince's proud saloon;
Purple & gold & spotless white,   20
And quivering shade, & sunny light,
    Blend with the emerald green.

She open'd for the mountain brook
A gently-winding, pebbly way
Into this placid, secret nook—   25
It's bell-like tinkling—list! you hear—

—'Tis never loud, yet always clear
  As linnet's song in May.

And we have other music here,
A thousand songsters through the year   30
  Dwell in these happy groves;
And in this season of their loves
They join their voices with the doves'
To raise a perfect harmony.

Thus spake I, while with sober pace   35
We slipp'd into that chosen place,
And from the centre of our Hall
The young ones gaz'd around;
Then like a flock of vigorous lambs
That quit their grave & slow-paced dams   40
  To gambol o'er the mead,

That innocent, fraternal Troop,
(Erewhile a steady listening groupe)
Off-starting—Girl & Boy—
In gamesome race, with agile bound   45
Beat o'er & o'er the grassy ground
As if in motion perfect joy.

So vanishes my idle scheme
That we through this long vernal day,
Associates in their youthful play   50
With them might travel in one stream.
Ah! how should we whose heads are grey?
  —Light was my heart, my spirits gay,
    And fondly did I dream.

But now, recall'd to consciousness   55
With weight of years of changed estate,
Thought is not needed to repress
Those shapeless fancies of delight
That flash'd before my dazzled sight
  Upon this joy-devoted morn.   60

Gladly we seek the stillest nook
Whence we may read as in a book
A history of years gone by,

Recall'd to faded memory's eye
By bright reflexion from the mirth 65
Of youthful hearts, a transient second birth
    Of our own childish days.

Pleasure unbidden is their Guide—
Their Leader,—faithful to their side—
Prompting each wayward feat of strength, 70
The ambitious leap, the emulous race,
The startling shout, the mimic chace
The simple half-disguisèd wile
Detected through the fluttering smile.

A truce to this unbridled course 75
Doth intervene—no need of force—
We spread upon the flowery grass
The noon-tide meal—each Lad & Lass
Obeys the call; we form a Round
And all are seated on the ground. 80

The sun's meridian hour is pass'd:
—Again begins the emulous race,
Again succeeds the sportive chace,
And thus was spent that vernal day
Till twilight check'd the noisy play; 85
Then did they feel a languor spread
Over their limbs—the beating head
Was still'd, the busy throbbing heart,
    And silently we all depart.

The shelter of our rustic Cot 90
Receives us, & we envy not
The palace or the stately dome,
But wish that *all* had such a home.
Each Child repeats his nightly prayer
That God may bless their parents' care 95
To guide them in the way of truth
Through helpless childhood, giddy youth.

The closing hymn of chearful praise
Doth yet again their spirits raise,
And 'tis not now a *thoughtless* joy; 100

For tender parents, loving friends,
And all the gifts God's bounty sends,
Feelingly do they bless his name

That homage paid, the Young retire
With no unsatisfied desire;   105
Theirs is one long, one steady sleep,
Till the sun, tip toe on the Steep
In front of our beloved Cot
Casts on the walls his brightest beams.
Within a startling lustre streams;   110
They all awaken suddenly
As at the touch of magic spell,
Or as the pilgrim at the bell
That summons him to matin prayer.

And is it sorrow that they feel?   115
(Nay—call it not by such a name)
The stroke of sadness that doth steal
With rapid motion through their hearts
When comes the thought that yesterday
With all its joys is pass'd away   120
The long-expected happy day!

An instant—and all sadness goes,
Nor brighter looks the half-blown rose
Than does the countenance of each Child
Whether of ardent soul or mild;   125
The hour was fix'd—they are prepared,
And homeward now they must depart,
And, after many a brisk adieu,
On ponies trim, & fleet of limb
Their bustling journey they pursue.   130

The fair-hair'd, gentle, quiet Maid,
And She who is of daring mood,
The valiant, & the timid Boy
Alike are rouz'd to hardihood
And where so e'er the Troop appear   135
They scatter smiles, a hearty cheer
Comes from both Old & Young,
And blessings fall from many a tongue.

They reach the dear paternal roof,
Nor dread a cold or stern reproof   140
While they pour forth the history
Of three days' mirth and revelry.
Ah Children! happy is your lot,
Still bound together in one knot
Beneath your tender Mother's eye!   145
—Too soon these blessed days shall fly
And Brothers shall from Sisters part.

And trust me, whatsoe'er your doom,
Whate'er betide through years to come,
The punctual pleasures of your home   150
Shall linger in your thoughts—
Dearer than any future hope,
Though Fancy take her freest scope.
For Oh! too soon your hearts shall own
The past is all that is your own.   155

And every day of *Festival*
Gratefully shall ye then recal,
Less for their own sakes than for this
That each shall be a resting-place
For memory, & divide the race   160
Of childhood's smooth & happy years,
Thus lengthening out that term of life
Which, govern'd by your Parents' care
Is free from sorrow & from strife.

NOTE: According to de Selincourt's biography, the holiday described in this poem occurred in July (371 n). The titles of versions (2) and (3), however, indicate a May date.

VERSIONS: (1) fair copy in Dorothy's hand pasted into Commonplace Book, in which the following is written after the poem: "*Finis*—and again I say tune up your musical pipes & put on your accommodating ears—be in good humour & forgive—bad metre, bad rhymes—no rhymes—identical rhymes & all that is lawless—As to dullness I leave that to take care of itself."; (2) fair copy in Dorothy's hand in Commonplace Book; (3) fair copy in Dorothy's hand in journal of September 25–November 1, 1826; (4) part fair copy, part repetitive copy in

Dorothy's hand in journal of June–September 1826 (pages have been cut out of the back of the journal, thereby cutting off the first thirty-four lines of this version); (5) part ink fair copy, part illegible pencil scrawl in Dorothy's hand in journal of June–September 1826; (6) parts of poem in Dorothy's hand in pencil, in journal of February 10–June 22, 1826; (7) fair copy of last five stanzas of poem in Dorothy's hand in journal of September 25–November 1, 1826

   title Irregular Stanzas / Holiday at Gwerndovennant—May 1826 (2) (3) (6); *omitted* (4) (5) (7)
  1–34 *omitted* (4)
  11–121 *omitted* (7)
  1 vernal] summers day (6)
  2 social] merry (6)
  3 forty] fifty (6)
  4 we] I (6)
  5 Hall] Hall^x *at bottom of page* ^{x}a green plot within a Dell near the cottage (2)
  14 we] who (3)
  15 here] she (2)
  16 Is guardian of this happy ground. (2)
  21 quivering] gentle (6)
  21–22 *in right margin* (quivering shadow sunny light) (2)
  27 always] is it (2); brisk & (3)
  29–34 *omitted* (6)
  35–47 *in pencil, difficult to read*

> Thus spake I while we slipped
> Into the centre of our Hall
> Then like a troop of frolic lambs
> That quit their grave and slow-paced dams
> To frolic o'er the hills
> In gamesome race with agile bound
> Your [?] dear   *version trails off here* (6)

  37 And] Then (2)
  39 Then] And (2)
  40 quit their grave] leave their steady (2)
  41 gambol] frolic (4)
  43 steady] quiet (2)

46 o'er & o'er] merrily (2)
48 scheme] dream (2)
54 And pleasure was my theme (2)
57 repress] suppress (2)
58 shapeless fancies of] images of wild (2)
60 this] that (2) (3)
64 faded memory's] Memory's fading (2)
66 transient] *omitted* (2) (3)
68 unbidden] unsought for (4)
69 Leader,—faithful to] prompter comes at (4)
70 Prompting] Crowning (4)
76 *omitted* (2)
78 The] Our (2)
81 The noontide hour is passed away; (2)
between 97 *and* 98   And that whenever Death shall come / They may
be fitted for that home / Where holy angels dwell (4)
100 And] But (4)
between 100 *and* 101   For gentle nights for happy days (4)
104–164

Nor is it sorrow that they feel
Call it not by such a name
Theirs is one long quiet sleep
Till the sun tiptoe on the steep.
Casts in the walls his brightest beams
Within a startling lustre streams
And all at once the youthful troop
Are wakeful and alert
And is it sorrow that they feel
Ah call it not by such a name
An instant & all sadness goes
Nor brighter looks the half-blown rose
Than does the countenance of each child
Whether of ardent mood or mild.

The homage paid the young retire
With no unsatisfied desire
Theirs is one long, one quiet sleep
Till the sun tiptoe on the steep
In front of our beloved Cot
Casts on the walls his brightest beams
Within a startling lustre streams

They all awaken suddenly
As at the touch of magic spell
Or as the pilgrim at the Bell
That summons him to matin prayer.

And is it sorrow that they feel
Ah! call it not by such a name
The stroke of sadness which doth steal
When comes the thought that yesterday
Into their hearts—that yesterday
With all its joys is passed away
The long-expected happy day
An instant & the feeling goes
Again each buoyant spirit flows
To the bright stream of Joy
Their fancy has no narrow scope
With rapid motion thru their hearts.

The meek-eyed & the hardy Girl
The timid & the spirited Boy
The meek-eyed & the hardy Maid
Alike by hope & pleasure swayed
Are ready for another day
Of liberty though not of play, fleet
Of foot & trim & heart are ready at the door
And after many a brisk adieu
Their [?parting] journey they pursue
On ponies trim & fleet of limb
And where so'er the troop appear
The meek the gentle quiet maid
And her who loves each active sport

The valiant & the timid Boy
Alike are rouzed by hardihood
And whereso'er the troop appear—
They scatter smiles a hearty cheer
Comes from the old & young.
And blessings fall from many a tongue
Now Homeward must the troop
Homeward now they must depart
And this they do with jocund heart
The hour was fixed they are prepared
And homeward now they must depart (4)

104–156   *in pencil, much of it illegible*

The punctual pleasures of their home
Their early lot of joy to come
[*illegible line*]
Soon will they gather
[*four illegible lines*]
Their backward journey is a treat
Ponies are trimmed all spruce & neat
[*two illegible lines*]
And Brothers shall from sisters part
Pour forth the history

in ink

They reach the dear paternal roof
Nor dread a cold or stern reproof
While they pour forth the mystery
Of three days mirth & revelry
Ah children happy is your lot
Still bound together in one knot
Beneath your tender mothers eye
Too soon these blessed days shall fly
The punctual pleasures of your home
Their homeward journey is a treat
Ponies are trimm'd all spruce & neat
And after many a brisk adieu
Their bustling journey they pursue
The meek, the gentle quiet maid
And she who is of spirited mood
The vibrant & the timid Boy
Alike are rouzed by hardihood
And whensoever they appear
They scatter smiles—a hearty cheer
Comes from both old & young
And blessings fall from many a tongue

They reach the dear paternal roof
And there is seen a living proof
Scope is given [?]

in pencil

To voluble discourse
Each one explores these [?] hours

The [*rest of line illegible*]
Ah children happy is your lot
Still bound together in one knot
Beneath your parents eye
Too soon alas

   in ink

Shall mingle with all joys to have
Better than all your joys to care
With every future hope
However free is fancy's scope
Too soon your tender heart's will own
The past is all that is your own
And you will bless indulgent friends
For thinly sprinkled festivals
That do divide these happy hours
[*illegible line*]
And thus to memory [?]
The time of childhood's happiness
Then shall you gratefully bless.

   in pencil

The punctual pleasures of your home
Whatever be your lot
Shall linger in the years to come

And however large the [?] [?]
And soon [?]
The past is all that is your own
Then shall you bless that
Though Fancy [?] its scope

   in ink

And trust me, whatsoer your doom
Bring what they may years to come
The punctual pleasures of your home
Shall linger in your thoughts
Dearer than any future hope
However free be fancy's scope
For ah! too soon your hearts shall own
The past is all that is your own
Then shall you bless [?] these early days

And each glad day of festival (5)

116 not by such a] by another (2)
117 stroke of] random (2)   doth] will (2)
123 looks] is (2)
124 does] now (2)
127 now] straight (2)
131 The fair-hair'd] The meek, the (3)   quiet] placid (2)
137 Comes from both] Meets them from (2)
147 shall] must (2)
152 Dearer] More prized(2); More dear (3) (7)
153 take] have (2)
154 For Oh] And Ah (2)
156 every day of] each appointed (2)
163 care] love (2)

Irregular Verses

Ah Julia! ask a Christmas rhyme
Of *me* who in the golden time
Of careless, hopeful, happy youth
Ne'er strove to decorate the truth,
Contented to lay bare my heart   5
To one dear Friend, who had her part
In all the love and all the care
And every joy that harboured there.
―To her I told in simple prose
Each girlish vision, as it rose   10
Before an active busy brain
That needed neither spur nor rein,
That still enjoyed the present hour
Yet for the *future* raised a tower
Of bliss more exquisite and pure   15
Bliss that (so deemed we) should endure
Maxims of caution, prudent fears
Vexed not the projects of those years
Simplicity our steadfast theme,
No works of Art adorned our scheme.—   20
A cottage in a verdant dell,

A foaming stream, a crystall Well,
A garden stored with fruit and flowers
And sunny seats and shady bowers,
A file of hives for humming bees   25
Under a row of stately trees
And, sheltering all this faery ground,
A belt of hills must wrap it round,
Not stern or mountainous, or bare,
Nor lacking herbs to scent the air;   30
Nor antient trees, nor scattered rocks,
And pastured by the blameless flocks
That print their green tracks to invite
Our wanderings to the topmost height.

   Such was the spot I fondly framed   35
When life was new, and hope untamed:
There with my one dear Friend would dwell,
Nor wish for aught beyond the dell.
   Alas! the cottage fled in air,
The streamlet never flowed: 40
—Yet did those visions pass away
So gently that they seemed to stay,
Though in our riper years we each pursued a different way.

—We parted, sorrowful; by duty led;
My Friend, ere long a happy Wife   45
Was seen with dignity to tread
The paths of usefulness, in active life;
And such her course through later days;
The same her honour and her praise;
As thou canst witness, thou dear Maid,   50
One of the Darlings of her care;
Thy *Mother* was that Friend who still repaid
Frank confidence with unshaken truth:
This was the glory of her youth,
A brighter gem than shines in prince's diadem.   55

   You ask why in that jocund time
Why did I not in jingling rhyme
Display those pleasant guileless dreams
That furnished still exhaustless themes?
—I *reverenced* the Poet's skill,   60

And *might have* nursed a mounting Will
To imitate the tender Lays
Of them who sang in Nature's praise;
But bashfulness, a struggling shame
A fear that elder heads might blame   65
—Or something worse—a lurking pride
Whispering my playmates would deride
Stifled ambition, checked the aim
If e'er by chance "the numbers came"
—Nay even the mild maternal smile,   70
That oft-times would repress, beguile
The over-confidence of youth,
Even that dear smile, to own the truth,
Was dreaded by a fond self-love;
"'Twill glance on me—and to reprove   75
Or," (sorest wrong in childhood's school)
"Will *point* the sting of ridicule."

    And now, dear Girl, I hear you ask
Is this your lightsome, chearful task?
You tell us tales of forty years,   80
Of hopes extinct, of childish fears,
Why cast among us thoughts of sadness
When we are seeking mirth and gladness?
    Nay, ill those words befit the Maid
Who pleaded for my Christmas rhyme   85
Mirthful she is; but placid—staid—
Her heart beats to no giddy chime
Though it with Chearfulness keep time
For Chearfulness, a willing guest,
Finds ever in her tranquil breast   90
A fostering home, a welcome rest.
And well she knows that, casting *thought* away,
We lose the best part of our day;
That joys of youth remembered when our youth is past
Are joys that to the end of life will last;   95

    And if this poor memorial strain,
Breathed from the depth of years gone by,
Should touch her Mother's heart with tender pain,
Or call a tear into her loving eye,

She will not check the tear or still the rising sigh.　　　100
—The happiest heart is given to sadness;
The saddest heart feels deepest gladness.

Thou dost not ask, thou dost not need
A verse from me; nor wilt thou heed
A greeting masked in laboured rhyme　　　105
From one whose heart has still kept time
With every pulse of thine

NOTE: Dorothy's goddaughter, Julia Marshall, was the daughter of Jane Pollard Marshall, to whom Dorothy wrote so many of the early letters. Married to John Marshall, a Leeds linen manufacturer, Jane bore eleven children. In a letter of November 1829 Dorothy wrote, "To Julia give my best Love, and tell her that I tried out some Christmas verses for her; but could not make a finish of them.—" (5:176). Julia sent her own poems to Dorothy, who in a letter of October 1830 pledged to "repay her to the best of my power by pointing out what seems to me amiss in any of her poems. I must, however say that the simplicity with which in general she expresses herself in metre appears to me very extraordinary in so young a Writer" (5:332). A month later, Dorothy observed: "There is such rectitude of sentiment and feeling in whatever Julia writes that it is very satisfactory to read; and with respect to style and composition, her defects are marvellously few; and having the good sense not to be vain she will go on improving" (5:349). Julia married the Reverend Henry Venn Elliott when she was twenty-four and died in 1841 at the age of thirty-two.

VERSIONS: (1) fair copy in Dorothy's hand in Commonplace Book; (2) crossed out fair copy in Dorothy's hand in Commonplace Book, lined once diagonally through each of three pages; (3) fair copy in Dorothy's hand in Mary Jones Album.

title　To Julia Marshall—A Fragment (2) (3)
6　part] share (2)
16　*crossed out* (2);　　Bliss that we deem'd should long endure (3)
17–18　*omitted* (2) (3)
19–20　No costly work of studious art / Did in those visions bear a part; (2); No costly works of studious art / Did in those visions bear a part (3)

22   A pure unsullied household Well (2) (3)
31   —Besprinkled o'er with trees & rocks, (2) (3)
33   print] leave (2) (3)
39–55   *omitted* (2)) (3)
56   *Then, at that brilliant jocund time,* (2) (3)
58   pleasant guileless] guileless happy (3)
61   a mounting Will] the wish & will (2) (3)
63   them] those (3)
66   a lurking] a touch of (2) (3)
between 66 and 67 penciled in a dread lest playmates would deride (2)
75   Twill glance on me] Twill surely come (2) (3)
77   Will] Twill (2) (3)
78   Girl, I hear you] Julia, you may (3)
79   lightsome] pleasant (3)
83   we are seeking] all we ask is (2); all we seek is (3)
84–107   *omitted* (2) (3)

[*Innocent were the lives they led*]

Innocent were the lives they led
Those gentle spirits that are fled
    To God who reigns above
Two duteous Daughters they & kind
Sisters they were in heart & mind   5
    For they were full of love

Too weak afflictions rod to bear
By accident & by sorrow were
    In early noon of life

Removèd from this world of care   10
In heavenly blessings sweet to share
    From trouble free & strife

VERSION: working copy in Dorothy's hand in the journal of November 11, 1827–June 24, 1828.

Dorothy worked on this stanza on the facing page, but then evidently rejected it:

Too weak afflictions to bear
Sickness & sorrow—not despair
Blighted them in the noon of life
Composed they left this world of care
In heavenly happiness to share
Too pure for earthly strife

[*No more the Pastor with his flock*]

No more the Pastor with his flock
   Assemble here in prayer
No more the chapel bell or chimes
   Sound sweetly thro' the air

Deserted are these sacred walls   5
   Deep silence here does reign
That still small voice in spirit calls
   And whispers Hope to gain

A blessed Mansion in the skies
   That Land of promise fair   10
Thither by love inspired rise
   Above this world of care.

How pensive is this autumn day
   With quiet pleasure fraught
Here slowly I pursue my way   15
   And soothed in every thought

To break the Calm here is no sound
   All nature is at rest
Hence pious feelings, clear profound
   Settle within my breast.   20

VERSION: working copy in Dorothy's hand at the end of her journal for November 11, 1827–June 24, 1828. I do not believe Dorothy meant the line before the last two stanzas to set them off as a separate poem. The handwriting and subject matter point to one five-stanza poem rather than two poems. *Dorothy did not finally include the following stanza:*

To rest & calm is all
   All nature is at rest
Religious feelings most profound
   Now animate my breast

To D.

A thousand delicate fibres link
My heart in love to thee dear Maid
Though thine be youth's rejoicing prime
My lively vigour long decayed

Thou art a native of these hills   5
And their prized nursling still hast been
And thou repay'st their fostering love
As testify thy happy looks, thy graceful joyous mien.

This mountain land delights us both
We love each rocky hill;   10
I hither came in age mature
With thoughtful choice and placid Will.

And I have found the peace I sought
Which thou *un*sought hast found

NOTE: The poem's date is uncertain. "D" must be Dora Wordsworth.

VERSION: fair copy in Dorothy's hand in the Commonplace Book.

Floating Island at Hawkshead,
An Incident in the schemes of Nature

Harmonious Powers with Nature work
On sky, earth, river, lake, and sea:
Sunshine and storm, whirlwind and breeze
All in one duteous task agree.

Once did I see a slip of earth,   5
By throbbing waves long undermined,
Loosed from its hold;—*how* no one knew
But all might see it float, obedient to the wind.

Might see it, from the verdant shore
Dissevered float upon the Lake,   10
Float, with its crest of trees adorned
On which the warbling birds their pastime take.

Food, shelter, safety there they find
There berries ripen, flowerets bloom;
There insects live their lives—and die: 15
A peopled *world* it is;—in size a tiny room.

And thus through many seasons' space
This little Island may survive
But Nature, though we mark her not,
Will take away—may cease to give.   20

Perchance when you are wandering forth
Upon some vacant sunny day
Without an object, hope, or fear,
Thither your eyes may turn—the Isle is passed away.

Buried beneath the glittering Lake!   25
Its place no longer to be found,
Yet the lost fragments shall remain,
To fertilize some other ground.

M. D Wordsworth

NOTE: This poem was probably written in the late 1820s. James Butler has called my attention to a note regarding the poem that Herbert Hill (Southey's son-in-law) wrote in his copy of William Knight's *The English Lake District as Interpreted in the Poems of Wordsworth* (Edinburgh, 1878). On page 211, repeating some of Isabella Fenwick's note to the poem, Knight writes: "The *Floating Island* is in Derwentwater, on which Dorothy Wordsworth composed some lines which have a melancholy interest. Her brother tells us that she 'took a pleasure in repeating these verses, which she composed not long before the beginning of her sad illness.'" Hill pencils in: "I have heard her repeat it often. There was one Stanza which she habitually forgot, & W. used to prompt her. The exquisite tenderness of his tones & his whole manner struck me very forcibly. HH."

VERSIONS: (1) fair copy in Dorothy's hand in the Commonplace Book; (2) version, initialed D.W., published by William with his poems of 1842, with the headnote "These lines are by the Author of the Address to the Wind, & c. published heretofore along with my Poems."

title   Floating Island. (2)
3   storm] cloud (2)
9   verdant] mossy (2)

Lines intended for my Niece's Album.

Dear Maiden did thy youthful mind
Dally with emblems sad? or gay?
When thou gavest the word—and it was done,—
"My Book shall appear in green array."

Well didst thou speak, and well devise;   5
'Tis Nature's choice, her favored hue,
The badge she carries on her front,
And Nature faithful is, and true.

She, careful Warder, duly guards
The works of God's Almighty power,   10
Sustains with her diffusive breath
All moving things & tree & herb & flower

Like office hath this tiny Book;
Memorials of the Good and Wise,
Kind counsels, mild reproofs that bind   15
The Dead to the Living by holy ties,

Parental blessings, Friendship's vows,
Hope, love, and Brother's truth
Here, all preserved with duteous care,
Retain their dower of endless youth.   20

Perennial green enfolds these leaves;
They lie enclosed in glossy sheath
As spotless as the lily flower,
Till touched by a quickening breath

And it *has* touched them: Yes dear Girl,   25
In reverence of thy "gifted Sire"
A wreath for thee is here entwined
By his true Brothers of the Lyre

The Farewell of the laurelled Knight
Traced by a brave but tremulous hand,   30
Pledge of his truth and loyalty,
Through changeful years unchanged shall stand.

Confiding hopes of youthful hearts
And each bright visionary scheme
Shall here remain in vivid hues,   35
The hues of a celestial dream.

But why should *I* inscribe my name,
No poet I—no longer young?
The ambition of a loving heart
Makes garrulous the tongue.   40

Memorials of thy aged Friend,
Dora! thou dost not need,
And when the cold earth covers her
No praises shall she heed.

Yet still a lurking wish prevails   45
That, when from Life we all have passed
The Friends who love thy Parents' name
On her's a thought may cast.
                Rydal—May—1832

VERSIONS: (1) fair copy in Dorothy's hand in the Commonplace
Book, with a line drawn down the right of the page marking off the
first six stanzas and in the right-hand margin, in Dorothy's hand: "not
to be put in the album"; (2) fair copy pasted into the Commonplace
Book with the note "transcribed by L.H." and dated June 1832, the
version actually entered in Dora's album.

    title To Dora Wordsworth (2)
    1–28 *omitted* (2)
    12 *several variant alternatives in the Commonplace Book, among which,
it appears, Dorothy never made a choice* Tree, herb, and fruit, and splendid
flower. *or* Insect & bird, herb, fruit, and flower. *or* Tree, shrub, and
fruit, and herb & flower

begins with 33–36 followed by 29–32 (2)
44   praises] flattery
47   love] loved   Parents'] Father's (2)

Loving & Liking

You may not love a roasted fowl
But you may love a screaming owl
Or even a spotted slimy toad
That crawls from his secure abode,
His mossy nook in your garden wall,   5
When evening dews begin to fall
You may not love a dainty frog,
Scared by the Frenchman from his bog
When in a fricassee or Stew
He floats, or delicate ragout.   10
But you may love him in his pool
Where tho' he ne'er was put to school,
He swims by perfect law of Nature
A model for a human creature

Note: This fourteen-line poem, though incorporated in the longer poem that follows, merits separate publication.

Version: fair copy in Dorothy's hand in Commonplace Book.

Loving & Liking.
Irregular Verses
Addressed to a Child.—

There's more in words than I can teach,
But listen Child!—I would not preach;
Yet would I give some plain directions,
To guide your speech and your affections.

Say not you *love* a roasted fowl;   5
But you may love a screaming owl,

Or even a black unwieldy toad
That crawls from his secure abode
Within your mossy garden wall,
When evening dews begin to fall.   10

You may not love a dainty frog
Drawn as in France from fen or bog,
When in a fricassee or stew
Served up, or delicate ragout;
—But you may love him in his pool   15
Where, though he ne'er was put to school
He swims by perfect law of Nature,
A model for a human creature,
Glancing amid the water bright,
And sending upward sparkling light.   20

And when the Bird with scarlet breast
Hops round the carpet, a bold guest
Though Susan make an angry stir
To scare him as a trespasser
Do you step forth and take his part   25
Encouraged by a loving heart.

Nor blush if o'er that heart be stealing
A love for things that have no feeling
Nor can repay, by loving you,
Aught that your care for them may do: 30
The peeping rose, that first *you* spied
May fill your breast with joyful pride
And you may love the strawberry flower
And love the strawberry in its bower
But when the fruit on which you gazed   35
With pleasure to your lip is raised
Say not you *love* the delicate treat;
But *like* it, enjoy it, and thankfully eat.

Long may you love your pensioner mouse,
Though one of a tribe that torment the house,   40
Nor dislike, for her cruel sport, the cat,
That deadly foe of mouse and rat:
Remember she follows the law of her Kind;
And Instinct is neither wayward nor blind.
Then think of her beautiful gliding form,   45
Her tread that would not crush a worm,

And her soothing song by the winter fire,
Soft as the dying throb of the lyre.

I would not circumscribe your love;
It may soar with the eagle and brood with the dove   50
May pierce the earth with the patient mole,
Or track the hedgehog to his hole
Loving & liking are the solace of life
They foster all joy, & extinguish all strife.

You love your Father and your Mother,   55
Your grown-up, and your baby Brother,
You love your Sisters and your Friends,
And countless blessings which God sends.
And while these right affections play
You *live* each moment of your day;   60
They lead you on to full content
And Likings fresh and innocent.

That store the mind, the memory feed,
And prompt to many a gentle deed.
But *Likings* come, and pass away;   65
'Tis *Love* that remains 'till our latest day.
Our heavenward guide is holy love
And it will be our bliss with Saints above.

NOTE: Publishing the poem in 1836, William dated its composition
1832. A Fenwick note on the poem gives its background: Rydal Mount,
1832. It arose, I believe, out of a casual expression of one of Mr. Swin-
burne's children.—I.F. (*PW* 2:485).

VERSIONS: (1) working copy in Dorothy's hand in Commonplace
Book; (2) version published by William in 1836 with "Poems Founded
on the Affections"; plus fragments
  2   But] Yet (2)
  3   Yet would I] But only (2)
  7   And, if you can, the unwieldy toad (2)
  11–14

        Oh mark the beauty of his eye:
        What wonders in that circle lie!
        So clear, so bright, our fathers said

He wears a jewel in his head!
And when, upon some showery day,
Into a path or public way
A frog leaps out from bordering grass,
Startling the timid as they pass,
Do you observe him, and endeavor
To take the intruder into favour;
Learning from him to find a reason
For a light heart in a dull season. (2)

15   But] And (2)   his] the (2)
16–17   That is for him a happy school, / In which he swims as taught by nature, (2)
18   model] pattern (2)
21–26   *omitted* (2)
27   that] your (2)
29–30   *omitted* (2)
31   peeping rose, that first *you*] spring's first rose by you (2)
35   on which you gazed] so often praised (2)
36   With pleasure] For beauty (2)
42   That deadly foe] Deadly foe both (2)
54   Rock the cradle of joy, smooth the death-bed of strife. (2)
57   Sisters] sister (2)

fragments, in Dorothy's hand in Commonplace Book, now on facing pages, the page between having been cut out

Dear Child I would not still be teaching
Nor would I tire you with long preaching
Then kindly take my plain directions
To regulate your young affections

addressed to a Child
There's more in words than I can teach,
But listen, Child!—I would not preach;
Yet would I give some plain directions
To guide your speech & your affections

Say not you love a roasted fowl;
But you may love &c &c

That store the mind, the memory feed
And prompt to many a gentle deed
But *likings* come and pass away
'Tis *Love* remains till our latest day:

Our guide to Heaven is holy love;
It is our bliss with saints above

Our heaven-ward guide is holy love
And it will be our bliss with Saints above.

Loving & liking are the solace of life.
They foster all joy & extinguish all strife.

By liking a friendship may grow out of strife,
But love is the sunshine & starlight of life.

Loving and liking are the solace of life
They foster all joy and extinguish all strife

fragment in Journal, February 12, 1831–September 7, 1833

I would not circumscribe your love
It may soar with the Eagle & brood with the Dove
May pierce the dark earth with the patient mole
Or track the worm to its moss-covered hole
To love and to like is the solace of life
Rocking the cradle of Joy, is the [?]

Lines intended for Edith Southey's Album.

Composed in June 1832 in recollection of a request made by her
some years ago, & of my own promise till now unfulfilled.

Fair Edith of the Classic Hill
Pleads for a tributary Lay
In memory of her long-known Friend,
And I with willing heart obey.

The "Laureate's Child" though Edith be,   5
Queen regent of that honoured Mount,
Yet will she not disdain the verse
That issues from a lowly Fount.

For truth is all that she requires,
Truth steadfast, unadorned;   10

The studied phrase of flattery
She from her infant days has scorned.

And though the truth might rouze the *Bard*
To sound her praise in transport high,
Tell of her goodness and her grace   15
I would not wound her modesty.

Indeed it were a needless task
Is not the Maid by all approved
—Enough to say why she's *obeyed*—
Because she ever is beloved.   20

But let this page a record stand
Of tender love which may not die,
Friendship betwixt the Old and Young,
The growth of faithful sympathy.

. . . .

A strong cord draws me to the Maid,   25
And face to face I speak to *her,*
Uttering the pensive word, farewell,
While no unruly pangs my bosom stir.

. . . .

Edith, farewell: and trust me, friend,
All anxious hopes are now at rest;   30
The evening sun shines on my bed;
As bright the Calm within my breast.

Sickness and sorrow, grief and pain
Are precious to the humbled soul
For Mercy wounds with pitying love,   35
That can all wayward thoughts control.

"'Tis *God* that maketh soft the heart,
The Almighty that doth trouble me",
Loosening my bon'dage to this earth
By pain, by joy—an awful mystery!   40

And when with agony worn down,
So gently doth it pass away,
My shattered frame sinks into rest
As soothing as the light of day.

Thus God afflicts; thus heals the wound: 45
—And workings of benignant Power,

Gentle or terrible, we trace—
Through every passing hour.

Order prevails: and can there be
A soul so impious, so forlorn
As slight these witnesses of grace—
And more—the Word of Promise scorn?

If such there be, how blest the day
Of sickness, pain, or pining grief
If it inform the torpid sense,
And to far worse than sorrow bring relief!

The Warnings long vouchsafed to me
Prompted that tender thought; farewell;
And if blithe Health should e'er return
Oh, may I not in thanklessness rebel!

—Forgetful of the feverish strife
That wraps me up in stillest peace,
Or of the fearful rush of pain
That, if it last, the pulse of life must cease.

Forgetful of wise Nature's skill
To soothe, or rouze and elevate,
While she her daily task pursues,
And we submissive wait!

The Great, the Rich, in dazzling pomp;
And their next Followers in degree;
And such as, far removed from these,
With cold and hunger pine in misery;

Each lifts the veil that overspreads
Our wishes, objects, restless cares;
—How different the voice of each!
The *same* the meaning it declares,

That all our labours, our desires
Are senseless as a maniac's strife
Save such as lead the enduring soul
To one blest end, eternal life.

And he whose heart is truly wise
Must inwardly perceive
That when we part from kindred—Friends—
It is in weakness that we grieve.

Weakness, God pities and will heal;   85
Yet the poor Mortal here would stay,
"The wonders of this beauteous world,
How leave them?"—They, too pass away.

Oh, that *my* aim might still be fix'd
On objects that shall still endure!   90
But we are weak,—and health brings joy
That dazzles us—bedims the pure.

Feelings our holiest, and our best
Insure for what we *see* a fond regard;
And the *un*seen, the permanent,   95
Offers in vain the unknown reward.

We stifle memory's warning voice.
Heaven grant me power to hear it, & beware!
Would that I never might forget
What now still prompts my daily prayer.   100

Then pray with me that in the hour
When here on earth I must no longer dwell,
Must part from Friends, & this fair world,
I may in calmness speak the *last* farewell!

NOTE: Edith Southey (b. 1804), Robert Southey's daughter, married the Reverend John Wood Warner.

VERSIONS: (1) working copy in Dorothy's hand in the Commonplace Book; (2) fair copy in Dorothy's hand placed in the Edith Southey Album, preserved in the Bristol Central Library, between leaves 104 and 105; (3) fair copy in Dorothy's hand in the Edith Southey Album. The first six stanzas appear on leaf 78. The rest are in a letter placed between 105 and 106 that states: "I enclose a 'Continuation' of the lines addressed to you—or rather I should say the lines written at your request . . . I do not send these verses for their merit's sake, (if any they have except *truth* of feeling) but, being addressed to you, they are by right yours; and for my sake you will keep them in your Desk; and perhaps many a year hence they may, when they chance to meet your eye, call forth pleasing & tender recollections of one who has known and loved you from infancy."

title Lines intended for E. Southey's Album—composed in June 1832.— (2)   *omitted* (3)
  11 phrase] voice (2) (3)
  15 Tell] Still (2) (3)
  17–20 *omitted* (2)
  17 Indeed it were] And truly 'twere (3)
  22 which] that (2) (3)
between 24 and 25 Continuation (2) *continues on inserted sheet titled* continuation of the verses written by D Wordsworth in Edith Southey's Album. (3)
  44 soothing] cheering (3)
  53 there] these (2)
  58 that] the (2)
  61 *last word missing* (3)
  63 the] that (3)
  97–100 *omitted* (3)
  101 Then] Oh, (3)
  102 on earth] below (2)

Thoughts on my sick-bed

And has the remnant of my life
Been pilfered of this sunny Spring?
And have its own prelusive sounds
Touched in my heart no echoing string?

Ah! say not so—the hidden life   5
Couchant within this feeble frame
Hath been enriched by kindred gifts,
That, undesired, unsought-for, came

With joyful heart in youthful days
When fresh each season in its Round   10
I welcomed the earliest Celandine
Glittering upon the mossy ground;

With busy eyes I pierced the lane
In quest of known and *un*known things,
—The primrose a lamp on its fortress rock,   15
The silent butterfly spreading its wings,

The violet betrayed by its noiseless breath,
The daffodil dancing in the breeze,
The carolling thrush, on his naked perch,
Towering above the budding trees.   20

Our cottage-hearth no longer our home,
Companions of Nature were we,
The Stirring, the Still, the Loquacious, the Mute—
To all we gave our sympathy.

Yet never in those careless days   25
When spring-time in rock, field, or bower
Was but a fountain of earthly hope
A promise of fruits & the *splendid* flower.

No! then I never felt a bliss
That might with *that* compare   30
Which, piercing to my couch of rest,
Came on the vernal air.

When loving Friends an offering brought,
The first flowers of the year,
Culled from the precincts of our home,   35
From nooks to Memory dear.

With some sad thoughts the work was done,
Unprompted and unbidden,
But joy it brought to my *hidden* life,
To consciousness no longer hidden.   40

I felt a Power unfelt before,
Controlling weakness, languor, pain;
It bore me to the Terrace walk
I trod the Hills again;—

No prisoner in this lonely room,   45
I *saw* the green Banks of the Wye,
Recalling thy prophetic words,
Bard, Brother, Friend from infancy!

No need of motion, or of strength,
Or even the breathing air: 50
—I thought of Nature's loveliest scenes;
And with Memory I was there.

NOTE: In his biography of Dorothy, de Selincourt includes the following letter of May 25, 1832, from Dora Wordsworth to Edward Quillinan: "'I hope she [Dorothy] will sometime let me send you an affecting poem which she has written on the pleasure she received from the first spring flowers that were carried up to her when confined to her sick room—the 3 last stanzas which I remember I will steal for you. [Dora quotes the last three stanzas of the poem.] you must excuse limping measure. Aunt cannot write regular metre'" (387–390).

VERSIONS: (1) fair copy in Dorothy's hand in Commonplace Book; (2) fair copy written under journal entries at the end of the journal of February 12, 1831–September 7, 1833; plus fragments

title   omitted (2)
7   kindred] precious (2)
9   How joyfully in my day of strength (2)
10   When each season was fresh in its punctual round (2)
11   earliest] new-born (2)
16   spreading] trying (2)
21   Our] The (2)
24   Each claimant could hold our sympathy (2)
25   Yet] But (2)
26   rock, field] field, rock (2)
28   *splendid*] perfect (2)
29   No] Ah (2)
30   *that*] this (2)
35–52   *omitted* (2)
fragments
fair copy in Dorothy's hand in Commonplace Book

> A Prisoner in this quiet Room,
> Nature's best gifts are mine—
> Friends, books & rural sights & sounds,
> Why should I then repine?

Journal, February 12, 1831–September 7, 1833
Entry in July 1833

> A prisoner in this quiet room
> Nature's best gifts are mine
> Friends—books—& rural sights & sounds
> Why should I then repine

1833, written sideways down the page

A prisoner in this lonely room
No bondage do I feel
No prisoner am I
[?] [?] & gifts are mine
Nature's best gifts are mine
Tho friends look [?] at sights & sounds
Why should I then repine
And if perchance my feet shall come
Thoughts images of early youth

continued sideways down next page

Thoughts images of early youth
To this poor [?] Grace
Imprisoned in this lonely room
Ye gave a power I know not nor care [?]

No need of motion or of strength
Or even the breathing air
I thought of nature's lovliest haunts
And with Memory I was there

And gratefully I remembered oer
The years that are for ever gone
With greatful heart I numbered o'er
And all the blessings that remain
Friends kindred—[?] [?] of immortality growing
Strengthening as the Body decays—feelings kept down &
repressed by exuberant health & thoughts

underwritten at various angles on page

That fluttered in this feeble frame
To this hidden life
No need of motion or of strength

sideways in pencil and ink down last page of journal

With some sad thoughts the work was done
Unprompted & unbidden
But joy it brought to my hidden life
My *hidden* life
To my inner self no longer hidden
To my consciousness no longer hidden

Lines written (rather say begun*) on the morning of Sunday April 6th, the third approach of Spring-time since my illness began. It was a morning of surpassing beauty.*

The worship of this sabbath morn,
How sweetly it begins!
With the full choral hymn of birds
Mingles no sad lament for sins.

The air is clear, the sunshine bright.   5
The dew-drops glitter on the trees;
My eye beholds a perfect Rest,
I hardly hear a stirring breeze.

A robe of quiet overspreads
The living lake and verdant field;   10
The very earth seems sanctified,
Protected by a holy shield.

The steed, now vagrant on the hill,
Rejoices in this sacred day,
Forgetful of the plough—the goad—   15
And, though subdued, is happy as the gay.

A chastened call of bleating lambs
Drops steadily from that lofty Steep;
—I could believe this sabbath peace
Was felt even by the mother sheep.   20

Conscious that they are safe from man
On this glad day of punctual rest,
By God himself—his work being done—
Pronounced the holiest and the best

'Tis but a fancy, a fond thought,   25
To which a waking dream gave birth,
Yet heavenly, in this brilliant Calm,
—Yea *heavenly* is the spirit of earth—

Nature attunes the pious heart
To gratitude and fervent love   30
By visible stillne[?ss] the chearful voice
Of living things in budding trees & in the air above.

Fit prelude are these lingering hours
To man's appointed, holy task
Of prayer and social gratitude: 35
They prompt our hearts in faith to ask,

Ask humbly for the precious boon
Of pious hope and fixed content
And pardon, sought through trust in Him
Who died to save the Penitent.   40

And now the chapel bell invites
The Old, the Middle-aged, and Young
To meet beneath those sacred walls,
And give to pious thought a tongue

That simple bell of jingling tone   45
To careless ears unmusical,
Speaks to the Serious in a strain
That might their wisest hours recal.

Alas! my feet no more may join
The chearful sabbath train;   50
But if I inwardly lament
Soon may a will subdued all grief restrain.

No prisoner am I on this couch
My mind is free to roam,
And leisure, peace, and loving Friends   55
Are the best treasures of an earthly home.

Such gifts are mine: then why deplore
The body's gentle slow decay,
A warning mercifully sent
To fix my hopes upon a surer stay?   60

NOTE: In keeping with her tendency to rework her verse, Dorothy used the 1824 lines in the longer poem that describes her state in 1832. Knight printed the four-stanza version with this note: "These lines were published in *The Monthly Packet,* in July 1891, where the following note is appended by Miss Christabel Coleridge:—'Written *circa* 1852–3, and given to Mrs. Derwent Coleridge.' But Miss Edith Coleridge, and Mr. E. H. Coleridge, tell me that they think they 'belong to an earlier period.' Mr. Coleridge writes, 'I have heard Miss Wordsworth repeat the lines now printed, seated in her arm-chair, on the terrace at Rydal Mount'" (8:325).

VERSIONS: (1) fair copy in Dorothy's hand in the Commonplace Book, in which the following stanza at the end of the poem is lined through vertically: "And may I learn those precious gifts / *Rightly* to prize, and by their soothing power / All fickle murmuring thoughts repress / And fit my faltering heart for the last solemn hour."; (2) fair copy in Dorothy's hand in Commonplace Book of first five stanzas, plus one stanza penciled in at bottom of page; (3) fair copy in Dorothy's hand on notepaper pasted into Commonplace Book, consisting of four stanzas, signed and dated, "Rydal Mount, August 20th 1849. Addressed To Mr. Graham."; (4) fair copy in Dorothy's hand of four stanzas on notepaper pasted in Commonplace Book, signed, "Composed & written by D. Wordsworth."; (5) inscribed in Dorothy's hand on the flyleaf of *The River Duddon a Series of Sonnets* (London, 1820), "For Mr. Monkhouse." and signed "Dorothy Wordsworth, Rydal Mount, August 5, 1845"; (6) fair copy of four stanzas in Lilly Library, Indiana University; (7) four stanzas in Dorothy's hand and signed Dorothy Wordsworth in Coleridge Collection, Victoria University Library, Toronto; plus fragments

title On a most beautiful Sunday morning April 1824 (2); *omitted* (3) (4) (5) (6) (7)
3 hymn] hymns (5) (6)
5–48 *omitted* (3) (4) (5) (6) (7)
8 I hardly hear] I *hear* not even (2)
9 quiet] stillness (2)
14 sacred] holy (2)
17 call] voice (2)
21–60 *omitted, added in pencil, now barely legible, at bottom of page*

> Thus have ye passed one gladsome hour
> But [?earnest] youth exhausts its power
> The weary limbs, the panting breast
> The throbbing head
> Plead piteously for rest. (2)

50 sabbath] *omitted* (6)
52 Soon] Oh! (3) (4) (5) (6) (7)   subdued] resigned (6)
53 am I on this couch] on this couch I am (6)
54 *omitted* (4)
55 Friends] hearts (6)
59 warning] token (6)
at bottom Dorothy Wordsworth (6)
fragment in Mary Monkhouse Album preserved at Dove Cottage

No prisoner am I on this couch
My mind is free to roam;
And leisure, peace, & loving Friends
Are the best treasures of an earthly home.
                    Dorothy Wordsworth Senr
                    Rydal Mount—August 16th
                    1840

To Thomas Carr, My Medical Attendant

Five years of sickness & of pain
This weary frame has travell'd o'er
But God is good—& once again
I rest upon a tranquil shore

I rest in quietness of mind   5
Oh! may I thank my God
With heart that never shall forget
The perilous path I've trod!

They tell me of one fearful night
When thou, my faithful Friend,   10
Didst part from me in holy trust
That soon my earthly cares must end.

NOTE: Thomas Carr was the Ambleside surgeon who attended the Wordsworth family. Emily Merewether, for whom the fourth version was copied, was the daughter of Francis Merewether, a family friend who emigrated to Australia. Since the poem appears in a letter of 1835, Dorothy's own dating of 1836 in the copy for Emily Merewether must be incorrect. In her letter to Hannah Hoare, Dorothy wrote: "On that night Mr Carr left me because he could do no more for me, & my poor Brother went to lie down on his bed thinking he could not bear to see me die." After she quoted the poem in her letter to Edward Ferguson, she wrote: "True it is, & I doubt not Mr Carr was *surprized* the next morning to hear that I was alive."

VERSIONS: (1) fair copy in Dorothy's hand in letter to Edward Ferguson, dated "Rydal Mount 8 October, 1837" and preserved in the Wordsworth Collection, Cornell University; (2) fair copy in Dorothy's hand in letter to James Greenwood, dated "Rydal Mount October 1835" with the note "Copied by DW for Mr Greenwood" preserved in the Brown University Library; (3) fair copy in Dorothy's hand in letter to Hannah Hoare, dated September 1837, preserved at Dove Cottage; (4) facsimile of fair copy in Dorothy's hand on loose sheet, signed "D Wordsworth Senr" and dated "Nov. 7th 1837" preserved in the Wordsworth Collection, Cornell University; (5) fair copy in Dorothy's hand in Coleridge Collection, Victoria University Library, Toronto

title   To my good and faithful friend / Thomas Carr. (2); To my kind Friend & medical Attendant T. Carr / composed a year ago—or more. (3); To my faithful Friend & judicious Medical Attendant, Thomas Carr (4); To my kind Friend & faithful Physician, Thomas Carr. (5)
   3   good] kind   once] now (2)
   at bottom   N.B. The verses were composed a year ago. Now copied for Emily Merewether (4)

To Rotha Quillinan

Ah! Rotha, many a long long day
And many a night has worn away
Since last I saw thy chearful face
But God is kind; & I am blest
By his prevailing grace.   5
Though helpless, feeble are my limbs
My heart is firm, my head is clear,
And I can look upon the past without a pang,
                without a fear.
The past that to thy heart recals   10
Bright days of mirth & innocent glee,
And let this token of good-will,
The Rosebud drawn by James's skill
Upon this paper here to bloom
As in a never-fading prime.   15
My youthful Friend be unto thee
A record of that happy time.
                DW Sr.

NOTE: This poem was probably composed in the mid 1830s. A note on the manuscript identifies it as "Poor Miss Ws Poem written after her melancholy illness." Rotha was the younger daughter of Edward Quillinan, who married Dora Wordsworth after the death of his first wife. Rotha's mother suffered a mental collapse and later died after having been badly burned. Dorothy Wordsworth nursed her until the end. As William's godchild, Rotha spent a great deal of time at Rydal Mount. The James of this poem might be James Dixon, the gardener at Rydal Mount for almost thirty years.

VERSION: fair copy in Dorothy's hand in the Coleridge Collection, Victoria University Library, Toronto.

Lines to Dora H.

No fairy pen wherewith to write
No fairy prompter to indite
Waits Dora upon me
Yet on thy tiny spotless book
With playful fancy I can look   5
And with a spark of childlike glee
My tremulous fingers feeble hands
Refuse to labour with the mind
And that full oft is misty dul & blind
How venture then to draw a line   10
Over this delicate book of thine
The gorgeous insects gauzy wing
The butterfly's resplendent ring
Would fitliest deck its spotless leaves
Or violet nursed in April dew   15
A half blown rose of vermeil hue
Or humming bird from India's land
Portrayed by youthful lady's hand
Such cunning skill was never mine
Nor in my early years the line   20
Eer flowed in fancy's theme
Nor aim held I but simple truth
The wild growth of a happy youth
Now age my eyesight oft bedims
My failing strength my tottering limbs   25
Into a prison change this room

Though it is not a cheerless spot
A cell of sorrow or of gloom
No damp cold walls enclose it round
No heavy hinges grating sound   30
Disturb the silence & the calm
To the weak body health & balm
Free entrance finds the summer breeze
Mine eyes behold the leafy trees
The sky the clouds the gleaming showers   35
Craggs lakes & odoriferous flowers
And fond affections nestle hear
With faithful recollections dear
Children whose parents I on buoyant knee
Carressed & fondled in their infancy   40
With visions of a pure delight
Not needing aim from bodily sight
Thou Dora then among the first
Dost nurture joy & pious trust
I call to mind thy Mother's girlish grace   45
And the mild gladness of her face

The prayer I then breathed forth for her
Doth now again my bosom stir
I prayed that innocence might guide her youth
Along the paths of sacred truth.
                    Miss Wordsworth
                    June 1835—   Eliz. Hutchinson

NOTE: Dora H. is probably Dora Hutchinson, eighth child of George Hutchinson, Mary Wordsworth's brother. The Elizabeth Hutchinson who copied the poem is "Ebba," another of Mary's nieces, daughter of Thomas and Mary Hutchinson of Brinsop. She was Dorothy's god-daughter and a visitor at Rydal Mount through 1835.

VERSION: fair copy in Elizabeth Hutchinson's hand taped into the Commonplace Book, plus many fragments near end of journal of October 4, 1834–November 4, 1835

fragments
pencil fragments in Dorothy's hand, perfectly clear, written sideways down the page:

Free entrance finds the summer breeze
My eyes behold no leafy trees

No drear thick damp walls enclose it round
No damp cold walls enwrap it round

No iron hinges warning sound

fairly illegible

No damp thick walls enwrap it round
No iron hinges grating sound
Torments

doom

ink of two different colors, sometimes overwritten

No fairy pen wherewith to write
No fairy prompter to indite
Is ready at my call
Yet on thy pure unspotted book
With playful fancy I can look
And now with timid hope
Something of a childlike joy
My tremulous fingers feeble hands
Refuse to labour with the mind
And *that* too oft is misty dark & blind

No iron Bars no

written on page that has been cut off in middle

My failing thoughts my tottering limbs
Into a prison change this room
Yet it is not a cheerless place
A cell of sorrow or of gloom
Our heavenly fathers precious gifts
The sunshine & the [?]ing air

written sideways down the last journal page

But shall I dare to draw a line
Venture then draw
How shall I dare to impress

Upon this delicate Book of thine
The gorgeous insects gauzy wing
The Butterfly's resplendent wing
Would fitly dark its spotless leaves
The violet fresh with morning dew
Or half-blown rose of vermeil hue
Or that small Bird from India's land
Mimicked by youthful lady's hand.

[*When shall I tread your garden path?*]

When shall I tread your garden path?
Or climb your sheltering hill?
When shall I wander, free as air,
And track the foaming rill?

A prisoner on my pillowed couch   5
Five years in feebleness I've lain,
Oh! shall I e'er with vigorous step
Travel the hills again?
                    To Mr Carter DW
                    Novr 11—1835

NOTE: Hired by William to aid him in the clerical duties connected with the stamp distributorship, John Carter was also the Wordsworth's handyman for over forty years. In a letter of 1855, Mary Wordsworth wrote to Mary Hutchinson that Carter was one of those "present at the *Close*" (352).

VERSIONS: (1) fair copy in Dorothy's hand in the Commonplace Book; (2) fair copy in Dorothy's hand in Coleridge Collection, Victoria University Library, Toronto.

title   To Mr Carter (2)
postscript omitted (2)

Miss B. Southey

Fit person is she for a Queen
To head those ancient Amazonian Files
Or ruling Bandit's wife
Among the Grecian Isles

Or is she from far India's shore?   5
From Afric's golden Coast?
Nay she is fair as lily flower,
And might be British London's boast
            D Wordsworth Old Poetess
            October 7th 1836—

NOTE: The poem is addressed to Bertha Southey (b. 1809), daughter of Robert Southey and wife of Herbert Hill, who visited Rydal Mount in August 1836, the probable time of this poem's composition.

VERSIONS: (1) fair copy in Dorothy's hand in the Southey Album owned by Jonathan Wordsworth; (2) fair copy in Dorothy's hand in Coleridge Collection, Victoria University Library with the following written on the manuscript in pencil: "The occasion of this was, Bertha going into her room in a [?shewofy] dress, & Miss W. immediately quoted this stanza & afterward threw off the next—all she writes are done in like prompt manner"

To Sarah Foxcroft's Infant

I will not seek to fathom God's decrees
Nor look beyond the present happy time,
Trusting that, careless as the summer breeze
A hand divine will lead thee through thy prime.
            DW

Copied Novr 17—1836

VERSIONS: (1) fair copy in Dorothy's hand in Commonplace Book; (2) fair copy in Dorothy's hand in the Coleridge Collection, Victoria University Library, Toronto.

title   To Sarah Heming's Baby (2)
4   will] shall (2)
initials and date omitted (2)

To Christopher Rennison (her Maid's Father) Ravenstonedale

Long may'st thou roam the heathy hills
Round bonny Rusendale,
And to thy loving Children bring
Full many a sports man's tale!

And when at length thy race is run,   5
Thy daily task of duty done
Oh! mayst thou peacefully resign
The life which here is but *begun!*

NOTE: Members of the Wordsworth family occasionally hunted at Ravenstonedale. A card from Dobell's Antiquarian Bookstore, evidently where the Swarthmore manuscript was purchased, contains this reference to the poem: "Dear Miss Margaret, To make ammends for my carelessness I will copy for you another poem which I think you will like better than either the one you *have* already, or the other which I intended to send."

VERSIONS: (1) fair copy in Dorothy's hand in the Coleridge Collection, Victoria University Library, Toronto; (2) fair copy in Dorothy's hand at Swarthmore, signed and dated "Rydal Mount Sept. 3rd 1836"

title To Christopher Rennison. (2)
between 4 and 5   Such tales as cheer the dismal Mine— (2)
6   *omitted* (2)
8   which] that (2)

Christmas day

This is the day when kindred meet
Round one accustomed social fire:
If still survive the hoary Sire
In patriarchal age, beside his honour'd feet
His Children's Children claim the appropriate seat;   5
And if the Partner of his youthful days,
His dear supporter through the uncertain ways
Of busy life—if *she* be spared,
She who all joy, all grief has shared
Now is their happiness complete: 10
Their Children & their Children's Children meet
Beneath the Grandsire's reverenced roof,
Where faithful love through trying years has stood all proof.
Dorothy Wordsworth
January 5th 1837

VERSIONS: (1) fair copy in Dorothy's hand on four-by-six-inch sheet
of paper in Wordsworth Collection, Cornell University; (2) fair copy
in Dorothy's hand in the Commonplace Book; plus fragments

title   Fragments Xmas day (2)
on same page in Commonplace Book are two fragments

The youngest-born, the middle-aged assembled at their side

The lowliest is the proudest seat,
The foot-stool at the Grandsire's feet.

fragment near end of journal, February 12, 1831–September 7, 1833

The lowliest is the proudest seat
The footstool at the Grandsire's feet

A Tribute to the Memory of the Revd John Curwen

Yes! let the poor afflicted weep
The widow & the orphan mourn!
This stedfast friend, in death asleep
Can soothe no more the heart forlorn

His was the candid generous soul—   5
The liberal hand, the kinder heart;
And never did a death-bell toll
For one more free from worldly art.

And never was the cry of grief,
Disease, or poverty, or pain   10
Or supplication for relief
Addressed to his kind heart in vain.

But ready still, by night or day
Was he the poor man's prayer to hear,
The sufferer's anguish to allay   15
The desolate orphan's heart to chear.

The cherished Friends who knew his work
By firm esteem to him were bound
And gaiety & harmless mirth
In him a kind promoter found.   20

His long descent—his ancient line—
Too oft in men the cause of pride—
He counted naught!—his great design
Was to far nobler thoughts allied.

It was the spread of Christian love   25
And charity 'mongst small & great;
His lifelong aim was to remove
Dissension, enmity, & hate.

Although a carping few there be
Who slightingly his merits hold,   30
Yet hundreds more will say with me
A warmer heart death ne'er made cold.
        DWordsworth. March 3rd 1840

NOTE: The Curwens were a prominent Lake District family. John Wordsworth married Isabella Curwen.

VERSION: fair copy in Dorothy's hand in the Commonplace Book

Fragment Christmas day

Not calmer was that glorious night
When on the Syrian plain
The Shepherds saw the heavenly light
And heard the angelic strain
Glory to God and peace on earth   5
Good-will to Man—the promised Birth
The Expectancy fulfilled

NOTE: This and the next two poems are probably by Dorothy, but authorship cannot be definitely attributed to her.

VERSION: fair copy in Dorothy's hand in Commonplace Book opposite the poem "Christmas day"

[This flower, the garden's proudest boast]

This flower, the garden's proudest boast
Is destined, dearest Maid, for thee—
When Love & joy attend thee most
Ah! then thou wilt remember me.

Oh thank these pretty harmless doves   5
Such be your joys & such your loves
Oh! never yield to feverish strife
Then shall you lead a happy life!

VERSION: fair copy in Dorothy's hand in the Commonplace Book, on the same page as "Fragment Christmas Day," although the handwriting indicates the piece was written at a much later date. These stanzas may not be related to each other, but the handwriting indicates that they are.

To E.C.

I've marked thee from a little Child:
—Thy ways unfettered, yet not wild,
Obedient to the silent law
Of filial love, with placid awe,
Promised a vigorous active life   5

NOTE: E.C. is probably Elizabeth Cookson (b. 1797), the eldest daughter of the Kendal Cooksons. A frequent visitor in the Wordsworth household, she helped copy William's verse.

VERSION: fair copy in Dorothy's hand in the Commonplace Book.

APPENDIX TWO
Mary Jones and her Pet-lamb

This text is taken from a fair copy in Dorothy's hand appearing in a notebook inscribed "Dorothy Wordsworth Rydal Mount." Preserved at Dove Cottage, the seven-by-nine-inch volume also contains versions of five poems, the beginning of the Green narrative, and descriptions of walks with William including one taken in November 1805, the possible year of the story's composition. Perhaps "Mary Jones" is the story mentioned in Dorothy's 1806 letter to Lady Beaumont. In any case, the story must have been important to Dorothy; a copy in her hand—not well preserved and blotchy in places—appears in the Mary Jones Album, which dates from the 1820s.

Mary Jones and her Pet-lamb.
a Tale written to amuse John & Dorothy.

William Jones and Margaret his Wife lived at the farthest house in one of the Cumberland Dales, just at the foot of the mountains. It was a pretty place; Williams Father & Grandfather were born & had dwelt there all their lives; & they had planted trees round their cottage to keep off the cold winds that blew from the Mountains: and now the trees were grown tall and spreading, and made a pleasant shade in summer, and though the wind roared among their branches on boisterous winter nights, telling of the storm, they fenced the Cottage and kept it warm, and, while William & Margaret sate by their fire of peat and sticks with their little Daughter on her three-legged stool beside them they blessed God for their comfortable lot; and often talked with thankful and chearful hearts of the innocent lives their Forefathers had spent.

I have told you that William Jones's little Daughter used to sit by her Father & Mother on her stool in the winter's evenings: she had her own place in the chimney-corner; and every evening she read to them a chapter in the Bible, or often a story out of one of her little books; for when her Father went to the market town he seldom came home without a new book for Mary, because she took care of them, and though she had never been at school was a good scholar, and noticed so well what she read that she could tell over again many of the histories which she found in the Bible or in other books. Her Parents had no child but her; and they loved her dearly. She was her Mother's companion when her Husband was out in the fields; and often too she followed her Father; and sometimes went with him a long way up the mountains when he, with help of his Dog, gathered the sheep together; and he would call her his little Shepherdess. Their house was far from any other Dwelling, so that Mary Jones (having no Brothers or Sisters) had not any Companions like herself; yet she had playfellows; the great Sheep-dog fondled, & jumped about her; & she fed the Chickens & the Ducks, & they would flock round her whenever she went into the yard; and nobody had such sleek beautiful cats as little Mary. It was a pretty sight to see her by the blazing fire; often with one cat on her knee, another at her feet, and a pair of kittens playing beside her; she had pigeons, too, & they would peck out of her hand, and she loved to sit and watch the bees carry their burthens to the hive: she was not afraid of them, for, as she did not tieze them, they never stung her. One snowy morning in February her Father brought a young Lamb home in his arms. Its Mother had died, and the helpless creature was nearly perishing with cold. It could not stand; so a basket was brought to the fire, and it was put into it, and covered up with wool, and Mary watched over it the whole day, and fed it with warm milk. She dreamt about it at night; and pleased she was, the next morning, to see it stand upon the hearth; but its limbs tottered, and it bleated piteously. The Child continued to nurse it till it grew strong; and then it was truly her favorite Playmate: it followed her all about in house and field, so that you hardly ever saw Mary without her Lamb, except when she went to Church, and as the Church was at the foot of the Valley above three miles off, Mary and her Mother could only go thither when the weather was fine. One Sunday after noon, towards the end of the month of June, when she had been at Church she straightway ran to seek her Lamb: she had her hands full of flowers which she had gathered by the way to make a garland for its neck: she was used to play with such fancies, & the Lamb would stand still and patient while she was busied with her work; and, when the work was done, she in pride and love, would praise its beauty, and strength, and lusty size, burying her hands in its white warm fleece. As I have said, as soon as she came from

Church she went to seek for the Lamb; she called to it by its name, but it did not run to her as usual, & it was nowhere to be found. That evening both she and all the household went about searching every nook in the fields, but all in vain; and poor Mary, long after she was in bed, cried bitterly. The next morning she waked in sorrow, I believe for the first time in her life, for though she had had her little griefs as all Children will have, she never before felt a grief that a night's sleep did not wear away. She began to weep again upon her pillow; but soon, looking about, she saw the pleasant sunshine upon the hills, and, drying her tears, she dressed herself with a lighter heart, hoping now that the lost one would be found, or would come home.

Again she searched, and in vain; and, at noon she sate down very sad, and all that afternoon she was grave and silent, and did not stir from her seat. At supper-time, however, she bethought her that the Lamb had been brought from the mountains, & perhaps was gone thither again; so, without telling any body what was in her mind, she left her porringer of milk upon the table, put her piece of bread into her pocket, and, slipping out of doors, began to climb the mountain, and she had got to the very top without observing that the sun had long been sunk behind the hills on the other side of the Valley. She then sate down quite tired; but she looked about for her Pet lamb, and fancied she saw it jump down a Rock at a little distance: she shouted; & presently the Creature ran to her, & leaping up, put its paws round her waist. I know not whether the Child or her Lamb was more glad. Mary sate down to rest again, and took out her bread, & they feasted together: for she had eaten no supper till now. When this was done she began to think of going home again, and how pleased her Mother would be that the Lamb was found; but when she looked for her way down she was quite at a loss. It was not dark, but the day light was faded, and she could not see her Father's house, or the trees, or the fields; she wandered about & about, often stumbling over the rocks: little did it serve her now that she had been a stout climber by her Father's side. At last she sate down with the Lamb beside her, & if she was in trouble the night before, what must she have felt now! She could not go a step further for weariness & fear, and, almost broken-hearted at the thought that she should never more see her Father & Mother, she laid herself on the ground & wept aloud. The poor Lamb lay down close to her, as if it wanted to keep her warm, and after a long time the Child fell asleep.

Mary had not been gone many minutes from the house before her Parents missed her but they thought little of it at first because she was accustomed to stray by herself in the fields; however at 1/2 past nine o'clock when the Family were preparing to go to bed, the Mother said, "but where is little Mary?" & called for her at the door, and as Mary did not answer she went out into the fields to seek her, shouting all the while, and, when she had gone all over their own grounds and did not find her Child her heart misgave her: she returned to the house to fetch her Husband, & they passed a miserable night, wandering about, & scarcely knowing whither. Towards morning, without any hope of finding her alive, they went up the mountain, and just after the sun had risen they came to the spot where she had fallen asleep, & still lay with her arms clasped round the Lamb's neck, as the Babes in the Wood were lying when Robin Red-breast covered them with leaves. William & Margaret, almost out of their senses with fear to find her dead & cold, went to her, & touched her: and Oh! what comfort and joy they had to feel that that part of her body which was close to the Lamb was warm, and to hear her breathe sweetly!—one moment, they wept in thankfulness over their Child; but stayed not; The Father took her up in his arms without waking her, wrapped her in his coat and bore her homeward, the Mother by their side, & the Lamb following.

By happy chance (poor thing! she had been too wretched to *think* about what she was doing) Mary had lain in the midst of a large plot of hether (perhaps the toil of wading through it had caused her to drop down there!) and the hether was so thick and dry that the damp from the ground could hardly reach her; and surely the Heavens looked graciously upon her helpless state; for it had been the mildest night of all the year; and now the morning was serene and beautiful. When they had reached the house the Mother softly undressed her; and Mary did not awake till nine o'clock the next morning. At her first waking she knew not where she had been, and hardly knew where she then was; for all that had passed was like a dream; but soon she cried for joy to find herself in her Mother's arms.

The Father & Mother fervently thanked God for having preserved their Child, and she, from that day, never strayed from home unknown to them & was a very dutiful and good Girl, and continued to be a comfort to her Parents, and after she was grown up to be a Woman, took care of them when they were infirm and old.

The Pet-lamb became a fine Ewe and brought forth many Lambs, and the Father said that, in memory of that night, it should never be killed by knife, so it lived on many years, and died of old age in the field close to the house, and was buried under a rose tree beside the bee-hives.

SELECTED
BIBLIOGRAPHY

By and about Dorothy Wordsworth

It may be helpful to describe briefly those manuscripts and published studies that make up the textual, biographical, and critical history of Dorothy Wordsworth. The *Bulletin of Bibliography,* 40, no. 4, 252–255 contains a fairly substantial Dorothy Wordsworth bibliography. What follows both expands and comments upon that list. I give full bibliographical references here for texts not included in my Selected List, which contains those works to which I actually refer in the course of my discussion.

EDITIONS
Fragments of the Grasmere journals were first included in the 1851 *Memoirs of William Wordsworth* by Christopher Wordsworth. J. C. Shairp's edition of *Recollections of a Tour Made in Scotland (A.D. 1803)* appeared in 1874, going through three editions by 1894 and even evoking poems from admiring readers. The first extended edition of Dorothy's writing was William Knight's 1897 *Journals of Dorothy Wordsworth* in two volumes; a one-volume edition came out in 1924. In his prefatory note, Knight tells the reader he includes only some of the "numerous trivial details" in the journals because "there is no need to record all the cases in which the sister wrote, 'To-day I mended William's shirts,' or 'William gathered sticks,' or 'I went in search of eggs,' etc. etc." (vii–viii). In his *Journals of Dorothy Wordsworth,* 2 vols. (1941 and three later reprints), Ernest de Selincourt includes a greater amount of more carefully edited material than does Knight, although he too is selective, even omitting some of the passages found in Knight. Mary Moorman's 1971 edition of the Grasmere and Alfoxden journals is the current standard text. *George & Sarah Green, A Narrative,* edited by de Selincourt, appeared in 1936. In *The Poetry of Dorothy Wordsworth* (New York: Columbia UP, 1940), Hyman Eigerman presents selections from the jour-

nals that he has arranged in verse form. The London Folio Society's *Dove Cottage: The Wordsworths at Grasmere,* ed. Kingsley Hart (1966) contains the Grasmere journals, selected letters, and some fine photographs of the area. Dorothy's letters are found in *The Letters of William and Dorothy Wordsworth,* 6 vols., 2nd edition, 1967–1982. These volumes have been edited: by Chester L. Shaver, *The Early Years, 1787– 1805;* by Mary Moorman and Alan G. Hill, *The Middle Years, 1806– 1820;* and by Alan G. Hill, *The Later Years, 1821–1850.* A brief account of Dorothy's published poetry will be found with her collected poems in the first appendix to this book.

BIOGRAPHIES

Many figures of the romantic period wrote about Dorothy, perhaps most tellingly Coleridge, De Quincey, and Samuel Rogers, who met her traveling in Scotland in 1803 and described how she organized the trip while the men talked; Rogers encouraged her to publish her "most excellent" recollections of the tour—*Recollections of the Table-Talk of Samuel Rogers,* ed. Alexander Dyce (London: E. Moxon, 1856), 208– 209. Dorothy Wordsworth's life is of considerable interest to twentieth-century scholars. In reviewing *Dorothy Wordsworth* by Robert Gittings and Jo Manton (Oxford: Clarendon, 1985), Norman Fruman points to the "virtues" of this "old-fashioned 'Life and Letters'" while outlining some of the questions to which a life of Dorothy might address itself (*TLS,* June 28, 1985, 711–713). Several biographies are now in preparation, but certainly Ernest de Selincourt's *Dorothy Wordsworth* (1933, rpt. 1965) stands as a sympathetic, readable, reliable, and scholarly biography. Catherine Macdonald Maclean's *Dorothy Wordsworth: The Early Years* (New York: Viking, 1932), deals somewhat sentimentally with the first part of Dorothy's life, but the book is a vital treatment. Maclean's telling of the early life narrates how Dorothy used nature, people, and writing to maintain her balance with the world.

These are the most important biographical studies, but several others may be noted to demonstrate the kinds of treatment her life has received. Aside from the sketch by J. C. Shairp in the preface to his edition of *Recollections of a Tour Made in Scotland,* Edmund Lee's *Dorothy Wordsworth: The Story of a Sister's Love* (London: J. Clarke, 1886) is the first biography. Drawing on the observations of Dorothy's contemporaries, Lee shows "how a younger sister consecrated her life to her brother's good, relinquishing for herself everything outside him in such a way that she became absorbed in his own existence" (17). Lee includes some of Dorothy's poems and also some of the public responses to the few pieces published during her lifetime. More recently, Elizabeth Gunn's *A Passion for the Particular* (London: Gollancz, 1981) offers a rather emotional biographical treatment.

Many biographers concentrate as much on William and Coleridge as they do on Dorothy. I mention those works which treat Dorothy more or less equally. Amanda Ellis's *Rebels and Conservatives* (Bloomington: Indiana UP, 1967) sketches the lives of William and Dorothy and a number of their friends, especially through their reactions to the French Revolution. *Dorothy and William Wordsworth: The Heart of a Circle of Friends,* by Sean Manly (New York: Vanguard, 1974), is a popular biography. In *William Wordsworth of Rydal Mount* (London: J. M. Dent, 1939), Frederika Beatty tells the story of Wordsworth and his circle in the last decade of his life, mentioning Dorothy only briefly. Still, the contemporary accounts she marshals give a most interesting picture of Dorothy after 1840. Helen Ashton, who calls her *William and Dorothy* (New York: Macmillan, 1938) "a novel," describes the brother-sister relationship by quoting and paraphrasing "very freely from Dorothy Wordsworth's adorable journals" (3). This book grew out of Ashton's *I Had a Sister: A Study of Mary Lamb, Dorothy Wordsworth, Caroline Herschel, and Cassandra Austen* (London: L. Dickson, 1937). *Farewell the Banner* by Frances Winwar (New York: Doubleday, Doran, 1938), is primarily a biography of Coleridge that makes frequent references to Dorothy and William. The subtitle of this book is *Three Persons and One Soul,* the phrase (often repeated in studies of Dorothy) attributed to Coleridge, who is said to have used it to describe his early relationship with William and Dorothy. It may be useful to recall that Ruth Aldrich finds no evidence that Coleridge actually wrote the phrase; she believes the words are probably a garbled version of a letter written in November 1801 to Godwin: "—A great change from the society of W. and his Sister—who tho' we were three persons it was but one God—" ("The Wordsworths and Coleridge: 'Three Persons,' but *not* 'One Soul'" *SIR* 2 [1962]:61–63).

Since the publication of F. W. Bateson's *Wordsworth: A Reinterpretation* (London: Longmans, 1954), the possibility of an incestuous relationship between William and Dorothy has been much discussed. Bateson argues that Wordsworth married to cure himself of his love for his sister and that his decline in poetic power resulted from the rupture of his relationship with Dorothy. In a lecture given in 1970 and reproduced in *Essays by Divers Hands* (37 [1972]:75–94), Mary Moorman answers Bateson and the theories that have come from his book by discussing the excellence of the poetry William was able to produce after his marriage and by defining the particular attractions William and Dorothy had for each other, sexuality not among them. The controversy reappears in the *TLS* from August through December 1974, initiated by the publication that year of Molly Lefebure's *Samuel Taylor Coleridge: A Bondage of Opium* (London: Gollancz, 1974), which also deals with the relationship. Another series of letters on the topic appears in *TLS* during April and May 1976.

CRITICISM

Critical discussions of Dorothy Wordsworth often have tended to shift focus from her art to her life. Some books, however, have dealt with her writing. In telling "a story about the activities of six people, three of them extraordinary, during the year from November 1801 to October 1802" (vii), William Heath's *Wordsworth and Coleridge* entails more than straight biography. Heath's textual analysis of the Grasmere journal shows how that work reflects Dorothy's ambivalent feelings about William's marriage. Patricia Ball's *The Science of Aspects: The Changing Role of Fact in the Work of Coleridge, Ruskin, and Hopkins* (London: Athlone, 1971) also includes some analysis of several journal passages. In "Dorothy Wordsworth and the Picturesque" John R. Nabholtz establishes the relationship of Dorothy's descriptions of natural scenes to the eighteenth-century tradition of the picturesque. Rachel Mayer Brownstein provides one of the first critical analyses of Dorothy's writing, considering her as a phenomenological writer whose major subject is the passage of time (*MLQ* 34 [1973]:48–63). Elizabeth Hardwick's discussion of Dorothy first appeared in "Amateurs: Dorothy Wordsworth & Jane Carlyle" (*NYRB,* Nov. 30, 1972) and then as a chapter in *Seduction and Betrayal: Women and Literature* (New York: Vintage, 1975). At least two critics write essays comparing the Grasmere journals to the journals of another author. George Mclean Harper in "Eugénie de Guérin and Dorothy Wordsworth" (*Atlantic Monthly* [May 1923]) finds Dorothy "the most permanently interesting woman writer of her generation in England" (656). All young women should read Dorothy Wordsworth, Harper insists, and take her as a model upon which to mold their own characters. In comparing her journals to the diaries of Francis Kilvert, a *TLS* reviewer distinguishes between Dorothy's genius and Kilvert's lesser talent ("Deep in Kilvert Country," August 19, 1960).

Whether or not we accept Harper's paternal exhortation, many of us would certainly agree with the *TLS* reviewer. More and more is being written about Dorothy Wordsworth. Alec Bond's "Reconsidering Dorothy Wordsworth," given first as a talk at the 1975 Wordsworth

Conference in England and printed in the *Charles Lamb Society Bulletin* ([July–October 1984], 194–207), points to many of the themes and motifs around which Dorothy structures her writing. The Winter, 1978 issue of the *Wordsworth Circle* contains several pieces on Dorothy Wordsworth, among which Carl Ketcham's elegant description of her unpublished, late journals is particularly noteworthy. Margaret Homans's *Women Writers and Poetic Identity* and Alan Liu's "On the Autobiographical Present: Dorothy Wordsworth's *Grasmere Journals*" indicate the more complex direction studies of Dorothy's writing are taking. One final item: Several witnesses reported a strange lady walking through Alfoxden house; she wore white crinolines before World War II and now wears black. In "The Ghost-Lady of Alfoxden," (*CE*, 1956), Leland Lileles follows local wisdom in speculating that the ghost is Dorothy Wordsworth.

Selected List

Austen, Jane. *Jane Austen's Letters, 1796–1817*. Ed. R. W. Chapman. Oxford: Oxford UP, 1978.

Cameron, Kenneth Neill. *Shelley: The Golden Years*. Cambridge: Harvard UP, 1974.

Chodorow, Nancy. *The Reproduction of Mothering*. Berkeley: U California P, 1978.

Cixous, Hélène. "The Laugh of the Medusa." Trans. Keith Cohen and Paula Cohen. *Signs* 1 (1976): 875–894.

Coleridge, Samuel Taylor. *The Collected Letters of Samuel Taylor Coleridge*. Ed. Leslie Griggs. Oxford: Clarendon, 1956–1971.

———. *Poetical Works*. Ed. E. H. Coleridge. London: Oxford UP, 1912.

Cooper, James Fenimore. *The Pioneers*. New York: Signet, 1964.

Cooper, Susan Fenimore. *Rural Hours*. New York: Putnam, 1876.

——— [Amabel Penfeather]. *Elinor Wyllys; or, The young folk of Longbridge*. Philadelphia: Carey and Hart, 1846.

Culler, Jonathan. *The Pursuit of Signs*. Ithaca: Cornell UP, 1981.

De Quincey, Thomas. *The Collected Writings*. Ed. David Masson. Edinburgh: Adam & Charles Black, 1889.

De Selincourt, Ernest. *Dorothy Wordsworth: A Biography*. Oxford: Clarendon, 1933.

Douglas, Ann. *The Feminization of American Culture*. New York: Avon, 1977.

DuPlessis, Rachel Blau. "For the Etruscans." In *The New Feminist Criticism*. Ed. Elaine Showalter. New York: Pantheon, 1985, 271–291.

Foster, Edward Halsey. *The Civilized Wilderness: Backgrounds to American Romantic Literature*. New York: Macmillan, 1976.

Friedman, Michael, *The Making of a Tory Humanist*. New York: Columbia UP, 1979.

Fuller, Margaret. *Memoirs of Margaret Fuller Ossoli*. Ed. R. W. Emerson, W. H. Channing, and J. F. Clarke. Boston: n.p., 1852.

———. *Summer on the Lakes*. New York: Haskell House, rpt., 1970.

———. *Woman in the Nineteenth Century*. Freeport: Books for Libraries Press, rpt., 1972.

Gilbert, Sandra, and Susan Gubar. *The Madwoman in the Attic*. New Haven: Yale UP, 1979.

———, eds. *The Norton Anthology of Literature by Women*. New York: Norton, 1985.

Gillett, Eric. *Maria Jane Jewsbury*. London: Oxford UP, 1932.

Gilligan, Carol. *In a Different Voice*. Cambridge: Harvard UP, 1982.

Heath, William. *Wordsworth and Coleridge*. Oxford: Clarendon, 1970.

Hemans, Felicia. *The Poetical Works*. Philadelphia: Thomas T. Ash, 1836.

Homans, Margaret. *Women Writers and Poetic Identity*. Princeton: Princeton UP, 1980.

Irigaray, Luce. *Ce sexe qui n'en est pas un*. Paris: Editions de Minuit, 1977.

Kolodny, Annette. *The Lay of the Land*. Chapel Hill: U North Carolina P, 1975.

Kristeva, Julia. *La Revolution du langue poétique*. Paris: Editions du Seuil, 1974.

Lamb, Charles, and Mary Lamb. *The Letters of Charles and Mary Anne Lamb*. Ed. Edwin W. Marrs, Jr. Ithaca: Cornell UP, 1978.

Levin, Susan M. "Subtle Fire: Dorothy Wordsworth's Prose and Poetry." *Massachusetts Review* 21 (1980): 345–363.

Liu, Alan. "On the Autobiographical Present: Dorothy Wordsworth's *Grasmere Journals*." *Criticism* 26 (1984): 115–137.

McCarty, Mari. "Possessing Female Space: 'The Tender Shoot.'" *Women's Studies* 8 (1981): 367–374.

Miller, Jean Baker. *Toward a New Psychology of Women*. Boston: Beacon, 1976.

Moorman, Mary. *William Wordsworth: A Biography*. Oxford: Clarendon, 1957.

Morley, F. V. *Dora Wordsworth, Her Book*. London: Oxford UP, 1924.

Nabholtz, John R. "Dorothy Wordsworth and the Picturesque." *Studies in Romanticism* 3 (1964): 118–128.

Onorato, Richard. *The Character of the Poet*. Princeton: Princeton UP, 1971.

Opie, Iona and Peter. *The Oxford Dictionary of Nursery Rhymes*. Oxford: Clarendon, 1951.

Parrington, Vernon Louis. *The Romantic Revolution in America, 1800–1860*. New York: Harcourt, 1927.

Poovey, Mary. "My Hideous Progeny: Mary Shelley and the Feminization of Romanticism." *PMLA* 95 (1980): 332–347.

Robinson, David M. "Margaret Fuller and the Transcendental Ethos: *Woman in the Nineteenth Century*." *PMLA* 97 (1982): 83–98.

Shelley, Mary. *Frankenstein*. New York: Signet, 1965.

———. *Journal*. Ed. F. L. Jones. Norman: U Oklahoma P, 1947.

———. *The Last Man*. Lincoln: U Nebraska P, 1965.

Shelley, Percy Bysshe. *The Complete Works of Percy Bysshe Shelley*. Ed. Roger Ingpen and Walter E. Peck. New York: Gordian P, 1965.

Showalter, Elaine, ed. *The New Feminist Criticism*. New York: Pantheon, 1985.

Trilling, Lionel. "The Fate of Pleasure: Wordsworth to Dostoevsky." *Romanticism Reconsidered*. Ed. Northrop Frye. New York: Columbia UP, 1963.

Urbanski, Marie Mitchell Olesen. *Margaret Fuller's "Woman in the Nineteenth Century."* Westport: Greenwood P, 1980.

Volney, Constantin François. *Oeuvres choisies*. Paris: Lebrigue Frères, 1834.

Wordsworth, Dorothy. *George and Sarah Green*. Ed. Ernest de Selincourt. Oxford: Clarendon, 1936.

———. *Journals of Dorothy Wordsworth*. Ed. Ernest de Selincourt. Hamden, Connecticut: Archon, 1970.

———. *Journals of Dorothy Wordsworth*. Ed. Mary Moorman. London: Oxford UP, 1971.

Wordsworth, Mary. *The Letters of Mary Wordsworth, 1800–1855*. Ed. Mary E. Burton. Oxford: Clarendon, 1958.

Wordsworth, William. *The Poetical Works of William Wordsworth*. Ed. Ernest de Selincourt. Oxford: Clarendon, 1954.

———. *The Prelude*. Ed. Jonathan Wordsworth, M. H. Abrams, and Stephen Gill. New York: Norton, 1979.

Wordsworth, William, and Samuel Taylor Coleridge. *Lyrical Ballads*. Ed. W. J. B. Owen. London: Oxford UP, 1969.

Wordsworth, William, and Dorothy Wordsworth. *The Letters of William and Dorothy Wordsworth*. Ed. Alan G. Hill, Mary Moorman, and Chester L. Shaver. Oxford: Clarendon, 1967–1982.

INDEX